RACIAL EQUITY ON COLLEGE CAMPUSES

SUNY series, Critical Race Studies in Education
———————
Derrick R. Brooms, editor

RACIAL EQUITY ON COLLEGE CAMPUSES
CONNECTING RESEARCH AND PRACTICE

EDITED BY
ROYEL M. JOHNSON, UJU ANYA,
AND LILIANA M. GARCES

Published by State University of New York Press, Albany

© 2022 State University of New York

All rights reserved

Printed in the United States of America

No part of this book may be used or reproduced in any manner whatsoever without written permission. No part of this book may be stored in a retrieval system or transmitted in any form or by any means including electronic, electrostatic, magnetic tape, mechanical, photocopying, recording, or otherwise without the prior permission in writing of the publisher.

For information, contact State University of New York Press, Albany, NY
www.sunypress.edu

Library of Congress Cataloging-in-Publication Data

Names: Johnson, Royel M., editor. | Anya, Uju, editor. | Garces, Liliana M., editor.
Title: Racial equity on college campuses : connecting research and practice / Royel M. Johnson, Uju Anya, Liliana M. Garces.
Description: Albany : State University of New York Press, [2022] | Series: SUNY series, Critical Race Studies in Education / Derrick R. Brooms, editor | Includes bibliographical references and index.
Identifiers: LCCN 2021041303 (print) | LCCN 2021041304 (ebook) | ISBN 9781438487076 (hardcover : alk paper) | ISBN 9781438487083 (ebook)
Subjects: LCSH: Racial justice in education—United States. | Discrimination in higher education—United States. | Educational equalization—United States. | Minorities—Education (Higher)—United States. | Minority college students—United States.
Classification: LCC LC212.42 .R345 2022 (print) | LCC LC212.42 (ebook) | DDC 378.1/980973—dc23/eng/20211109
LC record available at https://lccn.loc.gov/2021041303
LC ebook record available at https://lccn.loc.gov/2021041304

10 9 8 7 6 5 4 3 2 1

Contents

FOREWORD vii
    Estela Mara Bensimon

PREFACE xi

ACKNOWLEDGMENTS xv

INTRODUCTION 1
    Royel M. Johnson, Uju Anya, and Liliana M. Garces

Part I: University Leadership

CHAPTER 1
Advancing Racial Equity in Faculty Hiring through Inquiry 21
    Román Liera

CHAPTER 2
Leveraging Campus-wide Leadership Collaborations for Equity 43
    Amanda Taylor and Evelyn Ambriz

CHAPTER 3
The Role of Boards in Advancing the Equity Agenda 61
    Felecia Commodore, Raquel M. Rall, and Demetri L. Morgan

Part II: Teaching and Learning

CHAPTER 4
(Re)Shaping Higher Education Classrooms with
Inclusive Pedagogies 85
    *Paula Adamo, Liliana Diaz Solodukhin, Janiece Z. Mackey,
    Adrienne Martinez, and Judy Marquez Kiyama*

CHAPTER 5
Developing Intersectional Consciousness: A De/colonial
Approach to Researching Pedagogy in the Higher Education
Context   103
  Mildred Boveda

CHAPTER 6
From the Theater to Higher Education: Using Movies to
Facilitate Intergroup Racial Dialogues   121
  Ericka Roland

Part III: Student and Campus Life

CHAPTER 7
Reimagining Institutionalized Support for Undocumented and
DACA College Students: A Critical Approach   141
  Susana M. Muñoz and Stephen Santa-Ramirez

CHAPTER 8
Rethinking Postsecondary Education Access and Success to
Advance Racial Equity for Rural Black Students   167
  Darris R. Means, Aaron T. George, and Jenay Willis

CHAPTER 9
Beyond "Woke Play": Challenging Performative Allyship in
Student Affairs' "Diversity, Equity, and Inclusion" Programming   189
  Ali Watts

ABOUT THE EDITORS   213

ABOUT THE CONTRIBUTORS   215

INDEX   221

Foreword

The struggle for racial equity in the United States has ebbed and flowed often over the years. But what we're experiencing now is different. The energized leadership of the Black Lives Matter movement and the increasing support it is receiving from all segments of society, along with the horror we feel as witnesses to anti-Black crime by police, the rise of white supremacism, and the ravages COVID-19 has wrought on Black, Latinx, Indigenous, and Asian American communities, make it hard to imagine that the urgency for racial equity will die down.

As I read *Racial Equity on College Campuses*, I was often reminded of a time, twenty years ago, when I founded the Center for Urban Education at the University of Southern California, when the trend was to speak about *diversity* and not about *equity*. At that time, "equity" was viewed suspiciously. For some it conjured an image of disruptive activism and advocacy, whereas "diversity" was more encompassing, providing a vision of "all students" benefiting. Twenty years ago, when I chose to focus on equity as a matter of institutional accountability and practitioner learning, I did so as a symbol of reclaiming the spirit and intent of the civil rights movement: justice for racially minoritized groups whose "minoritized" status came about as a result of enslavement, colonization, and territorial occupation. It is gratifying now for me to see that the title of this book is centered specifically on racial equity and makes clear that "equity for all students" is whitewashing.

The editors of this book—Royel M. Johnson, Uju Anya, Liliana M. Garces—accurately portray the complexity of higher education institutions and discuss teaching and learning, student campus life, and leadership, the three core areas of academic organizations. Every chapter in this book effectively argues why racial equity must be integrated into the processes of teaching, leadership, and campus life to transform best intentions into solid actions. Higher education practitioners and leaders as well as policymakers need to clearly understand that racial equity is the debt higher education owes for its history of exclusionary practices. Too often, equity and/or racial equity has been invoked in a vacuum and disconnected from practice. Practitioners and leaders who participate in professional development activities that promote racial equity often complain that they don't know what to do to make racial equity actionable.

Fortunately for them, this book goes beyond simply promoting and arguing for the acceptance of racial equity as a worthy and necessary goal of every higher education institution; it also shows *how to do it* with authentic scenarios of how race, racism, whiteness, anti-Blackness, and antiracism play out on colleges campuses of all kinds. The authenticity of the scenarios and experiences provided throughout every chapter were made possible by the joint cooperation and authorship of scholars and practitioners—a truly admirable accomplishment for this book. In higher education, we often lament that our scholarly work does not impact practice and policy as we wish it would. This book shows that partnerships are fruitful when the intellectual power asymmetries that elevate academic production as superior and downgrade knowledge derived from practice as empirically unproven are discarded. The book, in addition to providing a clear pathway to racial equity in the everyday work of faculty, leaders, and staff, also provides a model of knowledge co-creation.

To their credit, the authors also manage to cover a great deal of unexplored territory in the domain of racial equity, including research methods, inclusive pedagogies in higher education classrooms (a topic that has been understudied in higher education), innovative methods for teaching about race and racism, DACA students, rural Black students (another unexplored topic because *rural* is often thought of as *white*), the dangers of equity-lite, the use of action research methods to change hiring practices, and a variety of topics under the umbrella of leadership.

Also admirable is the editors' success in bringing together a critical mass of Black, Latinx, and multiracial scholars and practitioners into a collaborative process. Many of the authors are assistant professors, others are recently promoted to the rank of associate, and others are graduate students and postdocs. A few are even from the realm of administrators and community organizers. The professional and experiential differences of the contributors have clearly made it possible to turn out a book that makes racial equity resonate to the instructor, the president, the director of student support services, the trustee, and, yes, to students too.

We are in the midst of what feels to me a true turning point in educational equity. Higher education must seize this moment and exercise genuine moral leadership to finally accomplish racial equity. As we chart this course, the ideas and actions detailed here in *Racial Equity on College Campuses* can help show the way ahead.

—Estela Mara Bensimon
University Professor & Dean's Professor in Educational Equity
Rossier School of Education, University of Southern California

Preface

In this era, indelibly marked by growing racial tensions and public and overt forms of bigotry and hatred, especially in higher education, access to research-based findings that can be translated into concrete recommendations for promoting racial equity on college campuses takes on heightened importance. *Racial Equity on College Campuses* answers this call to action, marshalling the expertise of 19 scholars and practitioners to inform the everyday practices of institutional actors across various areas of campus life. Racial equity, as defined in this book, refers to a condition in which one's educational opportunities, experiences, and outcomes are not contingent on one's race or ethnicity. Thus, achieving racial equity requires an explicit acknowledgment of and commitment to addressing the pervasive ways in which ideologies of white supremacy permeate institutional policy, practice, and culture.

This edited volume originated from a national convening we held February 7–9, 2019, on the Penn State University Park campus, funded through the Spencer Foundation's Small Conference Grant program. The two-day convening, titled *Envisioning Racial Equity on College Campuses: Bridging Research-to-Practice Gaps for Institutional Transformation*, sought to develop strategies for addressing the persistent research-to-practice gap that exists between higher education scholarship and the daily praxis of practitioners working in curriculum and instruction, student and campus life, and institutional leadership—three core areas of higher education. Thus, it brought together 23 racially diverse practitioners and educational scholars "to advance racial equity research in higher education and identify strategies to strengthen its accessibility and relevance for practitioners" (Johnson & Watts, 2019).

The chapters in this book are derived from research briefs that were originally submitted by authors for presentation at the conference. Given the focus of the convening, higher education practitioners were featured prominently throughout the symposium, serving as discussants during scholarly breakout sessions and offering direct feedback to presenters about how their work could be strengthened and tailored to better inform institutional policy and practice. Contributors to this volume also had the opportunity to benefit from insights shared during practitioner-centered panels about areas of higher education research that require more focused attention. Thus, *Racial Equity on College Campuses* is distinct from other books on this topic, in that the final chapters benefited from the close and careful review and feedback of practitioners working in the functional areas of higher education around which this volume is organized. Another distinct feature of this book is the structural similarity of the chapters included, which aims to increase its accessibility—each chapter opens with an introduction followed by a brief synthesis of major themes and conclusions from theoretical and empirical scholarship and closes with a robust set of actionable recommendations for institutional policy and practice.

The intended audience for this book is wide and varied. It is our hope that it will, first and foremost, serve as a resource for institutional administrators, faculty, and staff who seek empirically based recommendations to guide their practice, especially in the areas of curriculum and instruction, student and campus life, and university leadership. For those who teach at the graduate level, especially those in higher education and student affairs programs, this text might serve as a companion to books used in courses on issues related to race and racism, equity and diversity, and student affairs/university administration and leadership, to name a few. Researchers, especially those in graduate school and early in their careers, might also turn to the book as an exemplar or model for how they might translate findings from their research into actionable recommendations for practice and policy.

Finally, as with all projects of this kind, this book has some limitations. It is far from exhaustive in its coverage of the wide-ranging issues related to racial equity in higher education. However, where it lacks in the breadth of coverage, we strive to make up for it in depth, with the samples of racial equity-related issues that are included.

Reference

Johnson, R. M., & Watts, A. (2019, March 5). Bridging the gap: Advancing racial equity in higher education by connecting research to practice. A

Community of Higher Education Scholars: The Official Blog of AERA Division J. http://aeradivisionj.blogspot.com/2019/03/bridging-gap-advancing-racial-equity-in.html

Acknowledgments

An undertaking of this kind is not possible without the time, support, and care of an extensive network of people. We are grateful for the financial resources we received from the Spencer Foundation's Conference Grant program, which was the genesis of this project. And for the support of our program officer at Spencer, Matt Holsapple, for seeing the value in this work.

A very special thank-you also goes to Ali Watts and Evelyn Ambriz, our amazingly talented graduate students who wore multiple hats over the duration of this project, including that of conference planners, editorial assistants, and most importantly, thought partners. Your support was invaluable to us throughout the process of developing this work.

Thank you to our colleagues at Pennsylvania State University and University of Texas at Austin; Derrick Brooms, editor of the series in which this book will be featured; Rebecca Colesworthy, acquisitions editor at SUNY Press; and to all of the authors who contributed to this book. Finally, thank you to our close friends and family for generously sharing your time with us as we worked to bring this important project to a close. Your patience and understanding is much appreciated.

Introduction

ROYEL M. JOHNSON, UJU ANYA, AND LILIANA M. GARCES

Shortly following the historic 2008 presidential election of Barack Obama—the United States' first Black president—there were declarations from popular media sources, political pundits, and scholars alike that the country had arrived at a post-racial status (Burnham, 2009; Canason, 2009). This idea—or rather this illusion—of racial progress in our country was completely turned on its head when the electoral college selected Donald J. Trump as president, a candidate whose campaign in large part was based on the "racist idea" (Kendi, 2017) that our country's greatness was tied to our success in excluding Mexican immigrants through the construction of a wall on the border. When asked to make sense of how our country could elect someone who openly engaged in racist, sexist, and xenophobic rhetoric, author, journalist, and television commentator Howard Bryant (2020) noted that Trump's election was a backlash, a repudiation of half a century of Black progress and the election of a Black president.

Since the election of President Trump there has been a noticeable spike in the number of reported hate crimes across the country. Indeed, empirical evidence indicates that Trump's rise to power has emboldened white Americans, among others, to openly express and engage in racist ideas and behaviors (see, e.g., Edwards & Rushin, 2018). This "Trump effect," as some have described it, has also been observed on college and university campuses. Data from the Department of Education indicate that the number of *reported* hate crimes (referring to offenses motivated by biases of race, national origin, ethnicity, sexual orientation, gender, or disability) in higher education increased by 44 percent from 2016 to

2018 (U.S. Department of Education, n.d.). At the same time, we have also observed a rise in activism, with students protesting a host of issues related to race and racism on campuses (Eagan et al., 2015; Linder et al., 2019; Ndemanu, 2017; Wheatle & Commodore, 2019). Consider the following examples just from 2019:

1. Students at the University of Oklahoma held an emotional rally in January, covered their mouths with duct tape, and marched with signs reading "Enough Is Enough" after a series of blackface incidents on campus were met with limited administrative response (Mangan, 2019).

2. The University of Georgia's chapter of the NAACP held an open discussion on race in March to push for an administrative response after a video went viral on social media of white fraternity members mocking slavery by pretending to hit one another with belts and demanding that others "pick my cotton, n--" (Sicurella, 2019).

3. In August, student groups and faculty supporters at the University of Mississippi protested the campus administrative response after a photo was posted to social media of three white students carrying guns in front of a bullet-riddled sign dedicated to the murder of civil rights icon Emmett Till (Mathias, 2019).

4. The University of Arizona experienced two protests opposing racist incidents in fall 2019—the first in September, when the Arizona Black Student Union and hundreds of other students demonstrated against the campus police response to a racist verbal and physical assault of a Black student by two white peers (Anderson, 2019), and the second in November when members of the university's Native Students Outreach, Access and Resiliency group (and supporters) demanded apologies and accountability in response to culturally offensive and othering comments by university president Robert C. Robbins (Ontiveros, 2019).

5. Students at Georgia Southern University protested in October 2019 after classmates burned copies of a book

by a visiting Cuban American speaker—Jennine Capó Crucet—after she made critical comments about white privilege and escalating discrimination against immigrant communities (Balingit, 2019).

6. In November 2019, approximately 300 students at Syracuse University staged a multiday #NotAgainSU sit-in on campus in response to a rash of racist incidents—including graffiti with slurs against African American, Asian, and Jewish students found in residence halls and academic buildings, and an incident where white fraternity members yelled racist slurs at a passing Black student (Randle, 2019). A second sit-in that began in February 2020 resulted in the university temporarily suspending 30 students for violating campus disruption rules. Significant online backlash resulted in the administration revoking the suspensions after a week (Associated Press, 2020).

These examples represent just a handful of a growing number of high-profile, race-related incidents in higher education that university faculty, staff, and administrators are grappling to respond to through reforms to institutional policies and practices that shape teaching and learning, student and campus life, and university leadership. The examples described previously also, however, underscore the sobering reality that race (still) matters, and racism (still) festers on our nation's college and university campuses, just as it does in our broader society. Thus, the "Trump effect" in higher education is a mere symptom of deeper, long-standing, systemic issues in our country related to race and racism that are reinforced through discourse, policy, and practice. For instance, just recently, the Supreme Court *again* deliberated the constitutionality of race-conscious policies in postsecondary admissions in *Students for Fair Admissions Inc. v. Harvard University et al.* (see Garces & Poon, 2018). Although in the end, the court decided in favor of Harvard's approach to considering race in admissions, the continued attacks on these policies in higher education are emblematic of our country's resistance to accepting responsibility for its long-standing history of race-based exclusion and discrimination, which continue to negatively impact patterns of postsecondary participation and degree completion, especially for Black and Latinx students.

Despite a considerable increase in college enrollment rates for racially minoritized groups, data indicate that Black and Latinx students are still more likely to be concentrated at two-year, for-profit, and less-selective public institutions than their white peers (Espinosa et al., 2019, p. 37). These institutions tend to have lower degree completion rates (Ginder et al., 2018) and much higher loan default rates (Miller, 2017) than other colleges and universities, thus limiting students' ability to realize the economic returns of going to college and earning an undergraduate degree (Jones & Nichols, 2020). Generally, however, postsecondary degree attainment rates vary significantly by race and ethnicity across institutional types. Recent data published in a report by the American Council on Education indicate that in 2017, Asian American adults had the highest level of educational attainment, with 55.4 percent holding a bachelor's degree or higher, followed by white adults at 38 percent. By contrast, Native Hawaiian and Pacific Islander (25.2%), Black (24.2%), Native American (20.5%), and Latinx (17.3%) rates of attainment were significantly lower (Espinosa et al., 2019, p. 8). It is important to note, however, that while aggregate statistics on Asian Americans suggest that they have the highest level of degree attainment, this figure masks significant ethnic disparities within this racial group (Museus et al., 2015), particularly for those who identify as Laotian (12%), Hmong (12%), Cambodian (14%), and Vietnamese (27%) (Asian American Center for Advancing Justice, 2011, p. 31).

To mitigate disparities and address equity gaps in the postsecondary education experiences and outcomes among white and racially minoritized students, education researchers have advanced several promising frameworks, concepts, and a host of recommendations to guide institutional policy and practice. Consider, for instance, Museus's (2014) culturally engaging campus environments (CECE) model, which offers insight into the environmental factors that maximize student engagement and success among racially minoritized students. Strayhorn (2012, 2018) advanced a theoretical model of college students' sense of belonging, which has been used widely by higher education leaders, faculty, and student affairs practitioners, among others, to structure curricular and co-curricular opportunities and experiences for minoritized students in ways that are inclusive and affirming for all students. Smith (2011, 2015) developed an institutional diversity framework outlining the aspects of colleges and universities that must be engaged to foster diversity. And the Equity Scorecard out of the Center for Urban Education at the

University of Southern California was developed as a framework to guide practitioner inquiry into institutional policies and practices that exacerbate racial inequities on campus (Bensimon & Malcolm, 2012; Dowd & Bensimon, 2015).

Despite these advancements, along with the voluminous contributions from empirical research over the past 30 years (e.g., Allen, 1992; Fleming, 1984; Garces & Jayakumar, 2014; Harris & Bensimon, 2007; Harper & Hurtado, 2007; Harper et al., 2009; Hurtado et al., 1999; Museus & Park; 2015; Park, 2018; Solorzano, 1998; Stewart, 2013; Strayhorn & Johnson, 2013; Waterman, 2012), remarkable research-to-practice gaps exist in higher education (Kezar, 2000). Maxey and Kezar (2016) argue that many practitioners and policymakers "rely more on personal experience, practical knowledge, and anecdotal evidence in responding to the challenges they face" (p. 1046). This is not surprising given the fact that many practitioners and policymakers face increasingly complex and fast-paced conditions for decision-making, unique local challenges, and accountability demands for immediate results (e.g., Cohen & Garet, 1991; Kezar, 2000). And researchers, unfortunately, often overlook the complexities and challenges associated with applying or implementing recommendations from their work to institutional policy and practice, particularly in the area of racial equity, and at white-serving institutions that in large part remain resistant to structural and systemic change.

To address this gap between research and practice in the area of racial equity, the collection of chapters featured in this book is undergirded by a concept we refer to as translational racial equity research-practice (TRERP). This concept refers to the process in which practitioner-informed, scientific discoveries that center race, racism, and other interlocking systems of oppression are translated into institutional practice and policy interventions that aim to improve the material conditions of racially/ethnically minoritized people. Dominant research-to-practice perspectives have assumed a linear relationship in which insights from research flow unidirectionally into practice settings (Stein & Coburn, 2010) like college and university campuses. TRERP, on the other hand, recognizes practitioners, especially those of color, as part and parcel to knowledge production. The hyphen (-) in "research-practice" signifies a complex, mutually constitutive relationship, a nexus, in which insights from each influence the other. Our conceptualization of TRERP is informed by elements of critical race theory (Bell, 1993; Ladson-Billings & Tate, 1995), research on organizational change for racial equity (Bensimon & Malcolm, 2012; Dowd & Bensimon, 2015; Stewart, 2018), and scholarship on the relationship between research and practice (Stein & Coburn, 2010). The following propositions form the basis for TRERP:

1. Understanding and interpreting social phenomena is necessary but insufficient for *changing* the material conditions of Black, Indigenous, People of Color (BIPOC) in higher education and society more broadly. Racial equity research in higher education must be rooted in a transformative paradigm that challenges and dismantles structures and practices that promote white supremacy and reproduce race-based disparities. We advocate for what Denzin (2015) refers to as "ethically responsible activist research" (p. 32)—work that makes a difference in the lives of institutionally marginalized people.

2. Racial equity "problems" in higher education must be framed and represented in their full context (e.g., legacy of discrimination, role of systems/structures in producing inequities) to ensure equity-minded policy and practice recommendations (Dowd & Bensimon, 2015; Hankivsky et al., 2012; Johnson et al., 2021).

3. Practitioners who "work on the ground," especially BIPOC, are essential to the formulation and identification of racial equity "problems" worthy of scholarly attention. Indeed, practitioners are valuable co-constructors of knowledge whose expertise is important for the development of translational racial equity research and its implementation across various areas of educational practice.

4. Racial equity research-practice in higher education must anticipate and account for the ways in which white supremacy and other interlocking systems of oppression operate to mitigate and undermine organizational change. For instance, diversity and inclusion discourses and programs are often used as a tool by university leaders to appease their constituents (e.g., BIPOC students), while maintaining the status quo and avoiding institutional change (Iverson, 2007; Stewart, 2017).

5. To realize racial equity in higher education, multifocal strategies and reforms are needed that fundamentally alter how colleges and universities function, a process that Kezar (2014) refers to as transformational change. Similarly, translational racial equity research-practice emphasizes dismantling oppressive structures and the adoption of humanizing and dignity-affirming policies, practices, and processes.

The authors included in this volume address a small sample of salient problems that demand the collective attention of college and university leaders, administrators, and faculty who envision a future for higher education that is more racially diverse, inclusive, and equitable. Through the promising and actionable recommendations and strategies presented in each of the chapters, we hope to aid education stakeholders in moving from "equity talk to equity walk" (McNair et al., 2019). That is, to accepting personal and institutional responsibility for, and committing to address, systemic inequities disparately impacting racially minoritized communities on college and university campuses.

Overview of Chapters

Racial Equity on College Campuses is organized into three major parts: (1) University Leadership, (2) Teaching and Learning; and (3) Student and Campus Life. Part 1 considers the role of college and university leadership in advancing racial equity and offers actionable recommendations and considerations for transformative change. Part 2, Teaching and Learning, zeros in on the role and potential of classroom curriculum, as well as instructional practices and dispositions, in facilitating transformative change for racial equity. In part 3, Student and Campus Life, the scope is broadened to consider the experiences of racially minoritized students on campus generally, and how institutional resources, human and financial, can be marshalled to meet the diverse needs of students.

Across all three areas of the book, authors expertly connect theory and research to practice, with critical attention to the complexities associated with implementing and enacting their recommendations. The chapters in the book focus primarily on historically white institutions (HWIs) due to their historical legacies of racism and settler colonialism (see Anderson, 1988; Dancy et al., 2018), though their content is likely relevant across other institutional contexts. We also note that HWIs have been the primary sites of the growing number of racist incidents around the country, demonstrating their urgent need for clear and actionable recommendations to support their transformation into racially inclusive and equitable environments.

University Leadership. Part 1 of this book explores how issues of racial equity can and should be addressed at the level of institutional leadership and policymaking. Grounded in conversations with governing boards, hiring committees, and administrative leaders, these chapters stress that equity-minded leadership (at all levels) is a requirement for meaningful institutional transformation.

- In the opening chapter of this part, Román Liera takes up the specific institutional task of faculty hiring by tracing the myriad ways that hiring practices center white norms and send overt and covert signals that racially minoritized applicants are not welcome or competitive. "Best practices" for hiring diverse faculty often fail, Liera argues, because they do not take into account local organizational barriers or sufficiently interrogate departmental, disciplinary, or institutional discourses. In order to dismantle these barriers, he proposes a process of inquiry that guides hiring committees through an interrogation of their strategies for selecting and preparing committee members, recruiting applicants, drafting job announcements, outlining hiring criteria, and assessing candidates. He concludes with recommendations for how campuses and departments might address racial disparities in faculty hiring by encouraging committees to question gaps between their stated values of diversity/inclusivity and their enacted practices that persist in centering dominant cultural (white, male, middle-class, etc.) experience.

- In "Leveraging Campus-wide Leadership Collaborations for Equity," Amanda Taylor and Evelyn Ambriz present an insightful discussion of the power and potential of campus-wide collaborations for racial equity. Specifically, this chapter focuses on exploring the phenomenon of diversity and inclusion councils made up of faculty, staff, administrators, and students that are often commissioned after racist incidents or moments of increased student activism on campus. In order for these councils to be more than public relations gestures, the authors argue, careful attention must be paid to the recruitment of members, the power differentials between invited groups, and strategies for ensuring that the councils engage in meaningful work toward racial equity that can be maintained and institutionalized. The chapter draws insights from the Presidential Council for Diversity and Inclusion at American University (where Taylor serves as assistant vice president for diversity, equity, and inclusion) in framing its recommendations for forming, fostering, and facilitating campus-wide leadership councils engaged in equity work.

- In "The Role of Boards in Advancing the Equity Agenda," Felicia Commodore, Raquel M. Rall, and Demetri L. Morgan close out the part with discussion of a population that is often left out of conversations about racial equity efforts on campus—members of the board of trustees. An equity-minded board has the power to institutionalize equity efforts and to provide necessary supports when these efforts are challenged, but individual board members are rarely socialized to see equity as central or even relevant to their work. Troublingly, boards also continue to be predominantly white, male, and drawn from business and industry. The authors argue, however, that boards have a fiduciary duty of loyalty, care, and obedience to the mission of the institution, which in turn means that they have a duty to uphold, promote, and guide the institution's espoused racial equity commitments. Defining equity as a fiduciary duty allows the authors to reimagine the work of the board—including strategic planning, examination of institutional data, funding and budget allocation, hiring and accountability, and stakeholder management—and provide recommendations for how these tasks might be turned toward combating racial disparities and continued forms of exclusion and oppression.

Teaching and Learning. Part 2 of the book focuses on the classroom and other contexts of instructional interactions and pedagogical training. It draws from the experiences of faculty, instructors, and teacher education practitioners who report continued and escalating challenges in their efforts to create equitable curriculum and pedagogy in the time of Trump. In this part, the practitioners considered are not limited to those who exclusively work as instructors, nor are teaching and learning conceptualized as occurring solely within formal classrooms. Thus, pedagogical strategies are presented for promoting racial equity across diverse learning contexts.

- In the opening chapter of this part, Paula Adamo, Liliana Diaz Solodukhin, Janeice Z. Mackey, Adrienne Martinez, and Judy Marquez Kiyama argue that, despite increased focus on racial equity in higher education, curriculum and pedagogy remain elitist and structured by "rules" that are raced, classed, and gendered. Their chapter, "(Re)Shaping Higher Education Classrooms with Inclusive Pedagogies," explores the power of naming and transforming these traditional rules and norms by embracing inclusive practices that reflect the histories, knowledge, contributions, and lives of racially minoritized students. The authors provide examples from their own teaching practices to provide embodied context for their review and conclude with questions to guide instructors looking to (re)shape their classrooms for inclusive praxis.

- In "Developing Intersectional Consciousness: A De/colonial Approach to Researching Pedagogy in the Higher Education Context," Mildred Boveda encourages researchers and instructors alike to develop the intersectional consciousness and competence necessary to grapple with the multiple, interrelated systems of oppression that affect students' lives within and beyond the classroom. She offers overviews of two protocols that she and colleagues have developed over the course of a multiyear study of teacher education and special education programs. The intersectional competence measure helps instructors measure their preparation and capacity to engage in pedagogy that recognizes systemic oppressions, while the intersectional consciousness collaboration protocols give guidance in how to put that knowledge and preparation into practice. Boveda concludes by posing a series of reflective prompts for researchers and faculty to engage in de/colonial ethics regarding power, positionality, and complicity within the hegemonic structures of Westernized, essentialist, and otherwise oppressive ways of being and knowing.

- Finally, Ericka Roland closes this part with a discussion of how scenes from popular films addressing racial issues (like *Get Out*, *Crash*, and *The Hate You Give*) can be used as cultural artifacts to facilitate dialogues among diverse groups of college students. Her chapter, "From the Theater to Higher Education: Using Movies to Facilitate Intergroup Racial Dialogues," draws on personal reflection on her own experiences using the film *Dear White People* in the classroom and research on intergroup racial dialogue to introduce a seven-step process for selecting and introducing films as curricular/pedagogical content, and for facilitating risky and authentic intergroup dialogues that foster critical self-reflection, stimulating discussion, and equitable outcomes.

Student and Campus Life. The final part in this book focuses on issues and topics addressed by practitioners working in student affairs and student services roles directly impacted by racist incidents, student activism, and the persistent tensions of the "Trump effect." Practitioners who informed the discussions in this part were particularly concerned about student experiences outside of the classroom, and the direct interpersonal and systemic challenges of the current moment. They addressed challenges in campus climate and the potential for student affairs professionals to do more than merely promote diversity by also serving as social justice advocates and allies for transformational change. Chapters in this part examine the issues raised by demographic differences between practitioners and the students they serve and the results of mismatches in experience and understanding. The part also highlights questions related to populations that are both underserved and less often treated as significant constituencies, such as undocumented students and Black students from rural areas.

- Susana M. Muñoz and Stephen Santa-Ramírez's chapter, "Reimagining Institutionalized Support for Undocumented and DACA College Students: A Critical Approach," opens by recognizing that one symptom of the "Trump effect" has been the exacerbation of overtly anti-(im)migrant climates on many college campuses. This type of climate (and the political rhetoric and state actions that inform it) demands that campus practitioners interrogate and reimagine new ways of building institutional support for undocumented and Deferred Action for Childhood Arrivals (DACA) students. Using case studies from their own campuses—Colorado State University and Arizona State University, respectively—the authors present strategies for supporting students with immediate need, while also working to create transformative change toward four interrelated concepts of justice: labor, intersectional, reparative, and epistemic.

- Darris R. Means, Aaron T. George, and Jenay Willis interrogate another troubling postelection narrative in "Rethinking Postsecondary Education Access and Success to Advance Racial Equity for Rural Black Students." The authors observe that, following the 2016 election, journalists and education scholars alike turned significant attention to rural voters without college degrees who overwhelmingly voted for Trump. Research and funding sources have been directed to college access and success programs for rural students in subsequent years, but little attention has been paid to the diversity of experiences and backgrounds of these rural students. Too often *rural* has been presumed to mean *white*. Means and colleagues shift this focus, therefore, to explicitly center the access and success of rural Black students and provide recommendations for how policy and practice might shift to center the communities, experiences, knowledges, and practices of this underserved population.

- In "Beyond 'Woke Play': Challenging Performative Allyship in Student Affairs' 'Diversity, Equity, and Inclusion' Programming," Ali Watts expresses concern about (white) liberal inclinations in the Trump era to perform "woke" political consciousness without making deeper, and often riskier, commitments to activism and institutional change. In particular, she explores the complicity of Student Affairs departments and graduate programs in promoting a performative and surface-level approach to racial equity that leaves practitioners ill-prepared to engage in systemic critique and deconstruction of systems of oppression, exclusion, and erasure. The chapter ends with a series of recommendations based on the American College Personnel Association's (ACPA) "Strategic Imperative for Racial Justice and Decolonization" that help practitioners move beyond "woke play" to the serious work of institutional transformation.

As racial tensions mount around the country, especially in our nation's colleges and universities, that aim to undermine progress toward racial equity, access to research-based findings that can be translated into concrete recommendations for practitioners is increasingly important. We hope that the collection of chapters featured in this book add to the proverbial arsenal of tools and strategies that can be deployed in the work of many, whatever their context may be, such that they are a threat to the forces that conspire to maintain the status quo.

References

Allen, W. (1992). The color of success: African-American college student outcomes at predominantly white and historically Black public colleges and universities. *Harvard Educational Review, 62*(1), 26–45.

Anderson, G. (2019, September 17). A racist attack at Arizona. *Inside Higher Education.* https://www.insidehighered.com/news/2019/09/17/arizona-students-criticize-university-police-response-alleged-assault

Anderson, J. D. (1988). *The education of Blacks in the South, 1860–1935.* University of North Carolina Press.

Asian American Center for Advancing Justice (2011). *A community of contrasts: Asian Americans in the United States, 2011.* https://www.advancingjustice-la.org/sites/default/files/ENTERED_Community_of_Contrasts_2011.pdf

Associated Press (2020, February 20). Syracuse University lifts suspensions of racism protesters. *ABC News.* https://abcnews.go.com/US/wireStory/syracuse-university-lifts-suspensions-racism-protesters-69106461

Balingit, M. (2019, December 30). "A tale of two schools": At Georgia Southern, a book-burning ignites questions anew about race. *Washington Post.* https://www.washingtonpost.com/local/education/a-tale-of-two-schools-at-georgia-southern-a-book-burning-ignites-questions-anew-about-race/2019/12/30/363bdf80-f01b-11e9-89eb-ec56cd414732_story.html

Bell, D. (1993). Racism is permanent thesis: Courageous revelation or unconscious denial of racial genocide. *Capital University Law Review, 22*(3), 571–587.

Bensimon, E. M., & Malcolm, L. (2012). *Confronting equity issues on campus: Implementing the equity scorecard in theory and practice*. Stylus.

Bryant, H. (2020). *Full dissidence: Notes from an uneven playing field*. Beacon Press Books.

Burnham, L. B. (2009). *Changing the race: Racial politics and the election of Barack Obama*. Applied Research Center.

Canason, J. (2009, November 12). Lou Dobbs for president! The former CNN host sounds like he's running for office—and if so, he's a GOP nightmare. *Salon*. http://www.salon.com/2009/11/13/lou_dobbs/

Cohen, D., & Garet, M. (1991). Reforming educational policy with applied social research. In D. S. Anderson & B. J. Biddle (Eds.), *Knowledge for policy: Improving education through research* (pp. 123–140). Falmer.

Dancy, T. E., Edwards, K. T., & Davis, J. E. (2018). Historically white universities and plantation politics: Anti-Blackness and higher education in the Black Lives Matter era. *Urban Education, 53*(2), 176–195.

Denzin, N. K. (2015). What is critical qualitative inquiry? In G. S. Cannella, M. S. Perez., & P. A. Pasque (Eds.), *Critical qualitative inquiry: Foundations and futures* (pp. 31–50). Left Coast Press.

Dowd, A. C., & Bensimon, E. M. (2015). *Engaging the "race question": Accountability and equity in US higher education*. Teachers College Press.

Edwards, G. S., & Rushin, S. (2018). The effect of President Trump's election on hate crimes. *SSRN*. https://ssrn.com/abstract=3102652

Eagan, K., Stolzenberg, E. B., Bates, A. K., Aragon, M. C., Suchard, M. R., & Rios-Aguilar, C. (2015). *The American freshman: National norms fall 2015*. Higher Education Research Institute, UCLA. https://www.heri.ucla.edu/monographs/TheAmericanFreshman2016.pdf

Espinosa, L. L., Turk, J. M., Taylor, M., & Chessman, H. M. (2019). *Race and ethnicity in higher education: A status report*. https://www.acenet.edu/events/Pages/Race-and-Ethnicity-in-Higher-Education-A-Status-Report.aspx

Fleming, J. (1984). *Blacks in college: A comparative study of students' success in Black and in white institutions*. Jossey-Bass.

Garces, L. M., & Jayakumar, U. M. (2014). Dynamic diversity: Toward a contextual understanding of critical mass. *Educational Researcher, 43*(3), 115–124.

Garces, L. M., & Poon, O. (2018). *Asian Americans and race-conscious admissions: Understanding the conservative opposition's strategy of misinformation, intimidation & racial division*. Civil Rights Project. https://www.civilrightsproject.ucla.edu/research/college-access/affirmative-action/asian-americans-and-race-conscious-admissions-understanding-the-conservative-opposition2019s-strategy-of-misinformation-intimidation-racial-division/RaceCon_GarcesPoon_AsianAmericansRaceConsciousAdmi.pdf

Ginder, S. A., Kelly-Reid, J. E., & Mann, F. B. (2018). *Graduation rates for selected cohorts, 2009–14; outcome measures for cohort year 2009–10; stu-*

dent financial aid, academic year 2016–17; and admissions in postsecondary institutions, fall 2017: First look (Provisional Data) (NCES 2018-151). U.S. Department of Education. National Center for Education Statistics. https://nces.ed.gov/pubsearch.

Hankivsky, O., Grace, D., Hunting, G., Ferlatte, O., Clark, N., Fridkin, A., & Laviolette, T. (2012). Intersectionality-based policy analysis. In O. Hankivsky (Ed.), *An intersectionality-based policy analysis framework* (pp. 33–46). Vancouver, British Columbia, Canada: Simon Fraser University, Institute for Intersectionality Research and Policy.

Harper, S. R., & Hurtado, S. (2007). Nine themes in campus racial climates and implications for institutional transformation. *New Directions for Student Services, 2007*(120), 7–24.

Harper, S. R., Patton, L. D., & Wooden, O. S. (2009). Access and equity for African American students in higher education: A critical race historical analysis of policy efforts. *Journal of Higher Education, 80*(4), 389–414.

Harris III, F., & Bensimon, E. M. (2007). The equity scorecard: A collaborative approach to assess and respond to racial/ethnic disparities in student outcomes. *New Directions for Student Services, 2007*(120), 77–84.

Hurtado, S., Milem, J., Clayton-Pedersen, A., & Allen, W. (1999). Enacting diverse learning environments: Improving the climate for racial/ethnic diversity in higher education. *ASHE-ERIC Higher Education Report, 26*(8). ERIC Clearinghouse on Higher Education.

Iverson, S. V. (2007). Camouflaging power and privilege: A critical race analysis of university diversity policies. *Educational Administration Quarterly, 43*(5), 586–611.

Johnson, R. M., Alvarado, R., & Rosinger, K. O. (2021). What's the "problem" of considering criminal history in college admissions? A critical analysis of "Beyond the Box" policies in Louisiana and Maryland. *Journal of Higher Education.* DOI:10.1080/00221546.2020.1870849

Jones, T., & Nichols, A. H. (2020). *Hard truths: Why only race-conscious policies can fix racism in higher education.* The Education Trust. https://s3-us-east-2.amazonaws.com/edtrustmain/wp-content/uploads/2014/09/14161442/Hard-Truths-Why-Only-Race-Conscious-Policies-Can-Fix-Racism-in-Higher-Education-January-2020.pdf

Kendi, I. X. (2017). *Stamped from the beginning: The definitive history of racist ideas in America.* Random House.

Kezar, A. J. (2000). Higher education research at the millennium: Still trees without fruit? *Review of Higher Education, 23*(4), 443–468.

Kezar, A. (2014). *How colleges change: Understanding, leading, and enacting change.* New York: Routledge.

Ladson-Billings, G., & Tate, W. F. (1995). Toward a critical race theory of education. *Teachers College Record, 97*(1), 47–68.

Linder, C., Quaye, S. J., Lange, A. C., Roberts, R. E., Lacy, M. C., & Okello, W. K. (2019). "A student should have the privilege of just being a student": Student activism as labor. *Review of Higher Education, 42*(5), 37–62.

Mangan, K. (2019, January 23). Another blackface incident sends U. of Oklahoma students reeling. *Chronicle of Higher Education.* https://www.chronicle.com/article/Another-Blackface-Incident/245538

Mathias, C. (2019, August 1). Outrage at Ole Miss over white students posing with bullet-riddled Emmett Till sign. *Huffington Post.* https://www.huffpost.com/entry/ole-miss-emmett-till-guns-sign_n_5d42fe86e4b0ca604e2e69ed

Maxey, D., & Kezar, A. (2016). Leveraging the Delphi technique to enrich knowledge and engage educational policy problems. *Educational Policy, 30*(7), 1042–1070.

McNair, T. B., Bensimon, E. M., & Malcolm-Piqueux, L. (2019). *From equity talk to equity walk: Expanding practitioner knowledge for racial justice in higher education.* Jossey-Bass.

Miller, B. (2017, October 16). New federal data show a student loan crisis for African American borrowers. *Center for American Progress.* https://www.americanprogress.org/issues/education-postsecondary/news/2017/10/16/440711/new-federal-data-show-student-loan-crisis-african-american-borrowers/

Museus, S. D. (2014). The culturally engaging campus environments (CECE) model: A new theory of success among racially diverse college student populations. In M. B. Paulsen (Ed.), *Higher education: Handbook of theory and research* (pp. 189–227). Springer.

Museus, S. D., Ledesma, M. C., & Parker, T. L. (2015). *Racism and racial equity in higher education.* Jossey-Bass.

Museus, S. D., & Park, J. J. (2015). The continuing significance of racism in the lives of Asian American college students. *Journal of College Student Development, 56*(6), 551–569.

Ndemanu, M. T. (2017). Antecedents of college campus protests nationwide: Exploring Black student activists' demands. *Journal of Negro Education, 86*(3), 238–251.

Ontiveros, V. (2019, November 6). Native American students demand accountability from Robbins after offensive comments. *Daily Wildcat.* https://www.wildcat.arizona.edu/article/2019/11/n-robbins-soar?fb_comment_id=2348429445276736_2348949425224738

Park, J. J. (2018). *Race on campus: Debunking myths with data.* Harvard Education Press.

Randle, A. (2019, November 27). Racial slurs, and the 15 days that shook Syracuse. *New York Times.* https://www.nytimes.com/2019/11/27/nyregion/syracuse-university-racism.html

Sicurella, S. (2019, March 28). Racist TKE video generates reactions and conversations across UGA's campus. *Red & Black.* https://www.redandblack.com/

uganews/racist-tke-video-generates-reactions-and-conversations-across-uga-s/article_6afba9fc-50f3-11e9-ba46-d314f6b6fe51.html

Smith, D. G. (2011). *Diversity's promise for higher education: Making it work*. Johns Hopkins University Press.

Smith, D. G. (2015). *Diversity's promise for higher education: Making it work* (2nd ed.). Johns Hopkins University Press.

Solorzano, D. G. (1998). Critical race theory, race and gender microaggressions, and the experience of Chicana and Chicano scholars. *International Journal of Qualitative Studies in Education, 11*(1), 121–136.

Stein, M. K., & Coburn, C. E. (2010). Reframing the problem of research and practice. In C. E. Coburn, & M. K. Stein (Eds.), *Research and practice in education: Building alliances, bridging the divide* (pp. 1–13). Rowman & Littlefield.

Stewart, D. L. (2013). Racially minoritized students at US four-year institutions. *Journal of Negro Education, 82*(2), 184–197.

Stewart, D. L. (2017, March 29). Language of appeasement. *Inside Higher Education*. https://www.insidehighered.com/views/2017/03/30/college s-need-language-shift-not-one-you-think-essay

Stewart, D. L. (2018). Minding the gap between diversity and institutional transformation: Eight proposals for enacting institutional change. *Teachers College Record, 120*(14), www.tcrecord.org/Content.asp?ContentId=22377.

Strayhorn, T. L. (2012). *College students' sense of belonging: A key to educational success for all students*. Routledge.

Strayhorn, T. L. (2018). *College students' sense of belonging: A key to educational success for all students* (2nd ed.). Routledge.

Strayhorn, T. L., & Johnson, R. M. (2014). Why are all the white students sitting together in college? Impact of *Brown v. Board of Education* on cross-racial interactions among Blacks and whites. *Journal of Negro Education, 83*(3), 385–399.

U.S. Department of Education. (n.d.). *Generate trend data: Campus safety and security*. https://ope.ed.gov/campussafety/Trend/public/#/answer/2/201/trend/-1/-1/-1/-1

Waterman, S. J. (2012). Home-going as a strategy for success among Haudenosaunee college and university students. *Journal of Student Affairs Research and Practice, 49*(2), 193–209.

Wheatle, K. I., & Commodore, F. (2019). Reaching back to move forward: The historic and contemporary role of student activism in the development and implementation of higher education policy. *Review of Higher Education, 42*(5), 5–35.

PART I
UNIVERSITY LEADERSHIP

1

Advancing Racial Equity in Faculty Hiring through Inquiry

ROMÁN LIERA

Scholars have proposed various practices to help higher education practitioners racially diversify the professoriate. Seminal work by Caroline Turner, Daryl Smith, and Frank Tuitt provides higher education practitioners with practices to actively recruit racially minoritized faculty and train search committee members to minimize the impact of in-group racial bias in hiring decisions (see Turner, 2002, for examples). Yet, despite these efforts, racial representation in tenured and tenure-track appointments remains overwhelmingly white (National Center for Education Statistics, 2016). The existence of racial inequity in the professoriate is even more alarming when considering that Asian American, Black, Latinx, Indigenous, and other racially minoritized groups constitute only 22 percent of associate professors and 16 percent of full professors (National Center for Education Statistics, 2016). In this chapter, racial equity refers to institutionalizing a system where racially diverse knowledge is equally embedded in educational practices, policies, and the cultural fabric of organizations. Only then are we likely to produce equal outcomes among racial groups and enable racially minoritized people to exist in environments free from discrimination and bias (Liera, 2020b). Faculty hiring is a process higher education leaders can leverage to advance racial equity.

Given their research, service, and teaching responsibilities, faculty play significant roles not only in shaping the priorities of higher education as an institution but in training and socializing future leaders (Tuitt et al., 2007). Tenured, full-time faculty members garner opportunities to situate themselves in positions of power. Often, through membership on high-impact committees, or positions as endowed chairs or directors of research centers, faculty access and distribute organizational resources to students, faculty colleagues, and administrative staff. Racial diversity in the professoriate matters because racially minoritized faculty are likely to use their research, service, and teaching to advance their university's aspirations for equity, diversity, and inclusion (Baez, 2000; Delgado, Bernal & Villalpando, 2002; Gonzales, 2018; Turner et al., 2008). However, existing faculty hiring structures are intertwined with the campus racial culture's dominant racial schemas, which shape behaviors and perspectives around what types of knowledge and knowers are valued and devalued (Liera, 2020a). Without transforming faculty hiring structures across US college and university campuses, the reproduction of racial inequality in hiring decisions will continue to exist.

In this chapter, I argue that the implementation of existing "best practices" is inadequate to racially diversify the professoriate because those practices were not designed to address the local organizational barriers that impede racial equity efforts at any given higher education campus. First, I review the literature on faculty diversity to identify essential practices proposed by scholars for higher education practitioners to racially diversify the professoriate. Then, I conceptualize inquiry and review literature on how such organizational efforts provide higher education practitioners with the localized knowledge to define problems that impede racial equity at their campus and to design data-informed practices to advance racial equity. I close the chapter with recommendations for higher education practitioners to design an inquiry-based intervention to focus on organizational-level data collection and use to develop hiring practices that can facilitate a more racially equitable hiring structure. This chapter's focus on practitioner knowledge to dismantle racist structures and transform them through multifocal strategies that humanize and affirm racially minoritized peoples reflects the propositions of the translational racial equity research-practice (TRERP) framework guiding this volume.

Literature Review

In the 2007 edition of *Higher Education: Handbook of Theory and Research*, Tuitt and colleagues argued that the misalignment of signals between higher education organizations and job applicants helps explain the lack of progress to racially diversify the professoriate. For example, faculty applicants interpret the signals they receive from search committees through job announcements, interview questions, and interactions to visualize the campus culture and the potential opportunities to grow and prosper professionally. Search committees rely on information they collect from job application materials and interviews to evaluate a potential hire's future productivity and overall contribution to their organization. The continuous exchange of signals between the organization and candidates can reproduce racial inequalities if search committee members and academic departments fail to invest time and resources to evaluate their organization's existing values and hiring structures (White-Lewis, 2020a). In other words, to prioritize racial equity through faculty hiring, faculty search committee members must interrogate their understandings of *merit* and *fit* (Liera & Ching, 2020; White-Lewis, 2020b). Additionally, faculty can intentionally design hiring practices that address organizational barriers that have impeded the hiring and retention of Asian American, Black, Latinx, Indigenous, and other racially minoritized faculty members (Liera, 2020b). In this section, I describe five hiring strategies that scholars have highlighted to increase recruitment and hiring opportunities of racially minoritized faculty.

SEARCH COMMITTEE COMPOSITION

Given the scarcity of racially minoritized faculty on US colleges and universities, racially diversifying the professoriate should be a university's top priority (Turner, 2002). The search committee's composition is critical to successfully hiring racially minoritized faculty. A diverse search committee increases the likelihood for access to different networks, perspectives, and values (Turner, 2002). With a diverse search committee, faculty can hold each other accountable to mitigate in-group biases that favor faculty applicants who reflect the racial majority. For example, search committees that have at least one racially minoritized faculty on the committee are more likely to hire a racially minoritized faculty member (Smith et al., 2004).

Higher education leaders can diversify search committees by recruiting racially minoritized students and racially minoritized faculty members from peer campuses. However, since racially minoritized faculty are often tasked and overburdened with the role of the diversity expert, all faculty should be involved in efforts to diversify the values and perspectives that mediate hiring decisions (Bilimoria & Buch, 2010). In addition to all faculty, administrators with positional power (i.e., department chairs, deans, provosts) need to support and make the hiring of Asian American, Black, Latinx, and Indigenous faculty an organizational priority (Liera, 2020a; Tierney & Sallee, 2010).

Those who organize search committees with the priority to advance racial equity should consider, and counter, the power dynamics that can impede such efforts. For example, if junior faculty are tasked with advocating for racial equity, then tenured and full professors who can support and validate junior faculty should be recruited as members of the committee (Liera, 2020a). Similarly, administrative and faculty leaders should invest time to prevent situations where racially minoritized faculty are tasked with the responsibility to integrate equitable hiring practices. A diverse search committee where everyone is responsible for equitable hiring will help create recruitment strategies, job announcements, and criteria that increase the likelihood of hiring a racially minoritized faculty member without overburdening minoritized faculty members on the committee.

ACTIVE RECRUITMENT

The labor market myth that there are not enough qualified racially minoritized faculty candidates often results in passive recruitment efforts. For example, search committee members who believe that top-tier universities are competing for the few qualified racially minoritized faculty candidates also believe that they cannot compete within the market (Smith, 2009; Tuitt et al., 2007). A consequence of believing in such a myth includes that search committee members do not invest time, resources, and energy to actively recruit racially minoritized faculty candidates. Although the growth of racially minoritized people with doctorates has grown at faster rates in some disciplines than in others, the use of active recruitment strategies can further help search committees diversify their hiring pools (Bilimoria & Buch, 2010; Turner, 2002). In most cases, a more racially diversified pool increases the chances that search committee members will more fairly judge racially minoritized applicants (Sackett et al., 1991). As such, a racially diversified hiring pool often increases the likelihood of a racially diverse shortlist and of an offer to a racially minoritized faculty candidate (Bilimoria & Buch, 2010).

Scholars who study faculty diversity have proposed various strategies for search committees to cast a broad net and reach a critical mass of racially minoritized faculty candidates. To create a racially diverse hiring pool, search committee members should expand their networks with racially diverse audiences. To do so, faculty should actively create networks with academic departments that graduate high numbers of racially minoritized students (both master's and doctoral levels) and with interest groups and national organizations with high amounts of racially minoritized members (Light, 1994; Smith, 2000; Turner, 2002). Some campuses have also invested in cluster hires to attract racially diverse faculty (McMurtrie, 2016; Muñoz et al., 2017; Smith et al., 2004; Turner, 2002). Additionally, engagement in active recruitment efforts signals to racially minoritized faculty candidates that the department is serious about equity, diversity, and inclusion. Along with active recruitment of racially minoritized faculty, intentional job announcements can also signal departmental values for equity, diversity, and inclusion.

JOB ANNOUNCEMENTS

Job announcements are typically the first form of contact between organizations and potential job applicants. Search committee members can use the job announcement not only to communicate qualifications for and expectations of the job but also to highlight their departmental and campus values (Liera & Ching, 2020; Sensoy & DiAngelo, 2017; Smith et al., 2004). Since job announcements are never neutral (Sensoy & DiAngelo, 2017), search committee members can mark the invisible cultural norms of a department (Smith et al., 2004) and signal to potential racially minoritized faculty applicants that the department values them and their work (Tuitt et al., 2007). For search committee members to effectively leverage job announcements through the use of specific and targeted language (Smith et al., 2004), they need to define equity, diversity, and inclusion before starting a search (Sensoy & DiAngelo, 2017). For example, Smith and colleagues (2004) analyzed 689 searches from three large public research universities. They found that hiring committees who used diversity indicators (i.e., experience and success working with racially diverse populations) within job postings or special-hiring interventions were more likely to hire a racially minoritized professor. Search committee members can also leverage any special designations their campus might have, such as status as a Hispanic-serving institution or an Asian American and Native American Pacific Islander–serving institution. For colleges that do not have such designations, they can emphasize their departmental or campus-wide commitments to support and work with local communities. Search committee members can also read literature on funds of knowledge and cultural-relevant practices to learn what racially minoritized faculty value and prioritize. Being equipped with such knowledge, search committees can design their job announcements to align with the values of racially minoritized faculty (Liera, 2020a).

IMPLICIT BIAS TRAINING

Although antidiscrimination legislation has raised awareness of and challenged explicit discriminatory behaviors, implicit bias continues to shape faculty hiring decision-making (Rivera, 2017). In faculty hiring, search committee members reproduce racial and gender inequity when they favor job applicants who reflect the racial and gender majority (Liera & Ching, 2020). That is, the favoritism and advantages whites provide to other whites can explain racial inequity (DiTomaso, 2015). In field and experimental studies, scholars have found that hiring committee members prefer the curriculum vitae (CVs) of candidates perceived to be white over those of candidates perceived to be racially minoritized (Beattie et al., 2013; Eaton et al., 2019). White evaluators favor white applicants even when the credentials and qualifications of racially minoritized candidates are on par or exceed those of white applicants (Bertrand & Mullainathan, 2004; Eaton et al., 2019). For example, Eaton and colleagues (2019) changed the names of eight identical CVs to manipulate how committees perceived the applicant's race and gender. They then asked 251 biology and physics professors to read one of the identical CVs to rate them for competence, hireability, and likeability for a postdoctoral position in their field. Eaton and colleagues (2019) found that faculty in both departments had racial and gender biases against hiring Black women and Latinx women and men. Faculty search committee members further diminish the qualifications of racially minoritized applicants if they did not earn their degrees at prestigious research universities, if their research or academic trajectory strays from field conventions, or if their appearance, presentation, interactive style, language, and other such characteristics are not deemed a good "fit" for the organization (Tuitt et al., 2007).

Considering the role of implicit bias in hiring decisions, university and college leaders have invested resources to implement implicit bias training, primarily for those who serve on search committees (Turner, 2002). Generally, implicit bias training should help faculty members consider the role of intercultural sensitivity (Kayes, 2006), become aware of and concerned about the effects of implicit bias, and participate in long-term interventions that teach them habit-breaking techniques (Devine et al., 2013). However, there is limited research on the impact of implicit bias interventions, and the scholarship that does exist focuses on gender diversity (Fine et al., 2014; Smith et al., 2015). Smith and colleagues (2015) conducted a randomized and controlled three-step intervention at a single university that focused on (1) increasing faculty members' competency of implicit bias, (2) enhancing their perceived autonomy to deal with implicit bias by providing concrete strategies to control it, and (3) improved their relatedness with the search by connecting search committee members to support staff during the process. They found that faculty who participated in the intervention were more likely to consider and select women for tenure-track positions compared to those who were in control groups.

COMMON STANDARDS

Faculty search committee members rarely define criteria to determine the desired characteristics and qualifications of a faculty candidate (Meizlish & Kaplan, 2008; Rivera, 2017; Tomlinson & Freeman, 2017). The lack of clearly defined evaluation criteria leads reviewers to rely on their default preferences and biases to make hiring decisions (Fujimoto, 2012; Rivera, 2017; Turner, 2002; Villalpando & Delgado-Bernal, 2002). In faculty peer review committees, professors tend to favor and positively assess applicants with similar identities to themselves (Lamont, 2009; Posselt, 2016; Rivera, 2017). When faculty prefer those with similar personal and professional backgrounds, they normalize white preference for whites as the default, which is embedded in white notions of *merit* and *fit* (Liera & Ching, 2020). Since subjectivity and value systems inform faculty evaluations (Lamont, 2009; Posselt, 2016), including faculty hiring (Rivera, 2017), clearly defined and standard criteria, including rubrics that prioritize racial equity will help mitigate implicit biases (Lee, 2014; Light, 1994; Moody, 2015; Turner, 2002). Ultimately, to racially diversify the professoriate, search committee members must use criteria that value the type of knowledge, practices, methods, and experiences racially minoritized faculty candidates embody (Turner, 2002). The criteria should help search committee members look beyond traditional understandings of research, teaching, and service (Liera & Ching, 2020).

For example, search committee members should align their hiring criteria with their organization's mission and values for equity, diversity, and inclusion. Such criteria will prioritize faculty candidates' experiences mentoring and teaching racially minoritized students and commitments to racial equity (Liera & Ching, 2020). Sensoy and DiAngelo (2017) caution search committee members not to treat equity, diversity, and inclusion efforts, including criteria, as add-on evaluation metrics. Search committee members should prioritize criteria for racial equity in job announcements, interview questions, evaluation rubrics, campus visits, and final hiring decisions.

Faculty search committee members should design and implement standard criteria through long-term interventions that provide them with an opportunity to understand their campus culture and campus racial climate (Light, 1994; Tierney & Sallee, 2010). They should develop such strategies to address organizational barriers that exist in the local context. In the next section, I define inquiry and synthesize literature that focuses on faculty learning how to advance racial equity through inquiry-based interventions, before outlining action steps to help disrupt inequities.

Inquiry-Based Intervention as a Lever for Racial Equity in Faculty Hiring

Bensimon (2007) argues that addressing racial equity requires inquiry-based interventions for practitioners to reflect on their concept of equity, their role as advocates for racially minoritized students, the extent to which their practices serve racially minoritized students, and the changes they can make to achieve racial equity. With roots in neo-Marxism and human rights activism, an inquiry is a process designed to bring together researchers and practitioners to develop a sense of shared ownership of research projects, collectively analyze social problems, and act to transform the local environment (Kemmis & McTaggart, 2000). This approach to inquiry aligns with TRERP's recognition that practitioners are involved in knowledge production that informs organizational change (this volume). According to the action research principles that undergird the inquiry process, practical reasoning is not about identifying the "right" solution to remedy a situation; instead, it is about educating practitioners, fostering an understanding of "the nature and consequences of their actions more fully" and "assist[ing] them in weighing what should be done as a guide to (but not a prescription for) action" (Kemmis & McTaggart, 2000, p. 584). Through a focus on actions and the reasoning behind them, an inquiry-based intervention has the potential to activate a reflective process through which practitioners can question whether and how their practices contribute to mitigating and undermining organizational change (Witham & Bensimon, 2012).

Similar to TRERP's second proposition, inquiry-based interventions provide practitioners with the tools and language to study how their practices and assumptions, and those of their colleagues, reproduce racial inequity (Bensimon & Malcom, 2012; Bragg et al., 2016; Dowd & Bensimon, 2015; Dowd et al., 2015; Dowd & Liera, 2019). Typically, inquiry-based interventions follow a similar inquiry cycle, including (1) identifying equity gaps in outcomes; (2) questioning practices, policies, and cultures; (3) purposefully changing practices, policies, and cultures based on the results of systematic inquiry; (4) and evaluating the effectiveness of changes (Center for Urban Education, 2016). For example, data disaggregated by race helps practitioners evaluate structures, programs, and offices that impede the success of racially minoritized students. Practitioners have used data disaggregated by race to identify where inequities exist and which practices have a direct (e.g., faculty expertise) and indirect (e.g., faculty hiring practices) impact on student outcomes (Dowd et al., 2015; Liera & Dowd, 2019; Peña, 2012). In addition to using equity-minded tools and language, practitioners participate in inquiry-based activities to map out the process of their practices and where they reproduce racial inequity (Dowd & Bensimon, 2015). Ching (2018) studied how participation in an inquiry-based intervention workshop on assessing course syllabi for equity-mindedness and cultural inclusivity fostered learning about the effect teaching practices and classroom environments have on racially minoritized students and racial equity for community college math faculty. In alignment with TRERP's fifth proposition, this body of research asserts that changes to practices that perpetuate racial inequity support the sustainability of organizational change efforts to advance racial equity.

In the context of hiring, equity-minded practices guide faculty search committee members to be race- and critical-conscious when considering who they want to hire and what they value in a potential faculty colleague. Liera and Ching (2020) proposed an equity-minded approach to reframe traditional understandings of *merit* and *fit* in administrative and faculty hiring. They argued that equity-minded conceptions of merit and fit focus on what administrator and faculty candidates do to advance racial equity for students and their campus and how they do so. For example, equity-minded merit criteria include experience teaching and mentoring racially minoritized students, ability to critically reflect on how campus practices reproduce inequalities, and expertise creating and leading initiatives designed to improve the campus culture for racially minoritized groups. With equity-minded fit, the focus is on hiring administrator and faculty candidates who reflect the racial diversity of the student body, and importantly, students' experiences, epistemologies, and social interests (Liera & Ching, 2020). Equity-minded hiring practices help search committee members assess whether faculty candidates are competent in equity-mindedness. According to Estela Bensimon, there are at least five equity-minded competencies. Equity-minded practitioners (1) understand the accountability and critical dimensions of equity, (2) reframe race-based inequities as a problem of practice and view their elimination as an individual and collective responsibility, (3) encourage positive race consciousness, (4) reflect on organizational practices and aim to make them more culturally relevant, and (5) strategically navigate resistance to equity efforts and aim to build buy-in among colleagues (Center for Urban Education, 2019).

In the rest of this section, I summarize an empirical study where I examined a group of tenure-track and tenured faculty members who participated in a long-term inquiry-based intervention to advance racial equity through their faculty hiring structure (see Liera, 2020b, for the research design and theoretical framework of the study). The significant findings of the study will help set the foundation for the recommendations I propose to support college and university leaders designing an inquiry-based intervention. With the support of researchers from the Center for Urban Education (CUE) at the University of Southern California, the university provost and two faculty leaders identified and invited 15 faculty members to participate in a 10-month inquiry-based intervention. CUE researchers designed seven workshops throughout 10 months for faculty to identify the ways their campus racial culture impeded the advancement of racial equity in faculty hiring. A critical inquiry activity required faculty to map out their faculty hiring process and identify areas where the process reproduced inequalities. The group of faculty mapped out their hiring process into three sections, including recruitment, interviews, and hiring decisions. Ultimately, the faculty made three major policy changes to their hiring process. First, all faculty participants in search committees will be required to take an implicit bias training. Second, each search committee will be required to have at least two faculty members with training on racial equity and equity-mindedness. Finally, search committee chairs will be required to provide written proof to the provost that their search committee took every measure to implement equity-minded language and templates. In the next section, I outline the different inquiry activities that helped faculty identify the necessary changes for them to advance racial equity through their faculty hiring process.

Equity-Minded Inquiry Activities

In this section, I outline six inquiry activities that helped faculty interrogate taken-for-granted practices and values that impeded their racial equity efforts. In questioning their hiring practices, they used an equity-minded lens to redesign various aspects of their hiring process, including recruitment, interviews, and evaluation rubrics to advance racial equity. Ultimately, the activities helped faculty develop multifocal strategies that helped them fundamentally alter how they recruited and hired faculty members.

DEFINING AND FRAMING RACIAL EQUITY IN FACULTY HIRING

Higher education practitioners often conflate equity with equality and diversity, which makes it feasible to move away from interrogating power dynamics and the campus racial culture (Bensimon & Malcom, 2012; Dowd & Bensimon, 2015). Investing time to clearly define racial equity and equity-mindedness in order to leverage faculty hiring as a vehicle for change will guide faculty to create practices to overcome organizational barriers. Practitioners who experience success in scaling-up their change efforts reflected on and defined the various components of the theory of change proposed by scholars who study organizational change (Kezar et al., 2015). Within this chapter, the theory of change is an inquiry-based intervention framed within the theoretical foundations of TRERP. Through the cycle of inquiry, faculty who use an equity-minded lens to question their unspoken hiring norms and practices develop the local knowledge to identify where and how in the search process racial inequities get reproduced. Given such knowledge, faculty make necessary changes to mitigate biases that perpetuate racial inequity in hiring decisions. A specific definition of racial equity that emphasizes institutionalizing racially diverse perspectives in the cultural fabric of an organization has helped faculty prioritize equity-mindedness throughout the multiple aspects of their hiring process. For example, faculty in Liera's (2020b) study rethought their racial equity efforts in faculty hiring as an action-oriented, organizational effort to use equity-minded language to create a more racially equitable campus culture. The framing of racial equity as an effort to embed racially diverse perspectives into the cultural fabric of an organization helped faculty focus their efforts beyond just having equitable outcomes. Thus, the faculty used an equity-minded framework, which reflects TRERP's propositions, to create hiring templates that prioritized equity-minded competencies and faculty who can advance their racial equity efforts.

ANALYZING THE FACULTY HIRING PROCESS FOR EQUITY GAPS

Scholars have found that higher education practitioners who apply a theory of change learned about the limitations of their implicit theories of change (Kezar et al., 2015), deficit mindsets (Bensimon & Malcom, 2012; Dowd & Bensimon, 2015), and existing practices (Ching, 2018). In addition to defining a common language, faculty should invest time to use TRERP's propositions to analyze the various aspects of their hiring structure. Mapping out the faculty hiring structure into smaller components provides faculty opportunities to identify where inequalities are reproduced throughout the hiring process. The activity should use the existing faculty hiring policy that facilitates the perspectives and behaviors of search committee members during their recruitment, evaluation, and decision-making. As they break the faculty hiring policy down, faculty can identify specific activities they can design to further interrogate unspoken and taken-for-granted hiring practices and routines. In the rest of this section, I outline four areas of the hiring process where faculty in Liera's (2020b) study engaged inquiry to help them prioritize equity-mindedness.

CREATING EQUITY-MINDED JOB ANNOUNCEMENTS

There are various benefits for faculty members to use an equity-minded lens to analyze their job announcements. For example, an equity-minded inquiry approach helps faculty reflect upon the messages they convey through job announcements, including what job announcements communicate about the college's values, identity, goals, and approach. Moreover, faculty members will also uncover hidden assumptions about students, which provides them with insight on how to embed equity-mindedness in job announcements and attract faculty applicants who hold equity-minded values. Liera and Ching (2020) proposed that inquiry into job announcements investigates the language used, with a specific focus on the presence or absence of equity-minded and deficit-minded terms, the location of these terms in the announcement, and the frequency with which they appear. They further present an equity word search worksheet that faculty can use to identify, count, and locate equity-minded and deficit-minded terms. Such an activity gives faculty members a systematic way to analyze whether job announcements convey a priority for hiring racially minoritized, equity-minded faculty, or whether they signal a desire for candidates whose backgrounds reflect majority racial groups.

In addition to implementing equity-minded language, faculty should also utilize the preferred qualifications and application materials to require that faculty applicants discuss their experiences with and commitment to racial equity. For example, search committee members should require faculty applicants to write about their experiences with and commitment to racial equity in their cover letter instead of within a separate equity, diversity, and inclusion statement. When they prioritize equity-mindedness in the cover letter, faculty search committee members signal to potential faculty applicants that they value equity and want a faculty colleague who will help them advance their equity goals.

IDENTIFYING IMPLICIT BIASES

Since individuals hold implicit associations and attitudes about racial groups, faculty search committees should design interventions to help them "debias" existing associations and attitudes, mitigate the effects of bias, and prevent biases from affecting behavior (Godsil et al., 2015). Faculty members in Liera's (2020b) study participated in an inquiry activity where they wrote on index cards examples of implicit biases that they have observed during faculty search committee meetings. As part of the activity, faculty worked in small groups to discuss the various ways implicit biases shaped hiring decisions. After small group discussions, faculty shared-out with the entire group and used the index cards as data to group the different types of biases. In faculty hiring, biases often operate through unspoken norms and taken-for-granted understandings of merit and fit. Specifically, traditional conceptions of merit and fit are reflections of white, male sociocultural norms. In addition to collecting organizational-level data on implicit biases in faculty hiring, faculty members can apply TRERP to redefine conceptions of merit and fit. Faculty members can role-play a faculty search committee where conversations are framed through existing biases of merit and fit. After the role-play, faculty should reflect on the types of qualifications and experiences they value in faculty candidates and how their expectations might be biased.

In their book chapter, Liera and Ching (2020) outlined questions search committee members can use to guide their inquiry into biases regarding merit and fit and how to reconceptualize it. They proposed search committee members complete the following sentences on separate sheets of paper: (a) "When considering a candidate's 'merit' for this position, I think about these qualities . . ."; (b) "When considering a candidate's 'fit' for this position, I think about these qualities . . ." (p. 125). After answering the questions, the faculty should group the responses for merit and the responses for fit, then separately discuss what they wrote for merit and what they wrote for fit. Liera and Ching (2020) also provided the following questions to structure the discussions: (a) "What do our responses suggest about the criteria for merit and fit that we associate with this position?"; (b) "In what ways do these criteria for merit and fit align with traditional conceptions? Equity-minded conceptions?"; (c) "Based on these criteria for merit and fit, who will likely surface as strong candidates for the position?"; (d) "How would these criteria for merit and fit impact candidates from racially minoritized groups?" (p. 127). Based on the discussions, participants in the exercise can construct merit and fit criteria for the position that incorporate the equity-minded competencies described in the previous section and that search committee members agree to use in their evaluation of candidates.

ALIGNING INTERVIEW QUESTIONS WITH RACIAL EQUITY GOALS

Interviews are an essential component of the hiring process. It is during the interview that faculty candidates can speak to the qualifications they believe make them worthy for the position and demonstrate qualities that make them suitable for the job specifically and the organization more generally. However, what candidates are able to share during the interview depends on the questions search committee members ask. For example, if search committee members do not ask faculty candidates about their experiences working with racially minoritized students, then candidates do not have an opening to speak about their commitment to racial equity. Similar to mapping out the faculty hiring process, faculty in Liera's (2020b) study mapped out their interview goals, interview questions, and equity goals. The faculty created a table to map how core interview questions aligned with their interview goals. The inquiry activity of mapping interview questions with interview and equity goals helps faculty identify patterns in their questions and investigate whether their interview protocol prioritizes equity-mindedness and racial equity. In addition to interview questions about research, service, and teaching, faculty search committee members can develop questions to assess faculty applicants' competency for equity-mindedness. Interview questions should focus on whether faculty applicants understand the role of their professional and social experiences in their preparation to work in environments where equity is valued, are aware about the role of historical structural barriers racially minoritized groups encounter, have modified their teaching and advising approaches to meet the needs of racially minoritized groups, and have helped create a racially equitable work environment.

DESIGNING EQUITY-MINDED RUBRICS

Structured evaluation rubrics can minimize the impact of bias and increase transparency within hiring processes. Generally, quantitative ratings on evaluation rubrics should provide instruction on what type of response, behavior, and achievement corresponds to each rating level; while qualitative comments on evaluation rubrics should provide written assessments of candidate responses. An equity-minded rubric should include faculty candidates' commitment to work with racially diverse populations or to engage in efforts to advance racial equity as part of the minimum requirements when possible, or preferred qualifications at a minimum. Each criterion, specifically those assessing equity-minded competencies, should be clearly defined, including potential sources of evidence and rubric anchors. For example, faculty in Liera's (2020b) study created an equity-minded template where they included criteria to evaluate whether faculty candidates had the qualifications to mentor racially minoritized students, implement culturally relevant pedagogy, and advance the university's identity as a Hispanic-serving institution. Potential sources of evidence for mentoring racially minoritized students included: a track record of participation in activities aimed to reduce barriers in education and experience working with racially minoritized groups as documented on the CV, cover letter, research focus, teaching statement, publications, and letters of recommendation. To advance the university's racial equity goals, the faculty also defined quantitative anchors to minimize assessing faculty candidates who provided general statements of diversity as exemplary, proficient, or competent.

Search committee members should define the sources of evidence and anchors to distinguish faculty candidates with complex understandings of racial equity and qualifications to advance an organization's racial equity goals. For example, CUE has provided criteria for search committee members to screen faculty applicants for equity-minded competency, which may be helpful sources to draw upon. CUE proposed five criteria to assess faculty candidates' critical consciousness, self-reflection, sense of ownership to remove structural barriers, experience supporting racially minoritized groups, and use of asset-based approaches to interact with racially minoritized students (see Center for Urban Education, 2019).

Organizational Conditions to Design an Equity-Minded Inquiry-Based Intervention

In this section, I provide recommendations for higher education leaders to consider when deciding whether to invest in an inquiry-based intervention. As I provide recommendations, I acknowledge the various challenges that arise when designing an inquiry-based intervention for faculty members and high-level administrators to participate in across the silos of higher education organizations. Whether the organizational challenges consist of limited resources, including time and compensation, or outright resistance to change, higher education leaders should review the following recommendations in their decision to implement an inquiry-based intervention that models TRERP's propositions.

VISIBLE AND ONGOING LEADERSHIP SUPPORT

Campus-wide organizational change efforts benefit from the support of university and college leaders. Regarding faculty hiring, those in relative positions of power, including deans, department chairs, and search chairs, need to be committed to prioritizing equity-mindedness in faculty hiring as a leverage to create a more racially equitable campus culture. Administrative leaders can include a conversation, presentation, or update on racial equity efforts during departmental, college, or campus-wide meetings. Additionally, a provost, dean, or faculty governance chair can integrate workshops on racial equity and equity-mindedness in faculty hiring during faculty retreats.

The reality at most campuses is that not everyone will buy into changing faculty hiring, let alone prioritize equity-mindedness to hire more racially minoritized faculty members. With this in mind, those advancing racial equity through faculty hiring should strategize ways to publicize their efforts. Sharing the impact inquiry has had on learning and outcomes will help reach people from across campus, which can build the legitimacy of the process. Administrative leaders can also effectively utilize the campus newsletter to communicate about any racial equity efforts to the general campus population.

IDENTIFY AND SUPPORT FACULTY MEMBERS TO LEAD EFFORTS

Since tenure-track and tenured faculty members are gatekeepers of faculty hiring, leaders' identifying faculty who have expressed interest and have been committed to racial equity in any capacity will help establish a strong core of people to advance the work. In so doing, higher education leaders must acknowledge that changing organizational structures requires time and energy to negotiate existing systems of power. For these reasons, higher education leaders need to financially compensate faculty members who are tasked to prioritize and embed equity-mindedness in faculty hiring. Higher education leaders can also provide release time from teaching courses and committee work for faculty to invest their time in racial equity work.

ESTABLISH GROUND RULES

Whether faculty participate in cross-campus or departmental-level inquiry interventions, as a group, faculty should create ground rules to minimize potential tensions that will impede learning and organizational change. Faculty should design ground rules about honest conversations, within-group accountability, and confidentiality to build trusting relationships to support their racial equity efforts given existing organizational barriers of their campus. Trust is key to identify and change organizational barriers in faculty hiring that impede racial equity efforts. So, a primary goal of inquiry is to engage the same group of faculty members in the work from the beginning to the end of the hiring cycle. As with other campus conversations, faculty should design ground rules that will support their racial equity efforts through inquiry.

Conclusion

Calls for change in the racial demographics of the professoriate and in evaluations of faculty search committees are not new. In this chapter, I outlined "best practices" that administrative and faculty leaders could use as starting points to racially diversify their faculty bodies. Reflecting TRERP's propositions, I argued that inquiry-based interventions that centralize equity-mindedness provide administrators and faculty with the local knowledge to realize racial equity in faculty hiring.

References

Baez, B. (2000). Race-related service and faculty of color: Conceptualizing critical agency in academe. *Higher Education, 39*(3), 363–391.

Beattie, G., Cohen, D., & McGuire, L. (2013). An exploration of possible unconscious ethnic biases in higher education: The role of implicit attitudes on selection for university posts. *Semiotica, 197,* 171–201.

Bensimon, E. M. (2007). The underestimated significance of practitioner knowledge in the scholarship on student success. *Review of Higher Education, 30*(4), 441–469.

Bensimon, E. M., & Malcom, L. (2012). *Confronting equity issues on campus: Implementing the equity scorecard in theory and practice.* Stylus.

Bertrand, M., & Mullainathan, S. (2004). Are Emily and Greg more employable than Lakisha and Jamal? A field experiment on labor market discrimination. *American Economic Review, 94*(4), 991–1013.

Bilimoria, D., & Buch, K. K. (2010). The search is on: Engendering faculty diversity through more effective search and recruitment. *Magazine of Higher Learning, 42*(4), 27–32.

Bragg, D. D., McCambly, H., & Durham, B. (2016). Catching the spark: Student activism and student data as a catalyst for systemic transformation. *Change: The Magazine of Higher Learning, 48*(3), 36–46.

Center for Urban Education. (2016). An introduction to the Equity Scorecard. https://cue.usc.edu/files/2016/01/Introduction-to-the-EqS.pdf

Center for Urban Education. (2019). *Institute on Equity in Faculty Hiring at Community Colleges Toolkit.* Rossier School of Education, University of Southern California.

Ching, C. D. (2018). Confronting the equity "learning problem" through practitioner inquiry. *The Review of Higher Education, 41*(3), 387–421.

Delgado-Bernal, D., & Villalpando, O. (2002). An apartheid of knowledge in academia: The struggle over the "legitimate" knowledge of faculty of color. *Equity & Excellence in Education, 35*(2), 169–180.

DiTomaso, N. (2015). Racism and discrimination versus advantage and favoritism: Bias for versus bias against. *Research in Organizational Behavior, 35,* 57–77.

Dowd, A. C., & Bensimon, E. M. (2015). *Engaging the "race question": Accountability and equity in U.S. higher education.* Teachers College Press.

Dowd, A. C., Bishop, R., & Bensimon, E. M. (2015). Critical action research on race and equity in higher education. In A. M. Martínez-Alemán, B. Pusser, & E. M. Bensimon (Eds.), *Critical approaches to the study of higher education: A practical introduction* (pp. 174–192). Johns Hopkins University Press.

Dowd, A. C., & Liera, R. (2018). Sustaining organizational change towards racial equity through cycles of inquiry. *Education Policy Analysis Archives, 26*(65), 1–46.

Eaton, A. A., Saunders, J. F., Jacobson, R. K., & West, K. (2019). How gender and race stereotypes impact the achievement of scholars in STEM: Professors' biased evaluations of physics and biology post-doctoral candidates. *Sex Roles,* 1–15.

Fujimoto, E. O. (2012). Hiring diverse faculty members in community college: A case study in ethical decision making. *Community College Review, 40*(3), 255–274.

Godsil, R. D., Tropp, L. R., Goff, P. A., & powell, j. a. (2014). *Addressing implicit bias, racial anxiety, and stereotype threat in education and health care.* Perception Institute.

Gonzales, L. D. (2018). Subverting and minding boundaries: The intellectual work of women. *Journal of Higher Education, 89*(5), 677–701.

Kayes, P. E. (2006). New paradigms for diversifying faculty and staff in higher education: Uncovering cultural biases in the search and hiring process. *Multicultural Education, 14,* 65–69.

Kemmis, S., & McTaggart, R. (2000). Participatory action research. In N. K. Denzin & Y. S. Lincoln (Eds.), *Handbook of qualitative research* (2nd ed., pp. 567–605). Sage.

Kezar, A., Gehrke, S., & Elrod, S. (2015). Implicit theories of change as a barrier to change on college campuses: An examination of STEM reform. *Review of Higher Education, 38*(4), 479–506.

Lamont, M. (2009). *How professors think: Inside the curious world of academic judgment*. Harvard University Press.

Lee, C. D. (2014). *Search committees: A comprehensive guide to successful faculty, staff, and administrative searches*. Stylus.

Liera, R. (2020a). Equity advocates using equity-mindedness to interrupt faculty hiring's racial structure. *Teachers College Record, 122*(9), 1–42.

Liera, R. (2020b). Moving beyond a culture of niceness in faculty hiring to advance racial equity. *American Educational Research Journal, 57*(5), 1954–1994.

Liera, R., & Ching, C. (2020). Reconceptualizing "merit" and "fit": An equity-minded approach to hiring. In A. Kezar & J. Posselt (Eds.), *Administration for social justice and equity in higher education: Critical perspectives for leadership and decision-making* (pp. 111–131). Routledge.

Liera, R., & Dowd, A. C. (2019). Faculty learning at boundaries to broker racial equity. *Journal of Higher Education, 90*(3), 462–485.

Light, P. (1994). "Not like us": Removing the barriers to recruiting minority faculty. *Journal of Policy Analysis and Management, 13*, 164–180.

McMurtrie, B. (2016, September). How to do a better job of searching for diversity. *Chronicle of Higher Education.* http://www.chronicle.com/article/How-to-Do-a-Better-Job-of/237750

Meizlish, D., & Kaplan, M. (2008). Valuing and evaluating teaching in academic hiring: A multidisciplinary, cross-institutional study. *Journal of Higher Education, 79*(5), 489–512.

Moody, J. (2015). *Rising above cognitive errors: Improving searches, evaluations, and decision-making*. CreateSpace.

Muñoz, S. M., Basile, V., Gonzalez, J., Birmingham, D., Aragon, A., Jennings, L., & Gloeckner, G. (2017). (Counter)narratives and complexities: Critical perspectives from a university cluster hire focused on diversity, equity, and inclusion. *Journal of Critical Thought and Praxis, 6*(2), 1–21.

National Center for Education Statistics, U.S. Department of Education. (2016). Postsecondary education: Characteristics of postsecondary faculty. In *The condition of education 2016* (NCES 2016-144, pp. 222–225). Washington, DC: Author.

Peña, E. V. (2012). Inquiry methods for critical consciousness and self-change in faculty. *Review of Higher Education, 36*(1), 69–92.

Posselt, J. R. (2016). *Inside graduate admissions: Merit, diversity, and faculty gatekeeping*. Harvard University Press.

Rivera, L. (2017). When two bodies are (not) a problem: Gender and relationship status discrimination in academic hiring. *American Sociological Review, 82*(6), 1111–1138.

Sackett, P. R., DuBois, C. L., & Noe, A. W. (1991). Tokenism in performance evaluations: The effects of work-group representation on male-female and

white-black differences in performance ratings. *Journal of Applied Psychology*, 41(7–8), 263–528.
Sensoy, Ö., & DiAngelo, R. (2017). "We are all for diversity, but . . .": How faculty hiring committees reproduce whiteness and practical suggestions for how they can change. *Harvard Educational Review*, 87, 557–581.
Smith, D. G. (2000). How to diversify the faculty. *Academe*, 86(5), 48–52.
Smith, D. G. (2009). *Diversity's promise for higher education: Making it work*. Johns Hopkins University Press.
Smith, D. G., Turner, C. S. V., Osei-Kofi, N., & Richards, S. (2004). Interrupting the usual: Successful strategies for hiring diverse faculty. *Journal of Higher Education*, 75(2), 133–160.
Smith, J. L., Handley, I. M., Zale, A. V., Rushing, S., & Potvin, M. A. (2015). Now hiring! Empirically testing a three-step intervention to increase the faculty gender diversity in STEM. *Bioscience*, 65(11), 1084–1087.
Tierney, W. G., & Sallee, M. W. (2010). Do organizational structures and strategies increase faculty diversity? A cultural analysis. *American Academic*, 4(July), 159–184.
Tomlinson, G., & Freeman, S. (2017). Who really selected you? Insights into faculty selection processes in top-ranked higher education graduate programmes. *Journal of Further and Higher Education*, 1–14.
Tuitt, F. A., Danowitz Sagaria, M. A., & Turner, C. S. V. (2007). Signals and strategies in hiring faculty of color. In J. C. Smart (Ed.), *Higher education: Handbook of theory and research* (vol. 22, pp. 497–535). Springer.
Turner, C. S. V. (2002). *Diversifying the faculty: A guidebook for search committees*. American Association of Colleges and Universities.
Turner, C. S., González, J. C., & Wood, J. L. (2008). Faculty of color in academe: What 20 years of literature tell us. *Journal of Diversity in Higher Education*, 1(3), 139–168.
Villalpando, V., & Delgado-Bernal, D. (2002). A critical race theory analysis of barriers that impede the success of faculty of color. In W. A. Smith, P. G. Altbach, & K. Lomotey (Eds.), *The racial crisis in American higher education* (pp. 243–269). State University of New York Press.
White-Lewis, D. K. (2020a). Before the ad: How departments generate hiring priorities that support or avert faculty diversity. *Teachers College Record*, 123(1), 1–36.
White-Lewis, D. K. (2020b). The façade of fit in faculty search processes. *Journal of Higher Education*, 91(6), 833–857.
Witham, K., & Bensimon, E. M. (2012). Creating a culture of inquiry around equity and student success. In S. D. Museus & U. M. Jayakumar (Eds.), *Creating campus cultures: Fostering success among racially diverse student populations* (pp. 46–67). Routledge.

2

Leveraging Campus-wide Leadership Collaborations for Equity

AMANDA TAYLOR AND EVELYN AMBRIZ

Institutions of higher education, even those with inclusion-driven missions, often fall short of their goals to counter historic and entrenched policies and practices that exclude and marginalize people based on race, class, gender identity and/or expression, sexual orientation, and other structures of power (Bensimon et al., 2016; Templeton et al., 2016; Turner, 2003). Consistent with the translational racial equity research-practice (TRERP) framework guiding this volume, the role of those who "work on the ground," such as university leaders, is critical for helping dismantle structures and practices that reproduce race-based disparities. While the commitment of skillful university leaders is vital to create systemic change, traditional top-down leadership alone is not sufficient to dismantle the entrenched intersecting systems that sustain these oppressions (Astin & Astin, 2000; Hurtado et al., 1999; Williams, 2013). Shared leadership approaches and structures (Kezar & Holcombe 2017; Ishimaru & Galloway, 2014; Spillane et al., 2007), on the other hand, can help universities work toward equity. This chapter specifically focuses on how shared leadership structures can help advance racial

---

Note. The authors would like to thank the leadership team of American University's Presidential Council on Diversity and Inclusion (PCDI) for their helpful insights and feedback on this chapter, especially Eric Brock Jr., Rafael Cestero, Bridget Cooney, Consuelo Grier, Andrew Toczydlowski, and Ximena Varela.

equity, which we define as dismantling race-based disparities and challenging structures and practices that reproduce inequity and uphold the status quo. Such shared leadership is also key to addressing other forms of marginalization in higher education.

To facilitate such campus-wide shared leadership for racial equity, many universities engage in cross-campus collaborations, including diversity and inclusion councils. Although there are multiple forms of shared leadership collaborations in higher education, this chapter focuses explicitly on university-wide diversity and inclusion councils with close connections to the institution's president. These councils, often appointed by and reporting to the university president, are typically comprised of faculty, staff, administrators, and students who draw from their different campus perspectives and lived experiences to collaboratively lead campus-wide equity efforts (LePeau, 2015). While some research has begun to examine the structure and function of presidential diversity and inclusion councils (LePeau et al., 2019), key questions remain about how to best mobilize, utilize, and develop these collaborations to function inclusively, fully realize their potential impact, and sustain them over time. Moreover, little attention is paid to how to these collaborations can center and engage the expertise of students, particularly students of color, to ensure efforts to improve the campus racial climate resonate with those most impacted.

This chapter examines the strategic role of campus-wide shared leadership collaborations, specifically diversity and inclusion councils, to advance racial equity and pay special attention to student engagement in these efforts. The chapter begins with a brief overview of the literature on shared leadership collaborations for racial equity in higher education. It then articulates what is known about the existing structures and functions of diversity and inclusion councils and highlights the important role of student leadership. The chapter closes with recommendations for higher education leaders who seek to begin, sustain, and/or deepen the impact of these leadership collaborations to advance racial equity.

The Case for Leadership Collaborations for Equity

Leading for equity in higher education is a complex process, requiring a multipronged, cross-campus, and sustainable long-term approach (Hurtado et al., 1999; Milem et al., 2005). Though the unwavering support of the university president and of campus leaders is essential to advance equity, this work cannot be achieved by isolated efforts of individual community members and positional leaders (Bensimon & Neumann, 1993). Leadership for equity must be distributed across the organization so a range of organizational members, especially those whose voices might otherwise be marginalized, can contribute different perspectives, expertise, and insights to understanding the problem and creating innovative solutions that garner community buy-in, reduce unintended consequences, and increase equitable impact (Ishimaru & Galloway, 2014; Kezar, 2008; Kezar et al., 2008; Spillane et al., 2007).

Shared leadership approaches can also challenge normative beliefs, assumptions, and practices that sustain uneven power relationships and serve as barriers to trust and equal opportunity in the academy. Rather than assuming that knowledge is concentrated in a few (often predominantly white male) leaders "at the top," shared leadership approaches recognize that expertise necessary for equitable leadership is distributed across campus community members from a range of backgrounds. Shared leadership approaches bring people who might not otherwise meaningfully interact due to power and status differences into sustained and authentic relationships (Astin & Astin, 2000), challenging unconscious biases that perpetuate unfair practices and growing a more inclusive campus culture. Collaborative efforts value the production of innovative ideas that individuals could not achieve alone (Freeman, 1993), challenging higher education's entrenched individualistic culture that often rewards those who have already had more access to opportunity. Finally, shared leadership collaborations that distribute work across multiple people can also build institutional memory, regardless of administrative (or student) turnover (Holcombe & Kezar, 2017), making the long-term work necessary for equity initiatives more likely to continue over time.

Diversity and Inclusion Councils as Leadership Collaborations for Equity

Many universities have established diversity and inclusion councils to collaboratively lead campus-wide equity efforts (LePeau, 2015). Williams (2013) defines these collaborations as "diversity stakeholders who have formally joined forces to shape and in some instances implement a shared plan for the future relative to diversity in a particular organizational context" (p. 409). University presidents typically establish these councils to respond to on-campus racial crises or controversies, maintain compliance with federal regulations, and/or proactively address systemic issues of injustice and inequity on campus.

The precise focus of these collaborations varies depending on the developmental phase of the institution's diversity and inclusion efforts, though almost all aim to increase compositional diversity and advance campus-wide inclusion. Depending on their specific charge, these collaborative groups focus on three types of activities to varied degrees. First, diversity and inclusion councils can focus on strategic planning when charged with setting the institution's overall diversity agenda. Second, councils can have oversight of campus policies and procedures, when charged with campus climate assessment, updating human resources–related processes (e.g., recruitment and hiring), or revising institutional policies. Finally, councils can lead implementation of diversity training and campus-wide programming when charged with increasing awareness of bias reporting or nondiscrimination policies (LePeau et al., 2019).

Challenges to Shared Leadership Collaborations for Equity in Higher Education

Shared leadership collaborations like diversity and inclusion councils seem an intuitive approach for racial equity efforts in higher education, where cross-disciplinary approaches, multiple perspectives, and research teams—all forms of collaboration—are the gold standards for innovation and quality (Kezar & Lester, 2009). However, many cross-campus collaborations designed to enact racial equity do not fully engage the diverse perspectives of their participants and do not meaningfully challenge the entrenched power dynamics that sustain inequity (Holcombe & Kezar, 2017). Indeed, diversity and inclusion councils are not immune from the real and perceived cultural, status, and power dynamics in higher education that can make equitable collaboration challenging (LePeau, 2015).

Some of these challenges include divisions between student affairs and academic affairs units, deficit-oriented beliefs that students are apathetic (Kirshner & Ginwright, 2012) or oppositional (Slocum & Rhoads, 2009), and racist ideas that devalue contributions of people of color (Bensimon & Neumann, 1993). Without themselves engaging intentionally inclusive processes and practices, diversity and inclusion councils risk—counterintuitively—further excluding individuals from marginalized backgrounds and those with less power and status in the organization. Further, cross-university bodies that do not address existing power differentials among members tend to focus on surface-level cooperation—getting along, coordinating initiatives, sharing information, or achieving tasks with partners (Kezar & Lester, 2009), efforts that are unlikely to foster the deeper-level transformations necessary for system-wide equity (Kezar, 2008).

Strategies for Effective Higher Education Equity Collaborations

Contemporary scholarship begins to examine successful strategies that multistakeholder institution-wide partnerships, including diversity and inclusion councils, can employ to address the challenges to collaborative leadership in the academy and effectively drive campus-wide change. Importantly, diversity and inclusion councils are positioned to advance equity, focusing their efforts beyond increasing representational diversity on campus. They also work to create an inclusive institutional culture and advance structural changes to university policies, procedures, and practices (LePeau et al., 2019). Successful cross-campus collaborations are nimble enough to help the institution maintain a sustained focus on achieving equity goals, even amid inevitable leadership turnover, campus climate issues, and budget fluctuations (LePeau, 2015).

Key is that participants in successful collaborations recognize the institution's developmental stage in terms of diversity and inclusion efforts (Kezar, 2007). An early institutional stage is mobilization, which often involves building an initial diversity and inclusion plan; a mid-stage is implementation, which often includes energizing an existing diversity and inclusion plan and building support for the plan. Finally, a deeper institutionalization phase often involves routinizing efforts and building new reward and accountability structures to increase a diversity and inclusion plan's probability for long-lasting success (Kezar, 2007). Participants in cross-campus leadership collaborations must be skilled and flexible enough to respond to the leadership actions necessary for each institutional stage, including priority-setting, developing momentum, and consensus-building (Kezar, 2007).

Successful university-wide equity collaborations can take different forms and structures; however, they all bridge traditional divides between academic and student affairs, and between students, faculty, and administrators. To do so, collaborations must challenge status differentials between group members, modeling inclusion for the university community. Institutional leadership should codetermine the vision and mission for equity with collaboration participants. When selecting participants, institutional leaders should pay special attention to include traditionally marginalized and disenfranchised voices on campus—namely, administrators without a role-based leadership title and students, particularly those with marginalized identities. And though tensions may arise between members and established institutional norms and practices entrenched in the status quo, relationships among participants create space to voice concerns and find collaborative and strategic ways to move forward.

Role of Students in Institutional Collaborations for Equity

Importantly, in this chapter, we argue that students are vital collaborators as cross-campus teams work to codetermine the problem of racial inequity on campus, identify solutions, and evaluate impact. While much existing scholarship explores how and why students actively mobilize against university leadership in pursuit of racial equity on campuses (e.g., Gaston-Gayles et al., 2004; Slocum & Rhoads, 2009, students, and students of color in particular, bring key insights and expertise to campus climate discussions and valuable ideas for effective solutions. Additionally, students report less discrimination and bias at institutions that actively involve students in decision-making processes regarding campus climate (U.S. Department of Education, 2016, p. 3). Engaging students of color and other minoritized students in cross-campus equity efforts can also help correct the historic marginalization of these students from campus leadership development opportunities (Guthrie et al., 2013).

Further, involving students, and especially historically marginalized students, in decision-making for racial equity efforts increases organizational efficacy. When efforts to develop and implement equity-oriented solutions center the perspectives of students most negatively impacted by inequity on campus, institutions can help ensure policies, programs, and practices designed to advance equity truly resonate with the student experience. After all, those most knowledgeable about the student experience are students themselves; and students of color hold the deepest understanding of current campus climate issues impacting student communities of color. Meaningfully engaging students of color is also an important way to concretely reflect an asset-based approach that values the perspectives and contributions of students of color, and to directly counter problematic deficit orientations focused only on what students of color are "missing" or what they "need."

Finally, trust between students, faculty, and staff grows when students are engaged in meaningful, non-tokenizing work as partners in equity-focused campus collaborations. Students involved in truly collaborative endeavors also gain negotiation and communication skills as they express their ideas and perspectives (Menon, 2003), which are key leadership skills for living and working in a diverse and changing world (AACU, 2012; Astin & Astin, 2000). Faculty, staff, and administrators also learn new perspectives from and with students as they partner to problem solve and address equity challenges on campus.

Recommendations for Practice

The following recommendations aim to offer concrete ideas and strategies to support university leaders as they seek to build, support, and sustain the impact of equity-focused campus collaborations like diversity and inclusion councils. We draw from the body of empirical research described earlier in this chapter as well as our experiential knowledge, gained by serving in various higher education equity-focused administrative roles where we have built equity-focused collaborations with students, staff, and faculty. The first author is a white woman who is a senior administrator for strategic diversity and inclusion initiatives at a private liberal arts institution where she directly supports the president's council for diversity and inclusion. The second author is a Latina woman who has served as an assistant dean at a public-private liberal arts institution where she advised student activists and leaders of university-recognized organizations.

We organize recommendations as follows: create infrastructure for shared leadership structures, vision and goal setting by university leadership, build capacity for team members across campus, and promote strategies to create inclusive team dynamics.

BUILDING SHARED LEADERSHIP STRUCTURES

Name the elephant in the room (and across the campus). Leaders of equity-focused cross-campus collaborations must engage participants in direct conversations about how power and status dynamics operate to sustain racial inequity across campus, and—perhaps most importantly—how these dynamics are also likely to show up in their collaborative work given their varied roles as students, administrators, and faculty and their different identities and lived experiences. Collaboration leaders should discuss how power-based issues such as academic freedom can operate in collaborations, which can make staff and administrators feel more restricted than their faculty colleagues in what they can say. They should also address how student participants may worry that challenging a professor could impact their future academic opportunities. Collaboration participants should, together, determine what processes and procedures they will put in place during their regular meetings to pause, name, and reframe when these power and status differences show up and should also determine processes to hold each other accountable to these group agreements.

Consciously work to build relationships that counter biases. Once uneven power dynamics within the group are named, all collaboration members must engage in active work to build meaningful relationships that blur boundary lines between and among faculty, staff, students, and administrators. For example, building mentorship programs among members of diversity and inclusion councils can contribute to more authentic and trusting relationships between group members. It is also important that faculty and staff involved in mentoring relationships with students recognize the invaluable experiential knowledge that students carry (McCulloch, 2009). Teams may also consider engaging in intensive team-building activities, like off-site retreats, where they can explore and share their own values while they set institutional goals and priorities.

Make it meaningful. Ensure the work of equity collaborations is high-level, strategic, and goes beyond cooperation or shared implementation of fixed and predetermined goals. Shared leadership collaborations for equity must be charged to do more than just "check the box," divide the work, or report about ongoing efforts. Instead, these collaborations must provide an opportunity for participants to contribute to widespread initiatives for racial equity from conceptualization to implementation. This is especially important when it comes to engaging students in university-wide equity efforts. If limited to engagement with routine or procedural decision-making, students may interpret invitations for involvement as purely symbolic (Menon, 2003). A few opportunities for meaningful student participation include meetings with academic affairs leaders to discuss inclusion-related coursework or the development of new programs of study, opportunities to participate in hiring committees for mental health care roles, or meetings with the university board to share student-developed equity action plans. To honor the participants' efforts, consider offering an appointment letter from the president to lend credibility and further emphasize the importance of the work.

Build a shared purpose. It is easy to falsely assume that participants in university-wide equity collaborations have a shared sense of purpose and mission, especially if the group is working from an existing strategic plan that outlines the vision and rationale for racial equity work on campus. It is vital, however, that any collaborative group take the time necessary to engage in critical deliberation about the purpose of the group's work when the collaboration begins, when new members join, and continually throughout the implementation phase. For example, retreats or meetings can start with participants sharing what brought them to the work, and groups can establish expectations for ongoing check-ins about struggles (and successes) individuals may encounter as they work on challenging racial equity efforts.

Include a breadth of community members. Institution-wide collaborations should achieve a balanced membership of students, student affairs administrators and staff, and academic affairs representatives and faculty. Leaders who convene shared leadership collaborations should pay particular attention to include participants of color who may have otherwise been marginalized from university leadership roles and positions of influence. It is also important to consider direct alumni involvement in cross-campus collaborations, particularly alumni of color at various stages of their post-institution careers. Alumni can provide a distinctive insider-outsider perspective on the campus climate and, given their alumni status, are also well positioned to hold the institution accountable for achieving racial equity goals. Parents, and parents of color, are key stakeholders and can also serve as direct participants in institutional collaborations for equity.

Model inclusive application processes. To ensure an equitable representation of voices, transparent and inclusive application processes are imperative (LePeau et al., 2019). This requires institutions to move away from traditional nomination processes or role-based appointments based on perceived experience and expertise, processes that can reduce membership access and tokenize community members from marginalized groups. The terms, length of service, and nomination/application processes for institution-wide equity collaborations should be clear and transparent, and the rationale for the approach should be broadly communicated. An institution may consider a campus-wide electronic message, with selection criteria, to gather the information of interested individuals. Asking administrators with direct student engagement to nominate students and encourage students to self-nominate—whether they hold a leadership position or not—may also increase transparency and facilitate information dissemination. It is important to involve formal student, faculty, staff, and alumni governance organizations (especially those who represent affinity groups of color) as partners in the nomination process. For example, these shared governance structures can recommend a representative for appointment to the group or can widely distribute the membership application broadly through their constituencies. The selection process should use practices that counter unconscious biases and promote equity (e.g., use of a competency-based rubric rather than use of a traditional resume-based application evaluation).

Timing matters. When many different campus stakeholders are included in institution-wide collaborations, it is vital to carefully consider timing of meetings and communication structures to facilitate involvement from various stakeholders. For example, many alumni (and nontraditional students) may work outside of the university and during traditional 9–5 work hours. Meanwhile, "traditional" full-time students and faculty are often in class during 9–5 work hours, and their schedules fluctuate each semester. Staff, on the other hand, may be more readily available during traditional work hours and can often convene over the summer when many faculty and students are not physically on campus. To help ensure equal access to group meetings, meetings should have both in-person and virtual options and should vary in time and days of the week to offer possibilities for engagement from participants in various organizational roles. Collaboration leaders should also consider weekend meeting options with childcare, transportation support, and food options included. It is important to check in on an ongoing basis with collaboration participants to gather feedback, and to continue to be flexible as the personal and professional contexts of collaboration members change and evolve.

SETTING A SHARED VISION AND GOALS

Use data to assess the organization's unique equity needs and context. The structure, charge, composition, and strategic direction of an institution's diversity and inclusion work must align with the organization's developmental phase (Kezar, 2007). To determine their institutional phase, leaders must intentionally reflect on disaggregated data, and must use data in an ongoing way to assess and evolve their strategic approach. Collaboration and institutional leaders can start this work with a collaborative data-gathering and assessment tool, such as the equity scorecard (Harris & Bensimon, 2007) or the NERCHE rubric (NERCHE, 2016). Determining the institutionalization level of equity work will help dictate strategic priorities and next steps, so leaders should undertake assessment periodically. The first phase of this work often involves establishing a baseline, measured with standard data elements that will be consistently collected across the institution. As the work evolves and the context shifts, collaborations should revisit their charge, membership composition, and activities to continue advancing work toward transformational change.

Build the team's equity-focused data analysis skills. Teams must build skills to interpret and use disaggregated institutional data to focus their efforts (LePeau et al., 2019). External stakeholders, including a university's institutional research office, can help the group build the necessary data analysis and assessment skills to effectively leverage data to inform recommendations. The Data Wise project is also a powerful tool for increasing data literacy for equity-focused educational teams (Harvard University, n.d.).

Engage the governing board in conversations about racial equity work. It is important that university leaders engage the board in campus racial equity efforts, and that conversations are transparent about challenges and opportunities. Students engaged in campus collaborations may be uniquely positioned to lead these conversations by sharing honest feedback: they have likely built the requisite skills and contextual understanding to navigate what could be an intimidating environment, and they are not as deeply embedded within the institution's bureaucracy as some of their faculty and staff colleagues.

Develop a dynamic and interculturally competent communication

infrastructure. To engage the larger community in racial equity work and to make the group's work transparent, it is vital that university leaders engage the cross-campus collaborations in developing and executing a strategic communication strategy. This strategy must be multichannel and dynamic to address the numerous ways community stakeholders access information and receive messages, including generational preferences. For example, students are more likely to use social media platforms to gather and access information on diversity and inclusion initiatives, while faculty and staff may be more likely to use more traditional channels like email, print, and websites. The communication plan must also recognize how, given their cultural and power contexts, campus community members may interpret messages of diversity and inclusion in different ways. For example, an email that highlights an increase in the racial diversity of the student body might be interpreted as significant progress toward equity by some white community members; however, the same email might feel tokenizing, symbolic, and incremental to some community members of color if it does not also include a clear plan to improve the campus climate for an increasingly racially diverse student body. To help navigate this, cross-campus collaborations should be involved in the careful vetting of any campus-wide communications about racial equity, drawing on their diverse roles and lived experiences to help ensure the communications are effective and culturally responsive.

BUILDING CAPACITY

Mentor, and learn with, students engaged in the work. As students take on additional responsibilities through collaborative equity partnerships, they may face challenges balancing the demands of the collaboration work with schoolwork and other commitments. Formal or informal multigenerational mentorship structures within collaborations may function as a community of care for students. Mentors can support students should they encounter tensions with their peers as a result from participating in institutional shared leadership collaborations. Mentors can also provide students with knowledge of the institution's goals, policies, and practices while maintaining confidentiality.

Make the time. Institutional leaders should consider creating opportunities for members of equity collaborations to have some of their time freed to focus on the project, increase engagement and efficacy, and prevent burnout. This could take shape as course releases for faculty leaders, a stipend or specific work assignment for staff leaders, and/or an academic credit(s) for student leaders. These measures communicate the seriousness of, and university leadership's commitment to, the group's initiatives; it also creates enough time for participants to manage the demands of collaboration.

Provide and value administrative support. Managing campus collaborations takes a substantial amount of time, attention to detail, and logistical planning. Depending on institutional context, an institution may consider offering administrative support to help facilitate the collaboration. This increases each team member's time capacity to focus on strategic decision-making and deliberations. If dedicated administrative support is not available, departments could share existing resources or engage a graduate student assistant. Additionally, many of the administrative challenges in doing campus-wide equity work involve decentralized knowledge about the institution's bureaucratic structure (e.g., who to contact for demographic data, how to access space management systems for room reservations, how to properly expense reconciliations for food/supplies, etc.). So, students involved in cross-institutional equity collaborations, especially those who have not previously held campus leadership positions, often rely on administrative staff to navigate the institution and receive additional support. As such, it is important that university leaders value, recognize, and compensate (as feasible) staff for efforts to provide administrative support and guidance to students.

Invest in on-the-ground administrators. Student affairs practitioners can build bridges between students and high-level traditional campus leadership, as they support both stakeholder groups in unique ways. They advise students in communication with campus stakeholders and self-advocacy. Simultaneously, they help keep high-level administrators apprised of any building tensions within student communities. Midlevel administrators working in collaborations should be offered opportunities to further develop capacity for equity-focused student coaching, conflict resolution, and interest mediation through professional development funds, mentorship, and networking opportunities.

Prevent burnout. Equity work is challenging, especially given demanding academic and professional responsibilities for collaboration participants.

To combat burnout, leaders may consider setting term limits for active participation in collaborations, using self-care circles during or following particularly challenging periods, and using subgroups for key deliverables. The process of engaging in equity work can also trigger trauma from past experiences of racial injustice and microaggressions on campus. Collaboration leaders should directly engage participants, and students in particular, in exercises to manage stress and develop coping strategies, and leaders should provide mental health resources (Doble & Supriya, 2011).

SUPPORTING TEAM DYNAMICS

Teams need training too. For groups to work effectively and leaders to successfully guide collaborative teams for equity, they need teamwork and coalition-building skills as they negotiate intra-team dynamics and build relationships across campus to advance the equity goals at hand. Teams should develop their antiracist knowledge and skill base to ensure they are all cognizant of how to recognize and empower members of the team to identify, name, and challenge forms and structures of racism both within and outside of their group space (DiAngelo & Flynn, 2010). Teams should also learn and apply inclusive and equitable meeting practices (see Aorta Coop, 2017, for an anti-oppressive meeting guide), group processes, and decision-making (see Racial Equity Tools, n.d., for a comprehensive equitable planning process toolkit).

Celebrate victories (even small ones). Equity work is often seen and approached as "oppression talk," which can be particularly tiring and challenging, especially for individuals who daily encounter oppression. However, if the team celebrates one another's individual accomplishments and (even small) victories as they work toward fulfilling their vision and meaning of equity work, teams will grow closer together; and those celebrations can serve as signals and anchors for what is possible, which will further motivate the team.

Conclusion

Shared leadership initiatives are an important tool for higher education campus leaders to consider as they seek to advance campus-wide racial equity goals. When campus leaders engage students, faculty, and administrators in meaningful collaborations in which all members' perspectives are acknowledged, valued, and affirmed, they can build trust among stakeholders and improve the likelihood that racial equity initiatives will engage the expertise of individuals throughout the organization and ultimately be more successful. Campus-wide collaborations must also center student voices within strategic and high-level conversations to ensure equity efforts meaningfully reflect the perspectives and positively impact the experiences of the students they are designed to serve. The vision, goals, and composition of these collaborations should be clearly communicated across campus and with the governing board. Perhaps most importantly, teams put together for the purpose of shared leadership should focus on trust-building and communication; additionally, they must hold some real, not symbolic, influence within the institution.

Undoubtedly, the context of a particular institution—size, financial resources, history, demographics, and current institutional culture—will shape how and why these collaborations begin, how they are structured, and how quickly they will progress. However, all institutions have an opportunity to engage in these types of collaborations in varied ways. When working in concert with other strategic efforts, shared leadership collaborations are key resources in leading effective campus-wide initiatives for racial equity.

References

American Association of Colleges and Universities [AACU]. (2012). A national call to action: A crucible moment, college learning & democracy's future. https://www.aacu.org/sites/default/files/files/crucible/Crucible_508F.pdf

Aorta Coop. (2017). Anti-oppressive facilitation for democratic process. http://aorta.coop/portfolio_page/anti-oppressive-facilitation/

Astin, A. W., & Astin, H. S. (2000). *Leadership reconsidered: Engaging higher education in social change*. W. K. Kellogg Foundation. https://files.eric.ed.gov/fulltext/ED444437.pdf

Bensimon, E. M., Dowd, A., & Witham, K. (2016). Five principles for enacting equity by design. *Diversity & Democracy, 19*(1). https://www.aacu.org/diversitydemocracy/2016/winter/bensimon

Bensimon, E. M., & Neumann, A. (1993). *Redesigning collegiate leadership: Teams and teamwork in higher education*. Johns Hopkins University Press.

DiAngelo, R., & Flynn, D. (2010). Showing what we tell: Facilitating Antiracist education in cross-racial teams. *Understanding and Dismantling Privilege,*

1(1), 1–24. https://robindiangelo.com/2018site/wp-content/uploads/2016/01/Showing-what-tell.pdf

Doble, N., & Supriya, M. (2011). Student life balance: Myth or reality? *International Journal of Educational Management, 25*(3), 237–251. https://doi.org/10.1108/09513541111120088

Gaston-Gayles, J., Wolf-Wendel, L., Tuttle, K., Twombley, S., & Ward, K. (2004). From disciplinarian to change agent: How the civil rights era changed the roles of student affairs professionals. *NASPA Journal, 42*(3), 263–282. https://doi.org/10.2202/1949-6605.1508

Guthrie, K. L., Bertrand Jones, B., Osteen, L., & Hu, S. (2013). *Cultivating leader identity and capacity in students from diverse backgrounds: ASHE higher education report, 39*(4). Wiley Periodicals.

Freeman, R. E. (1993). Collaboration, global perspectives, and teacher education. *Theory into Practice, 32*(1), 33–39. https://www.jstor.org/stable/1476480

Harris, F., & Bensimon, E. M. (2007). The equity scorecard: A collaborative approach to assess and respond to racial/ethnic outcomes. *New Directions for Student Services, 2007*(120), 77–84. https://doi.org/10.1002/ss.259

Harvard University (n.d.). Data Wise: Educators collaborating so all students thrive. from https://datawise.gse.harvard.edu/

Holcombe, E., & Kezar, A. (2017). The whys and hows of shared leadership in higher education. https://www.higheredtoday.org/2017/05/10/whys-hows-shared-leadership-higher-education/

Hurtado, S., Milem, J., Clayton-Pederson, A., & Allen, W. (1999). *Enacting diverse learning environments: Improving the climate for racial/ethnic diversity in higher education*. Jossey-Bass.

Ishimaru, A. M., Galloway, M. K. (2014). Beyond individual effectiveness: Conceptualizing organizational leadership for equity. *Leadership and Policy in Schools, 13*(1), 93–146. doi:10.1080/15700763.2014.890733

Kezar, A. (2007). Tools for a time and place: Phased leadership strategies to institutionalize a diversity agenda. *Review of Higher Education, 30*(4), 413–439.

Kezar, A. (2008). Understanding leadership strategies for addressing the politics of diversity. *Journal of Higher Education, 79*(4), 406–441. https://muse.jhu.edu/article/241242/pdf

Kezar, A., Eckel, P., Contreras-McGavin, M., & Quaye, S. (2008). Creating a web of support: An important leadership strategy for advancing campus diversity. *Higher Education, 55*(1), 69–92.

Kezar, A. J., & Holcombe, E. M. (2017). Shared leadership in higher education: Important lessons from research and practice. American Council on Education. *Viewpoints: Voices from the Field*, 1–29. https://www.acenet.edu/news-room/Pages/Shared-Leadership-in-Higher-Education-Important-Lessons-from-Research-and-Practice.aspx

Kezar, A., & Lester, J. (2009). *Organizing higher education for collaboration: A guide for campus leaders*. Jossey-Bass.

Kirshner, B., & Ginwright, S. (2012). Youth organizing as a developmental context for African American and Latino adolescents. *Child Development Perspectives, 6*(3), 288–294. http://dx.doi.org/10.1111/j.1750-8606.2012.00243.x

LePeau, L. (2015). A grounded theory of academic affairs and student affairs partnerships for diversity and inclusion aims. *Review of Higher Education, 39*, 97–122.

LePeau, L. A., Hurtado S. S., & Williams L. (2019). Institutionalizing diversity agendas: Presidents' councils for diversity as mechanisms for strategic change. *Journal of Student Affairs Research and Practice,* 1–15. https://doi.org/10.1080/19496591.2018.1490306

McCulloch, A. (2009). The student as co-producer: Learning from public administration about the student-university relationship. *Studies in Higher Education, 34*(2), 171–183. https://doi:10.1080/03075070802562857

Menon, M. E. (2003). Student involvement in university governance: A need for negotiated educational aims? *Tertiary Education and Management, 9*(3), 233–246.

Milem, J. F., Chang, M. J., & Antonio, A. L. (2005). *Making diversity work on campus: A research-based perspective.* Association of American Colleges and Universities.

New England Resource Center for Higher Education (NERCHE). (2016). *NERCHE self-assessment rubric for the institutionalization of diversity, equity, and inclusion in higher education.* https://www.wpi.edu/sites/default/files/Project_Inclusion_NERCHE_Rubric-Self-Assessment-2016.pdf

Racial Equity Tools. (n.d.). How can we create an inclusive and equitable planning process? https://drive.google.com/file/d/1S6sMC5MDw5O5GkepD2NoetLs7_oJqrhM/view

Slocum, J., & Rhoads, R. (2009). Faculty and student engagement in the Argentine grassroots rebellion: Toward a democratic and emancipatory vision of the university. *Higher Education, 57*(1), 85–105. http://www.jstor.org/stable/40269108

Spillane, J. P., Diamond, J. B., & Murphy, J. F. (2007). *Distributed leadership in practice (Critical issues in educational leadership series).* Teachers College Press.

Templeton, E., Love, B., Davis, B. H., & Davis Jr., M. (2016). Illusion of inclusion: University policies that perpetuate exclusion of student of color. *Journal Committed to Social Change on Race and Ethnicity, 2*(1), 88–115. https://www.ncore.ou.edu/media/filer_public/4c/ee/4cee15dd-3745-418e-9e86-33f6ff8a5bbe/emerald_templeton_et_al_jcscore__spring_2016_.pdf

Turner, C. S. (2003). Race in the academy: Moving beyond diversity and toward the incorporation of faculty of color in predominantly white colleges and universities. *Journal of Black Studies, 34*(1), 112–125.

U.S. Department of Education, Office of Planning, Evaluation and Policy Development and Office of the Under Secretary. (2016). *Advancing diversity and inclusion in higher education.* http://www2.ed.gov/rschstat/research/pubs/advancing-diversity-inclusion.pdf

Williams, D. A. (2013). *Strategic diversity leadership: Activating change and transformation in higher education.* Stylus.

3

Equity as Leadership
The Role of Boards in Advancing the Equity Agenda

FELECIA COMMODORE, RAQUEL M. RALL,
AND DEMETRI L. MORGAN

The population of racially minoritized groups in higher education continues to grow and by 2030 will make up the majority of the higher education population (Vespa et al., 2018). Institutions must respond to these increases in demographic diversity with policies and practices that lead to more institutions embracing the pursuit for equity in terms of access and success of all constituents (Garces & Jayakumar, 2014; Museus, 2014). In this chapter, we define equity-centered decision-making as a critical and collaborative examination that pushes postsecondary education leaders to be intentional rather than passive agents of work that enhances inclusion, access, diversity, and social justice. Consistent with the translational racial equity research-practice (TRERP) framework presented earlier in this book, we assert that equity-centered institutions are ones that engage in decision-making and practices that execute and accomplish their institutional mission in ways that specifically advance racial justice informed by research and practice.

While scholarship lends some attention to institutional leadership's role in centering the pursuit of equity, the role of the board of trustees is rarely addressed (Rall et al., 2020). Yet trustee boards can (and should) play an integral role in promoting equity (Rall, 2021), as they play a major fiduciary role in the life of an institution and often work alongside presidents and chancellors in decision-making, strategic planning, and policy setting (AGB, 2015; Rall et al., 2018). Likewise, boards represent an institution's goals, values, and mission (Chait et al., 1996). And while institutional mission, values, and vision statements have grown to include or allude to issues of diversity, equity, and inclusion, there is a disconnect between these institutional goals and boards of trustees' work (Morphew & Hartley, 2006). Likewise, when examining research in the area of racial equity in higher education, there is little research that speaks to the role of governing boards (Rall et al., 2018). This disconnect between the practices of the board and the dearth of research can lead to challenges in the intentional institutionalization of these values and leaves equity efforts susceptible to being temporary rather than sustainable (Rall et al., Forthcoming). Barriers to sustainable efforts that promote equity are often structural, cultural, and political. However, governing boards and their members, due to power, position, policy, and politics, can remove many of these barriers (Barringer & Riffe, 2018). For this reason, trustees must be equipped with the tools and strategies needed to disempower and remove barriers to achieving equity.

In this chapter, we address the role of the board of trustees in institutional equity work. We first make the case for equity-centered board work: we argue that equity must be the foundation for the work of the board, not peripheral to its work and decision-making processes. After we establish the importance and necessity of equity-centered board practices and decision-making, we present a framework to demonstrate equity as a fiduciary duty of boards. We use this framework to break down how equity is central to, and practiced as, a duty of loyalty, of care, and of obedience. In establishing this importance, we advance the TRERP framework, as it speaks to the process through which practitioner-informed discoveries centering issues of racism and interlocking systems of oppressions are translated into policy and practice that aim to improve conditions for racially and ethnically marginalized persons in the institution's community (this volume). Trustees enacting their fiduciary roles devoid of equity can perpetuate racism and interlocking systems of oppression. Therefore, by integrating efforts to advance equity as part of a trustee's fiduciary role, trustees take on the posture of practitioners whose discoveries in their work can be translated into policy and practice that addresses issues for racially and ethnically marginalized people. Through these frameworks and their recommended application, trustees will be better positioned to play their part in the manifestation of more equitable higher education institutions.

Why Equity Matters in the Work of the Board

The board of trustees is an institutional entity that is often overlooked, understudied, and shallowly understood within higher education regarding the topic of equity (Barringer & Riffe, 2018; Pusser et al., 2006; Rall et al., 2018; Taylor & Machado, 2008). As an entity, the board of trustees holds great power but can also be a great distance from the day-to-day realities of campus life. The often-present chasm between boards and the daily realities of campus life is a result of a constant concern that boards may meddle in the day-to-day intricacies of management rather than work at the higher level of governance (Taylor & Machado, 2008). However, with recent public cases of problematic presidential hires and firings, institutional strategic planning, and financial solvency, scholars have given more attention to higher education boards of trustees (e.g., Fain, 2019; Lederman, 2019). Generally, an understanding exists that boards have a responsibility to uphold their fiduciary duty to their respective institutions and have significant input in long-term strategic planning and stabilization of the fiscal health of the institution (AGB, 2015; Lane, 2013; McLendon, 2003; Schmidt, 2014). Often, boards of trustees do not find themselves the focus of higher education conversations except when it comes to one of their biggest and most notable responsibilities: firing and hiring presidents.

Moreover, in recent years, institutions have found themselves in several headline-generating scandals that have slowly brought boards of trustees to the forefront. Conversations about access and climate for Black students at the University of Maryland College Park, issues regarding the targeting and retention of Black staff at the University of Alabama, or the denial of tenure to the only Latina professor on the tenure track at Harvard University have all put issues of equity at the forefront of higher education stakeholders' collective consciousness. Within this new level of awareness lies a question regarding the role of the board in not only preventing negative media attention for the institution but also in making decisions, setting agendas, and establishing policies that create institutions that are more equity-minded.

THE CHANGING ROLE OF BOARDS

When such stories regarding institutional negligence, scandal, racial tension, and lack of inclusion are present in media, the areas of development, recruitment, and enrollment may all be impacted. As such, boards and presidents find themselves currently under pressure to address issues of educational equity. Though boards and presidents are increasingly challenged to consider issues of educational equity, a great deal of confusion concerning what exactly equity means within the college and university context exists. Additionally, institutional leaders hold the question of how focusing efforts on educational equity contributes to broader institutional goals. Currently, campus stakeholders must navigate constantly shifting policies related to DACA, transgender bathroom bills, international travel bans, and a host of challenges to federal, state, and institutional practices that impact marginalized members of their campus communities. Board members must begin to address and discuss these issues of educational equity and inclusion as they engage in the work of the board. Focusing on these equity efforts is becoming an increasingly important element in stabilizing an institution's immediate and long-term health; therefore equity-centered decision-making is imperative.

Educational decision-makers can either aid or hinder institutions as they move toward more equitable conditions (Rall et al., 2020). Hence, it is more important than ever for trustees to establish more equitable policies and practices on their campuses. Historically, boards were mostly concerned with presidential hires and firings and the institution's fiscal health (AGB, 2015; Davies, 2011; Herron, 1969; Lane, 2013; McLendon, 2003). In addition, contemporarily, boards of trustees are underutilized and limited in activity in areas outside of development and protecting the institution from legal challenges and liabilities (Blanchard, 1967; Morgan et al., 2021b). However, as higher education and society have evolved, so have the reach, responsibilities, and impact of the board. Currently, boards are involved in institutional development, major administrative hires and appointments, institutional advocacy, political and policy issues (e.g., free speech, sexual assault, DACA), and must be able to understand and explain data within an era of higher education accountability (AGB, 2011).

BOARD DIVERSITY AND COMPOSITION

The role of the board, as well as the skill sets and perspectives of trustees necessary to ensure a high-functioning board, is shifting in ways that are difficult to discern. Hence there tends to be a fixation on board composition and whether it informs the work and outcomes of boards

(Johnson et al., 2013). While scholars have pointed to the importance of diversity in terms of social identities in achieving effective board outcomes (Taylor et al., 1991), board diversity continues to be an elusive challenge in higher education (Rall & Orué, 2020). Indeed, the demographics of board members are not changing on boards across US higher education in pace with the changing demographics of the nation at large. As previously mentioned, US racial demographics, as well as the racial demographics of student bodies at colleges, are changing. In 1976, 84.3 percent of enrolled college students were white, 9.6 percent Black, 3.6 percent Latinx, and 2.5 percent were from other racially minoritized groups (NCES, 2017). Now, 54.7 percent of college students are white, 13.4 percent are Black, 16 percent are Latinx, 6.4 percent are Asian, and less than 1 percent are Native American (NCES, 2017). Regarding gender, there has been a 9 percent increase in women attending college over the past 39 years (NCES, 2017). The average board member is an older white male who hails from the business industry (AGB, 2013, 2016). Additionally, public institution boards are an average size of 12 members, where nine are men and three are women. On average, nine members are white, two are Black, and one is a member of another racially minoritized group (AGB, 2011). It is extremely rare that a woman or person of color serve as the board chair (AGB, 2011). In an exploratory analysis of public institution boards, Commodore et al. (2018) found, when looking at a representative sample of public institutions, that 14.7 percent of board members were Black, 4.3 percent were Latinx, and 5.4 percent were of another racially minoritized group. Furthermore, upon the removal of minority-serving institutions from the sample, the representation of Black and Latinx board members dropped to 8.1 percent and 3.5 percent, respectively. In sum, college campuses are becoming more diverse by race and gender, but their boards of trustees are not. Governing boards interested in effective service to institutions in this next era of higher education must seriously work to achieve diversity in their membership composition.

Though these explorations of board composition and board diversity focus on race and, at times, gender, it is important to note that board diversity includes a spectrum of identities and ideologies. Board composition may seem inconsequential, but it impacts the work of the board. The lack of representation of diverse voices in the institution's decision-making process brings to question whether the board's processes are equity-centered or equitable in practice. For example, we might ask how the interests of marginalized and disenfranchised groups are being addressed if their voices are not part of decision-making bodies? What measures, standards, and processes are used and set as the norm for institutional governance and decision-making, and what perspectives are privileged in this process? How can boards develop strategic plans and institutional policies that are equity-minded if the board itself struggles with issues of diversity, equity, and inclusion within its composition? To be clear, structural diversity alone does not equate to equity; equitable mindsets from board members and equity-oriented decision-making are also necessary. Representation alone does not achieve equity just as diversity is not synonymous with inclusion.

ASSUMING A ROLE IN EQUITY

As the term "equity" becomes more commonplace in board discussions, trustees must familiarize themselves with issues of equity both broadly and specific to their respective institutions. In familiarizing themselves with these issues, boards of trustees must also attain access to research that speaks to how the work of the board can be more equity-centered. To this end, trustees interested in and committed to advancing the equity agenda need to ask some important questions including, but not limited to, the following (Rall et al., 2020):

1. How might board members take a more (pro)active role in advancing today's equity imperative?
2. How might institutions foster a more intentionally welcoming environment that encourages and supports an equity-centered campus, and how can boards ensure the institution is advancing appropriately on this front?
3. How is equity integral to board decision-making?
4. How can the board hold institutional stakeholders accountable to high standards of equity?
5. What does equity mean for *my* institution?

Importantly, contemplating equity is not the same as practicing equity. In the next section, we address how boards move past a mere consideration of equity for their work to, instead, practically exercise equity-centered governance and decision-making. We introduce a framework of equity as a fiduciary duty that boards can apply to their existing practices. We also provide recommendations for the practical application of this framework.

A Framework for Integrating Equity as a Fiduciary Duty

Though institutions should address how they serve students in a more equity-minded manner, little exists regarding work of the board that creates more equitable institutional practices and policies (Bensimon, 2006; Bensimon & Harris, 2012). Board members, under state statutory and common law, are fiduciaries and must act with care, loyalty, and obedience (AGB, n.d.) for their institution. AGB (n.d.) lays out the definition of a fiduciary in this way:

> A fiduciary is someone who has special responsibilities in connection with the administration, investment, monitoring, and distribution of property—meaning, the charitable or public assets of the institution, as well as intangible assets such as its reputation and role in the community. (para. 2)

This definition indicates that board members have a responsibility to engage in actions and decisions that are in the best legal, reputational, and financial interests of the institution. Often, direct connections exist between the board's fiduciary duties and tasks such as presidential hires and terminations, investments and acquisitions, and the enforcement of policies and protocols that protect the institution from liability (AGB, 2015; Davies, 2011; Schmidt, 2014). We propose a specific understanding of equity as a fiduciary duty (Rall et al., 2019): equity as a duty of care, equity as a duty of loyalty, and equity as a duty of obedience. Once we delineate how these three elements of fiduciary duty embody equity, we provide recommendations on how to apply the presented framework in practice.

EQUITY AS A DUTY OF CARE

According to AGB's Governance Brief on Fiduciary Responsibilities, the duty of care commonly requires board members to enact their roles and responsibilities "in good faith and using that degree of diligence, care, and skill which ordinarily prudent persons would reasonably exercise under similar circumstances in like positions" (2015, p. 4). Additionally, a board member must act in a manner that he or she reasonably believes to be in the best interests of the institution. Trustees must operate with intentional diligence to ensure the creation of environments conducive to high-level learning and high-level job performance. This deliberate diligence helps facilitate equitable access to both effective educational practices and welcoming campus climates.

Boards that desire said outcomes should engage in equity-minded governance and decision-making centered on the people, policies, and practices that implicitly and explicitly contribute to disparities in higher education. For example, if institutional data show that the Latinx student population has grown from 20 to 35 percent over the last ten years but has remained stagnant for Latinx tenure-track and tenured faculty, at less than 5 percent, in the same period, the board should pay attention. Boards may consider how strategic planning, budgeting, and institutional hiring policies can increase the latter percentage.

EQUITY AS A DUTY OF LOYALTY

The duty of loyalty assumes trustees will act in good faith and in a manner that prioritizes the interests of the college or university. We propose that prioritizing an institution's interest in inequitable practices and decision-making inherently represents an act of loyalty conducted in good faith. Said differently, when board members choose not to view equitable practices and decision-making as a priority in or central to their work, they run the risk of not approaching board duties in good faith. Board members need to push past their own self-interests to prioritize the public good. This perspective proves especially important for board members of public institutions. In the specific context of public colleges and universities, there is a heightened expectation that trustees act on behalf of the interests not only of the institution but also those of the state's citizens. For institutions with special missions or missions that focus primarily on the empowerment of historically marginalized populations, there is also an expectation to prioritize what will prove equitable and good for that population of students, as opposed to only self-interest.

It is not simple to center equity in board decision-making. It might be quite difficult, often due to a lack of tools that properly equip board members to engage in said practices. To center equity in board practices, first, board members must understand what equity means and why it is needed. Then, trustees must desire equity as a priority that guides their work. Once a comprehensive understanding and a willingness to move forward are established, then the effort to move equity from theory to practice is possible. Tia Brown McNair (2016) wrote in *The Time Is Now: Committing to Equity and Inclusive Excellence* that boards must commit to identify, examine, and dismantle pervasive "mindsets in higher education that serve as catalysts for marginalization, inequity, and intolerance. These mindsets impede the exploration and acceptance of difference as a core value in our democratic society and in effective educational environments" (para 4.). Boards can approach heightened accountability in this area practically: if they bolster diversity in board composition, multiple perspectives can enhance board accountability. Another practice to advance equity as the duty of loyalty is clarity around what metrics and outcomes the board will use to evaluate presidents and to assess the overall trajectory of the institution.

EQUITY AS A DUTY OF OBEDIENCE

The duty of obedience delineates the duty of board members to ensure the institution operates in accordance with, and for the advancement of, its purpose and mission within the confines of the law. In an era of accountability-based measures such as graduation rates, retention rates, and student loan default rates, this aspect of fiduciary duty is of great importance to board members. Increased calls for institutions to exhibit and report measures of effectiveness and efficiency have had an impact on the work of boards. Additionally, in an increasingly litigious society, it is necessary to help ensure that their respective institutions are not vulnerable to legal threats. Many institutions espouse a commitment to diversity and student success. A true commitment to the duty of obedience, focused specifically on achieving the institution's mission, thus requires that boards look within to ask themselves how well their institutions live up to their expressed commitment to equity. For example, does the diversity of the student body match the composition of faculty, staff, and upper-level administration? How might board decision-making processes consider an assessment of campus climate and the creation of new task forces or positions centered on equity in doing their work? Boards who approach their work and ask reflective questions through this equity-centered framework can orient their board to successfully contribute to equity through decision-making and policy creation that move their institutions toward a more equitable culture and practice.

Recommendations for Practice

Approaching equity as a fiduciary duty aids boards in (re)framing the duties of the board. In line with the TRERP framework, the processes through which colleges and universities function must be fundamentally altered to realize racial equity. One of these processes would be how boards of trustees engage in decision-making, strategic planning, and policy setting. As translational racial equity research-practice emphasizes, the adoption of policies, practices, and processes that are more mindful of people's lived realities is paramount. When boards take a position of equity as fiduciary duty, they engage in decision-making processes in this manner and construct policies that do the same. In this section, we outline three areas in which boards can integrate equity into their fiduciary duty: strategic planning, funding and budget allocation decision-making, and personnel hires and accountability measures. Through presenting these recommendations we hope to provide boards and institutional leaders with a foundation to engage in TRERP and ultimately engage in the work of the board in a way that anticipates and accounts for how interlocking systems of oppression stifle organizational change and widespread institutional effectiveness.

EQUITY-MINDED STRATEGIC PLANNING

Strategic planning is an important aspect to ensure the short-term and long-term health of an institution (Dooris, 2003; Richards et al., 2004; Wolf & Floyd, 2017). Allison and Kaye define strategic planning as:

> A systematic process through which an organization agrees on and builds key stakeholder commitment to priorities that are essential to its mission and responsive to the organizational environment. Strategic planning guides the acquisition and allocation of resources to achieve these priorities. (2015, p. 1)

There are many steps and stages to design a strategic plan. These include, but are not limited to: defining outcomes, identifying conditions for success, planning for data collection, anticipating other needed research, designing a strategic planning process, and creating an organization profile (Allison & Kaye, 2015). During the strategic planning process, boards often analyze the organization's strengths, weaknesses, opportunities, and threats (SWOT) to understand where the institution performs well, where it does not perform well, and to identify opportunities for improvement (Allison & Kaye, 2015; Dooris, 2003). Often in the SWOT stage of strategic planning, various performance and outcome measures are used to aid in the evaluation of the institution's effectiveness (Allison & Kaye, 2015; Voorhees, 2008). External pressures, such as outcomes baselines and goals set by state and federal legislators and agencies, often dictate these performance and outcome measures. Goals and aspirations internal to the institution may also influence the board's goals and measures. As state and federal agencies and legislators employ current performance measures to assess the current state of institutions, individual institutions also use these performance measures to develop and set new institutional goals and benchmarks. Given these practices, for boards aiming to set outcomes and performance measures that center diversity, inclusion, and equity, the strategic planning process is an ideal area to accomplish this goal (Morgan et al., 2021a) Focusing on equity and equitable outcomes guides the institution's strategic planning and allows boards to construct measurable assessment and accountability methods. Boards of trustees and those involved in the strategic planning process are able to facilitate institutional efforts to gather disaggregated and detailed data.

Furthermore, a concentrated focus on equity sets the stage for more equity-minded or equity-focused evaluative practices and processes. Once evaluation goals and measures are in place, boards can more easily communicate these equity-focused goals and measures with both internal and external stakeholders. Additionally, boards are able to signal to potential partners and donors that equity is central to institutional values. Ability to partner with and procure stakeholders can bolster institutional reputation, relations with external communities, and possibly finances, which all contribute to fulfilling the board's fiduciary duty.

Boards engaging in equity-minded strategic planning can approach the process leveraging the E.Q.U.I.T.Y acronym that presents different practices that can be employed (Critical Higher Education Collaborative, 2019b):

Examine Disaggregated Data to Identify Masked Areas of Inequity

Equity-centered strategic planning only occurs insofar as the board and other institutional leaders gather, evaluate, and interpret disaggregated data. Specifically, boards must receive data points grouped into different subpopulations across categories related to race, gender identity, sexual orientation, socioeconomic status, ability, and geographic background to engage in equity-centered strategic planning. Ideally, boards must also have data available that allow the ability to group and manipulate data across multiple identity categories (e.g., being able to examine differences between Black women and Black men versus the more standard only centering racial differences *or* gender differences) to thoroughly engage in an equity-centered process that is also mindful of intersectional realities (Crenshaw, 1991; Collins, 2015). Finally, outcomes and metrics of interest should be collaboratively defined in areas where there is the flexibility to do so. All institutions already gather enrollment, persistence, and graduation data but it may take additional efforts to capture data in disaggregated ways on student campus climate experiences or staff member experiences. The point here is that preceding strategic planning efforts, the board must ensure that quality, comprehensive, and granular data are available for examination.

Question Areas of Inequities

To engage in equity-centered strategic planning, boards must question and seriously inquire what inequities exist and persist at their respective institutions. Once identifying these existing inequities, boards should ask what are the factors related to these inequities and how may various instances of inequities be interrelated or intersectional? Once the board has access to and examines data, the board in collaboration with the president and other institutional leaders must begin a period of investigating areas of inequities. During this stage, the board should employ practices such as making sure data are reliable, interviewing or asking for reports from stakeholders most knowledgeable about or proximate to the documented inequity, and benchmarking the inequity against peer and aspirational institutions.

Understand How to Facilitate

Throughout the strategic planning process, boards must work to understand and negotiate their role in enacting equity in relation to the roles of other stakeholders. Centering equity and valuing stakeholders is imperative to a successful strategic planning process. Through centering equity in board practices, composition, and operations, boards can model inclusive and sensitive leadership (Ryan, 2007). Board members should be mindful of who is and who is not present within decision-making processes and work to systematically cultivate diverse perspectives. Board members can do this through taking a membership inventory. Questions that can be asked as part of the inventory are: What are the racial and ethnic demographics represented on the board? What various identities are represented on the board? What educational and vocational backgrounds are and are not represented on the board? What communities are and are not represented on the board? Once the answers to these questions are collected and interpreted, questions should be raised as to whether this board composition is representative of the current state and future aspirations of the institution. If it is not, board members should strategize and implement ways to aid the decision-making processes and work of the board to be more representative and inclusive of various stakeholders impacted by the institution and its operations. We also recommend that the board determine appropriate accountability mechanisms for those most responsible for operationalizing the strategic planning process and the strategic plan.

Tackle the Barriers

Inevitable in any planning process are challenges that can derail well-intentioned efforts. Boards must collaborate with other stakeholders and leaders in removing barriers for success within the strategic-planning process. Maintaining clear communication regarding their goals and providing counsel to various stakeholders on how to maneuver around or through various issues, when necessary, is important. Boards can schedule regular discussions with various internal and external stakeholders. Boards can also establish regular updates and insight into their processes with campus constituents through a quarterly correspondence or, specifically for private institutions, public accessibility to board meeting minutes and presentations.

Yield Resources

Throughout, and most importantly after, the strategic-planning process, boards must allot and make available equitable and adequate resources for the goals of the strategic plan to be realized. Yielding resources happens mostly through the budgeting process. In this next section, we discuss how boards can engage in equity-minded funding and budget practices.

EQUITY-MINDED FUNDING AND BUDGET ALLOCATION

A part of the strategic planning process involves proposing what resources are necessary to reach the board's stated goals. Though these resources can fit into various categories, financial resources play a major role. When examining an institution's budget, it is often easy to tell what areas are priorities based on budget allocations. Approving budgets and determining budget allocations are some of the major tasks of a board of trustees (AGB, 2015; Davies, 2011; Kezar, 2006), so boards have a unique opportunity to use budgets as tools for equity. Investment in and fund allocation towards initiatives and programs that exemplify equitable practices have a significant impact in moving the institution towards greater equity. If boards want to take the task of institutionalizing equitable practices seriously, they must financially support the efforts needed to do so.

Though boards are an important part of the budgeting process at institutions, their budgeting processes are often informed by budgets from different departments and divisions across the institution. Board members need to communicate through communication with the president of the institution and through public statements to campus stakeholders that budgets and resource allocation on every level need to be equity-minded and equity-centered for an optimal ability to be approved. Building financial reward structures into the budgeting process for departments, programs, and initiatives that take equity-minded approaches to accomplish institutional goals and mission is a possibility. This could take the form of reallocation of funds to include percentage bonuses for departments or divisions that engage in successful and measurable equity initiatives. These rewards may not always be monetary. Board members could approve of building space, increased faculty lines, or the approval of the addition of a program or a major. Boards can also work with the provost and president to develop evaluation mechanisms for upper-level administrators and deans that center issues of equity. In the same way boards can use their reward power regarding resources they also have the power to withhold or limit resources. Board members can consider not approving budget requests, budget increases, and space requests for departments, programs, and initiatives that do not show any effort to aid the institution in reaching its equity goals.

Fund allocation toward equity efforts may not be an easy task with other budgeting pressures from a strained funding environment, from competition for funding, and from the move toward outcomes-based funding in some states. Boards of public institutions, who desire to engage in equity-minded and equity-centered budgeting practices, located in states where the dominant political and economic ideologies may not align, may encounter a tension-ridden process. However, institutions must begin to move toward attempting to achieve equity and boards play a role in making that financially possible. Boards must take the initiative to at the very least place the discussion of equity-centered budgeting processes on the agendas of both board committee meetings and full board meetings. If a finance or budgeting committee is part of the board's governance structure, this committee should be working with the financial officers of the institution, the president, and the board chair to take existing budget models and budget drafting practices and find how issues and measures of equity can be interwoven. Once this work has been done it can be brought to the larger board for more drawn-out conversations regarding feasibility and possible implementation. Overall, just because it may not be possible to do currently does not mean a board should not aptly prepare to make the shift to equity-centered budgeting for future boards possible.

Other areas related to financial resources where boards must apply an equity mindset are fundraising, donor acquisition, and investment decisions. A healthy endowment is a goal for most institutions (Astin, 2012). Most higher education institutions are attempting to figure out how to grow their endowments and secure the financial health and futures of their institutions (Goetzmann & Oster, 2013; Weisbrod & Asch, 2010). In addition to existing challenges, boards who engage in equity-minded work must examine if investment portfolios, assets, and gifts align with goals centered on equity. Boards should take inventory of their assets and investment portfolios and ask the following questions: Does the mission of the source(s) of these assets, gifts, or investments align with the mission of our institution? Does the source(s) of these assets, gifts, or investments engage in equitable practices or espouse a value of equity, specifically racial equity? Does the source(s) of these assets, gifts, or investments engage in practices or espouse values that harm or would be perceived as harmful to marginalized communities to which campus stakeholders may belong? Will the acquisition, investment, or revenue received from these assets, gifts, or investments be able to support the institution in efforts to achieve equity and enable equitable practices, programs, and initiatives? Questions regarding harm, exploitation, and disenfranchisement in portfolio composition or gift procurement help facilitate a more equity-minded discussion in the fundraising and endowment area. Boards asking these and similar questions do well to begin the process of equity-minded decision-making regarding institutional finances.

It is important to align financial practices, such as gift procurement and new investments, with principles of equity. Boards must be watchful of the fiscal health of the institution. This vigilance includes not only ensuring the growth and maintenance of existing funds but, in an equity-centered practice, also working to align the funding investments of the institution with institutional goals, vision, and values. Also, this involves courting and partnering with donors whose missions and goals are equity-centered and equity-minded. Boards that attempt to be more equity-minded in their budgeting processes can request, fundraise, and set fees to build financial resources to support and sustain equitable practices, policies, and programming. Institutions that have eliminated fines and fees for overdue library books, due to their inequitable tax on underresourced students, is one example of an equity-minded fee structure. Another example that centers equity-mindedness may be budget reallocation to provide more support for marginalized groups who are retained or who persist at a disparate rate relative to their counterparts. Equity efforts should be intentionally designed toward institutionalization—using budgets and allocating financial resources to encourage or stimulate these practices aid the creation of an equity-minded institutional culture.

EQUITY-MINDED PERSONNEL HIRES AND ACCOUNTABILITY MEASURES

A high-functioning board is not involved in the day-to-day operations and departmental hires of an institution (AGB, 2012; Freedman, 2005; Kezar, 2006; Taylor et al., 1991). However, there are some important hires for which a board is responsible such as the college president. While the institutional context may influence governing practices (Minor, 2006,

2008), it is important for all institutional boards to be diligent in the selection of key upper administrators such as the president.

Though objectivity may be considered by board members to be a core component of optimal board decision-making, we argue that these presidential hire decisions are based on values, and rightly so (Commodore, 2018; Taylor & Machado, 2008). When focusing on presidential selection at three private HBCUs, Commodore found that as objective as board members attempted to be, their values still played a role in the way they engaged with the selection process (2018). The decision-making process at institutions, including presidential hiring (Commodore, 2018), reflects institutional values. A board that upholds the value of achieving equity must do its due diligence to recruit and select presidents and other key personnel who value equity and have records of engaging in practices that align with these values.

In conjunction with hiring, boards must have measures in place to hold presidents accountable for engaging in activity that supports the institutional value of equity. Boards should also work with presidents to set up accountability mechanisms for upper-level administrators. Strategically building a leadership team that has the mindset and ability to aid the institution in achieving equity, and formalizing ways to hold that leadership accountable, enables the board to be equity-minded in fulfilling their fiduciary duties. Boards can practice these approaches by embedding questions within recruitment and hiring practices and processes that allow for the evaluation and understanding of a candidate's awareness of equity issues and vision for equitable practices in presidential and senior-level positions. Also, boards should make it a top priority to retain senior leaders that demonstrate a commitment to, and a positive impact on, an equity-focused strategic plan. To work toward retention of equity-minded senior leaders, boards should design and implement tools to evaluate senior leaders in equity-related competencies. Boards must advocate for, establish, and communicate clear parameters, metrics, and benchmarks to hold senior leaders accountable for engagement in equity-focused work and support of an equity-focused strategic plan.

ADDITIONAL AREAS OF FOCUS

In addition to engaging in equity-minded strategic planning, equity-minded funding and budget allocation, and equity-minded personnel hire and accountability measures, we offer the following recommendations for boards to consider in attempting to practice equity as fiduciary duty.

Boards should discuss and work with institutional stakeholders to build a working understanding of equity in the context of their institutional mission, goals, and environment. Dialogue with stakeholders can occur through several mediums, whether it be town halls, open community meetings, open forums at board meetings, or conducting regular focus groups across campus. Boards can also use equity-minded decision-making to set and monitor institutional goals and progress. As previously mentioned, equity-minded assessment and goal monitoring occur through collecting data in a manner that allows for sophisticated disaggregation, and through establishing evaluations and metrics that are dynamic and equity-focused. The use of disaggregated data can inform board decisions across different demographic and stakeholder experiences. Boards must challenge members to shift from thinking about what specifically is an issue of equity to consider what *is not* an issue of equity. This mindset shift is buttressed by boards when they ensure the board solicits diverse perspectives—particularly input from marginalized populations and those populations different from the dominant norms—before making decisions. Intentionality in diversification of board composition, as well as in (re)structuring the organization and shared governance models and practices, sets a culture that encourages similar equity practices on all levels.

Conclusion

The work of an institutional board can, at times, be hard to generalize due to the major role of institutional context. There are unique characteristics and circumstances that an individual board must contemplate in their work, as each board must engage with a unique set of circumstances when contemplating how to ensure the life and sustainability of their respective institutions. As the higher education community strives to maintain more equitable colleges and universities, boards of trustees must be involved in this goal of more equitable colleges and universities. Boards are well positioned to set the standard regarding equity, to construct and implement equitable practices and policies, and to center equity in the mission of their respective institutions. With boards leading the way, higher education can begin to build institutions that are proactive in shaping themselves to better serve diverse student populations and communities.

References

Allison, M., & Kaye, J. (2015). *Strategic planning for nonprofit organizations: A practical guide and workbook*. John Wiley & Sons.

Association of Governing Boards of Universities and Colleges (AGB). (n.d.). Fiduciary Duties. https://www.agb.org/briefs/fiduciary-duties

Association of Governing Boards of Universities and Colleges (AGB). (2011). *2011 AGB survey of Higher Education governance*. AGB Press. http://agb.org/sites/agb.org/files/report_2011_governance survey.pdf

Association of Governing Boards of Universities and Colleges (AGB). (2012). When governance goes awry: What are the takeaways? https://www.agb.org/trusteeship/2012/9/when-governance-goes-awry-what-are-takeaways

Association of Governing Boards of Universities and Colleges (AGB). (2013). *Building public governing board capacity: Suggestions and recommendations to governors and state legislatures for improving the selection and composition of public college and university board members*. AGB Press.

Association of Governing Boards of Universities and Colleges (AGB). (2015). Board policies, practices, and composition highlighted in new AGB research. *Trusteeship*. https://www.agb.org/trusteeship/2016/mayjune/board-policies-practices-and-composition-highlighted-in-new-agb-research

Association of Governing Boards of Universities and Colleges (AGB). (2016). *AGB board of directors' statement on the fiduciary duties of governing board members*. http://agb.org/sites/default/files/u27174/statement_2015_fiduciary_duties.pdf

Astin, A. W. (2012). *Assessment for excellence: The philosophy and practice of assessment and evaluation in higher education*. Rowman & Littlefield.

Barringer, S. N., & Riffe, K. A. (2018). Not just figureheads: Trustees as microfoundations of higher education institutions. *Innovative Higher Education*, *43*(3), 155–170.

Bensimon, E. M. (2006). Learning equity-mindedness: Equality in educational outcomes. *The Academic Workplace*, *1*(17), 2–21.

Bensimon, E. M., & Harris, F. III. (2012). The mediational means of enacting equity-mindedness among community college practitioners. In E. M. Bensimon & L. E. Malcolm (Eds.), *Confronting equity issues on campus: Implementing the equity scorecard in theory and practice*. Stylus.

Blanchard, K. H. (1967). College boards of trustees: A need for directive, leadership . . . a study of college presidents and board chairmen and their relationships with their trustees. *Academy of Management Journal*, *10*(4), 409–417.

Chait, R. P., Holland, T., & Taylor, B. E. (1996). The new work of the nonprofit board. *Harvard Business Review*, Sept./Oct., 36–46.

Crenshaw, K. (1991). Mapping the margins: Intersectionality, identity politics, and violence against women of color. *Stanford Law Review, 43*(6), 1241–1299.

Critical Higher Education Governance Collaborative. (2019a). *Building better boards: The call for equity in board decision making.* https://www.chegc.org/infographic-page.

Critical Higher Education Governance Collaborative. (2019b, October). *Equity ready boards: Campus trustees as bridge builders.* Keynote conducted at the Massachusetts Department of Higher Education Annual Statewide Trustee Education Conference, Boston, MA.

Collins, P. H. (2015). Intersectionality's definitional dilemmas. *Annual Review of Sociology, 41*(1), 1–20.

Commodore, F. (2018). The tie that binds: Trusteeship, values, and the decision-making process at AME-affiliated HBCUs. *Journal of Higher Education, 89*(4), 397–421.

Commodore, F., Rall, R. M., & Morgan, D. L. (2018, November). Asleep at the wheel: Failure to achieve inclusion at the highest level of university control. *Association for the Study of Higher Education Annual Meeting.* Paper presented at ASHE annual meeting, Tampa, FL.

Davies, G. K. (2011). Perspectives: Changing roles of governing and coordinating boards. *Change: The Magazine of Higher Learning, 43*(4), 45–48. doi:10.1080/00091383.2011.585299

Dooris, M. J. (2003). Two decades of strategic planning. *Planning for Higher Education, 31*(2), 26–32.

Fain, W. (2019, October 30). Wayne State trustees push back on free college. *Inside Higher Ed.* https://www.insidehighered.com/quicktakes/2019/10/30/wayne-state-trustees-push-back-free-college

Freedman, J. O. (2005). Presidents and trustees. In R. G. Ehrenberg (Ed.), *Governing academia* (pp. 9–27). Cornell University Press.

Garces, L. M., & Jayakumar, U. M. (2014). Dynamic diversity: Toward a contextual understanding of critical mass. *Educational Researcher, 43*(3), 115–124.

Goetzmann, W. N., & Oster, S. (2013). Competition among university endowments. In *How the financial crisis and great recession affected higher education* (pp. 99–126). University of Chicago Press.

Herron, O. R. (1969). *The role of the trustee.* International Textbook.

Johnson, S. G., Schnatterly, K., & Hill, A. D. (2013). Board composition beyond independence: Social capital, human capital, and demographics. *Journal of Management, 39*(1), 232–262.

Kezar, A. (2006). Rethinking public higher education governing boards' performance: Results of a national study of governing boards in the United States. *Journal of Higher Education, 77*(6), 968–1008. doi:10.1353/jhe.2006.0051

Lane, J. E. (2013). Higher education system 3.0: Adding value to states and institutions. In D. B. Johnstone & J. Lane (Eds.), *Higher education systems*

3.0: *Harnessing systemness, delivering performance* (pp. 3–26). State University of New York Press.

Lederman, D. (2019). Alaska regents reject plan for "One University" accreditation. *Inside Higher Ed.* https://www.insidehighered.com/quicktakes/2019/12/06/alaska-regents-reject-plan-one-university-accreditation

McLendon, M. K. (2003). Setting the governmental agenda for state decentralization of higher education. *Journal of Higher Education, 74*(5), 479–515. doi:10.1353/jhe.2003.0038

McNair, T. B. (2016). The time is now: Committing to equity and inclusive excellence. *Diversity & Democracy, 19*(1), 4–7. https://www.aacu.org/diversitydemocracy/2016/winter/mcnair

Minor, J. T. (2006). A case of complex governance: A structural analysis of university decision-making. *Journal of the Professoriate, 1*(2), 22–37.

Minor, J. T. (2008). Groundwork for studying governance at historically Black colleges and universities. *Understanding Minority-Serving Institutions*, 169–182.

Morgan, D. L., LePeau, L. A., & Commodore, F. (2021a). Observable evidence and partnership possibilities for governing board involvement in diversity, equity, and inclusion: A content analysis. *Research in Higher Education*, 1–33. https://link.springer.com/article/10.1007/s11162-021-09651-x

Morgan, D. L., Rall, R. M., Commodore, F., Fischer, R. A., & Bernstein, S. (2021b). Hiding in plain sight: The potential of state-level governing boards in postsecondary education policy agenda-setting. *Journal of Higher Education, 92*(4), 570–595.

Morphew, C. C., & Hartley, M. (2006). Mission statements: A thematic analysis of rhetoric across institutional type. *Journal of Higher Education, 77*(3), 456–471.

Museus, S. D. (2014). The culturally engaging campus environments (CECE) model: A new theory of success among racially diverse college student populations. In M. Paulsen (Ed.), *Higher education: Handbook of theory and research* (29th ed., pp. 189–227). Springer.

National Center for Education Statistics (NCES). (2017). Higher education general information survey (HEGIS), "Fall Enrollment in Colleges and Universities" surveys, 1976 and 1980; integrated postsecondary education data system (IPEDS), "Fall Enrollment Survey" (IPEDS-EF:90); and IPEDS spring 2001 through spring 2016, fall enrollment component.

Pusser, B., Slaughter, S., & Thomas, S. L. (2006). Playing the board game: An empirical analysis of university trustee and corporate board interlocks. *Journal of Higher Education, 77*(5), 747–775.

Rall, R. M. (2021). Modeling equity-minded leadership amid crises: The call for higher education governing boards to lead the way. *Journal of Higher Education Management, 36*(1), 25–31.

Rall, R. M., Morgan, D. L., & Commodore, F. (2018). Invisible injustice: Higher education boards and issues of diversity, equity, and inclusivity. In R. Jeffries

(Ed.), *Diversity, equity, and inclusivity in contemporary higher education* (pp. 261–277). IGI Global. doi:10.4018/978-1-5225-5724-1.ch016

Rall, R. M., Morgan, D. L., & Commodore, F. (2019, February). Responding to the call for equity: What every board member should know. The Association of Governing Boards of Universities and Colleges. https://agb.org/blog-post/responding-to-the-call-for-equity-what-every-board-member-should-know/

Rall, R. M., Morgan, D. L., & Commodore, F. (2020). Towards culturally sustaining governance: Best practices of theory, research, and practice. *Journal of Education Human Resources, 38*(1), 139–164.

Rall, R. M., Morgan, D. L., & Commodore, F. (Forthcoming). *Bounded boards: A commentary on the limitations of knowledge and scope of research of boards of higher education.*

Rall, R. M., & Orué, V. (2020). I, too, am a lead(her): The power and possibilities of women of color on governing boards of higher education in California. *Journal of Higher Education Management, 35*(1), 32–39.

Richards, L., O'Shea, J., & Connolly, M. (2004). Managing the concept of strategic change within a higher education institution: The role of strategic and scenario planning techniques. *Strategic Change, 13*(7), 345–359.

Ryan, J. (2007). Inclusive leadership: A review. *Journal of Educational Administration and Foundation, 18*(1/2), 92–125.

Schmidt, B. C. (2014). *Governance for a new era.* https://www.goacta.org/images/download/governance_for_a_new_era.pdf

Taylor, B. E., Chait, R. P., & Holland, T. P. (1991). Trustee motivation and board effectiveness. *Nonprofit and Voluntary Sector Quarterly, 20*(2), 207–224.

Taylor, J. S., & Machado, M. D. L. (2008). Governing boards in public higher education institutions: A perspective from the United States. *Tertiary Education and Management, 14*(3), 243–260.

Vespa, J., Armstrong, D. M., & Medina, L. (2018). *Demographic turning points for the United States: Population projections for 2020 to 2060.* Current Population Reports, U.S. Census Bureau, 23-1114.

Voorhees, R. A. (2008). Institutional research's role in strategic planning. *New Directions for Higher Education, 2008*(141), 77–85.

Weisbrod, B. A., & Asch, E. D. (2010). The truth about the "crisis" in higher education finance. *Change: The Magazine of Higher Learning, 42*(1), 23–29.

Wolf, C., & Floyd, S. W. (2017). Strategic planning research: Toward a theory-driven agenda. *Journal of Management, 43*(6), 1754–1788.

PART II
TEACHING AND LEARNING

4

(Re)Shaping Higher Education Classrooms with Inclusive Pedagogies

PAULA ADAMO, LILIANA DIAZ SOLODUKHIN, JANIECE Z. MACKEY, ADRIENNE MARTINEZ, AND JUDY MARQUEZ KIYAMA

Despite postsecondary institutions making gains in their diversity and inclusion efforts, many continue to exercise elitist values in their teaching and learning practices (Burke et al., 2017) and, in doing so, perpetuate the rewarding of only certain forms of knowledge and learning. Transmission models (Nola & Irzik, 2005) or banking models (Freire, 1970/2000) of teaching and learning, which approach students as empty containers to transmit or transfer knowledge into, do not humanize classroom environments for minoritized students whose cultural knowledge may differ from dominant forms of teaching and learning. Minoritized student populations may not understand unspoken classroom norms (Rendón, 1994), classified as "recognition and realization rules" (Burke et al., 2017, p. 77). Such "rules," which are often raced, classed, and gendered, contain inherent power dynamics and missed opportunities for culturally responsive teaching and learning.

This chapter focuses on how educational spaces can be reshaped to build upon the cultural values, assets, and collective knowledge of racially minoritized student populations. Particular attention is paid to asset-based and liberatory frameworks that draw upon resources found in the families and communities of racially minoritized groups with the mutual goals of creating changes in how everyday pedagogical participation is structured and interrogating the ways in which teaching and learning is raced, classed, and gendered. The chapter covers theoretical foundations of culturally responsive pedagogy and humanizing instructional methods as a means to understand and integrate cultural knowledge. The inspiration for this chapter began well before the assembling of our written thoughts. The authors first came together in a graduate-level course focused on inclusive pedagogies. The classroom space afforded us the opportunity to practice frameworks, theories, and methods written about in this chapter. In doing so, we observed what Johnson and colleagues (this volume) suggest is the "hyphen" in the translational racial equity research-practice (TRERP) framework: "The hyphen (-) in 'research-practice' signifies a complex, mutually constitutive relationship, a nexus, in which insights from each influence the other" (p. 00). We share further insights from the course later in the chapter. Recommendations for the development of culturally responsive, racial equity-focused curriculum are included throughout the chapter.[1] We conclude with a set of guiding questions for incorporating inclusive pedagogies into higher education classrooms.

Culturally Responsive Curriculum: Theoretical Roots of Inclusive Pedagogies

Culturally responsive pedagogy includes the following three criteria: "an ability to develop students academically, a willingness to nurture and support cultural competence, and the development of a sociopolitical or critical consciousness" (Ladson-Billings, 1995, p. 483). In building critical consciousness, students should feel comfortable to question sociohistorical and sociopolitical contexts while also questioning knowledge construction within learning spaces (Ladson-Billings, 2017). Culturally responsive pedagogy situates learning opportunities within the social and cultural contexts in which students and their families live, work, and function in everyday life (Kiyama et al., 2017) and moves beyond simply acquiring knowledge or "data" on various societal groups (Osei-Kofi et al., 2004). Students' learning is enhanced when we invest time and energy into understanding their lived experiences (Osei-Kofi et al., 2004), draw upon their cultural ways of knowing and being (Brockenbrough, 2014; Ladson-Billings, 1995), while also pushing students to examine the sociohistorical and sociocultural practices that informed such ways of knowing (Weiler, 2003).

However, Ladson-Billings (2017) cautions against the "corruption of culturally relevant pedagogy," which academia has been guilty of when "student learning is translated as assimilation and narrow forms of success . . . and the goal of supporting students' critical consciousness is either distorted at best, or conveniently left out altogether at worst" (p. 142). In our work, we engaged in pedagogical practices that are grounded in racial equity and foster cultural responsiveness while holding the concept of "culture" from an anthropological perspective as suggested by Ladson-Billings (2017) and others (see González et al., 2005, for examples of how culture is incorporated through a funds of knowledge framework). We sought to practice inclusive pedagogies built from a cultural lens that is responsive to students' worldviews, epistemologies, ways of being, as well as recognized components of various groups (Ladson-Billings, 2017). Similarly, we followed the model of Osei-Kofi and colleagues (2004), who suggest that creating inclusive learning spaces must go beyond celebration of difference to recognize that teaching and learning is never apolitical, thus establishing a need to "confront higher education at the core" (p. 56). That is, inclusive pedagogies can be understood as one mechanism by which the principles of the TRERP framework are realized; they offer an opportunity to interrogate the cycle of higher education that reinforces oppression and inequity and offer us a tool by which to interrupt that cycle (Salazar et al., 2010).

A Practice of Reciprocity and Epistemological Equity

Student learning and *inclusive pedagogies require a practice of reciprocity* (Vélez-Ibáñez & Greenberg, 2005), modeled first by the professor and further developed by the students. This includes engaging in radical honesty (Williams, 2016) while building a space in which students' funds of knowledge[2] can be shared (Kiyama et al., 2017). In order to mitigate harmful ways of critical consciousness being experienced "through the prism of whiteness" (Ladson-Billings, 2017, p. 142), there must be the self-work of unpacking one's positionality alongside reciprocity within classrooms. Doing so can create enhanced academic success (Ladson-Billings, 1995; Salazar et al., 2010) and demonstrate student agency and active participation in the pedagogical process. Creating a reciprocal environment allows for spaces of self-reflection and awareness of one's racialized, gendered, and classed experiences and cultural knowledge, and the ways in which personal experiences and histories converge with academic theory and content, in which students and professors can exercise action and agency in their own learning without constraint or discrimination, or, in other words, engage in liberatory praxis (hooks, 1994, p. 148).

Students enter the university with their own forms of knowledge and community networks that support their success and sense of identity. In these networks, knowledge is reciprocally exchanged (Moll, 2014). Instructors can create humanizing classroom environments that recognize students as members of robust community networks with diverse knowledge (Moll, 2014). Validating classroom environments celebrate students' identities by developing a variety of pedagogical approaches that acknowledge different learning styles, incorporate diverse scholars within the curriculum, and invite instructors to enter as co-learners alongside students whose contributions create spaces for mutual learning (Rendón, 1994). Additionally, it encourages instructors to engage in the co-creation of course content by collaboratively working with students to develop curriculum and instructional methods (Bovill et al., 2016). Recognizing students are members of communities with intersecting identities and welcoming these identities into the classroom starts the process of humanizing the classroom.

The classroom is not insular from what may be happening outside the walls of the classroom or the grounds of the university campus. Higher education institutions and, similarly, the college classroom are microcosms of society (Kaldis, 2009). Faculty can reinforce a humanizing approach by inviting students to share what may be affecting their learning and how it relates to the course or day's topic. The immigration status of a student's parent(s), economic instability, familial problems, or political rhetoric can affect a student's learning. Acknowledging issues affecting students, with a quick check-in at the beginning of class, can spur conversation among students and encourage discussions on the pertinence of course readings and assignments to issues they or their communities face. Allowing time for this type of sharing requires some reciprocity from faculty, who should also share how their learning is being affected.

Reciprocity, as a means to humanizing classroom environments, requires eliminating elitist values within faculty and student interactions and relationships. In order to do so, faculty can practice *epistemological equity* as one method of enacting a humanizing environment and encourage the construction of spaces where various forms of knowledge can coexist (Sefa Dei, 2010). Celebrating a student's "multiple forms of knowledge, identities, locations, and ways of knowing" (Osei-Kofi et al., 2004, p. 56) is a way epistemological equity can be achieved. Once implemented, classroom interactions between faculty and students can extend further to enrich curricular and cocurricular learning for institution-wide learning opportunities.

Institution-wide learning can include research opportunities that uphold student knowledge and networks as assets that may inform a research study and serve to expand a faculty member's liberatory pedagogy. An example of reciprocity, epistemological equity, and liberatory pedagogy in action can be seen in Liliana Diaz Solodukhin[3] and Cecilia Orphan's 2018–2019 research exploring reciprocal research relationships between a white faculty member and Latinx student. In their findings, Diaz Solodukhin and Orphan (2020) demonstrate how reciprocity and epistemological equity was achieved when the faculty member invited the student to co-lead a community-based research project. The student, as a member of this community, set expectations for the study and outlined how they would like this research to support and benefit their community. The faculty member learned from the student that relationships would need to be mended and trust regained by the university for this community to engage in future community-based research. The community had a mistrust of institutional agents (Martinez-Cosio & Iannacone, 2007) based on negative interactions with university researchers in the past. Reciprocally, the student expanded their research and advocacy skills in preparation for a leadership role within their community during their program and after graduation. Much in the same way the participants in the study exemplify a reciprocal relationship, the researchers (Orphan and Diaz Solodukhin) also exemplify acts of reciprocity in how they approach their collaborative research project, demonstrating that teaching and mentoring reciprocity is not limited to classroom settings. This particular example also illustrates the third TRERP principle, "Practitioners who 'work on the ground,' especially BIPOC, are essential to the formulation and identification of racial equity 'problems' worthy of scholarly attention" (Johnson et al., this volume, p. 00). As seen here, the community knowledge and trust that the student (i.e., the on-the-ground practitioner) brought to this project not only advanced a research agenda aimed at addressing racial inequities; they also prevented possible racial harm.

Counter-Spaces of Resistance

Inclusive pedagogies make room for counter-spaces of resistance (Muñoz et al., 2014) and allow for students to *experience* culturally relevant pedagogy

(Ladson-Billings, 2017), *transform* the classroom to make Black Lives Matter (Tuitt et al., 2018), and *humanize* teaching and research practices (Paris & Winn, 2014). The classroom can provide ways to co-create, deconstruct, and reconstruct learning, and offers the space to "refuse" to share forms of knowledge and research (Tuck & Yang, 2014), while engaging in humanizing and decolonizing teaching and research methods.

Faculty openness to engage in reflexive understanding of their pedagogical approach, curricula, and self creates opportunities for more racially inclusive classroom environments (Salazar et al., 2010; Osei-Kofi et al., 2004). Academic and interpersonal validation that demonstrates concern for students and the establishment of meaningful relationships, and construction of co-learning opportunities where multiple perspectives and identities are valued can humanize the classroom for racially minoritized students (Rendón, 1994). While much has been written and published over the past several decades regarding the environments of postsecondary campuses in which students of color are minoritized, similar themes remain consistent in students' experiences of exclusion, racism, and overall toxic campus climates (Harper, 2013). College campuses are unique environments for students to examine, often for the first time intentionally, systems of oppression and the impact of such systems on particular communities. Likewise, students can explore how their own identities are related to these structures of embedded racism (Gaxiola Serrano et al., 2019).

With intentional instruction, students can build a critical consciousness and contribute to the student learning environment by sharing their own lived experiences (Delgado & Stefancic, 2001; Ladson-Billings, 1999; Solórzano, 1997; Quaye & Chang, 2011; Villalpando, 2003).

However, the commitment to elevating voices and experiences that have been historically excluded in the curriculum can have unintentional adverse impact on racially minoritized students. An ever-growing concern on college campuses is how the First Amendment is enacted and upheld especially when white students demonstrate acts of overt and covert racism that contribute to a toxic campus climate (Campbell, 2004). These acts are often protected by the First Amendment to avoid student conduct sanctions or placated as a learning opportunity for the students perpetuating the toxic racial environment, which directly impedes the learning of racially minoritized students (Cress, 2008; Campbell, 2004). In such scenarios, racially minoritized students are often called upon to participate in learning dialogues without regard to the emotional and physical toll of their participation (Campbell, 2004).

The research on the racial toxicity of predominately white campuses is robust. Yet, research regarding how racially minoritized students, particularly Black students, manage to productively navigate these campuses is scant (Harper, 2013). Racially minoritized students were not only historically excluded from college campuses but were often isolated and ignored, leading to the feelings of invisibility and disposability. Research indicates that Black and minoritized students outperform their white counterparts academically when faculty and administrators validate their intellectual competence and ability to thrive in competitive career environments (Bensimon, 2007; Rendón & Muñoz, 2011). Moreover, for racially minoritized students, inclusive pedagogies and practices can delicately honor their lived experiences, while being duly mindful of the potential tokenizing nature of sharing such experiences. By shifting pedagogical approaches and focusing on student validation, racially minoritized students show increased retention and degree attainment rates (Cress, 2008). The counter-spaces of resistance can serve as a reprieve from a hostile campus environment so racially minoritized students can fully connect with and own their narratives as tools to survive and thrive in a climate that can be burdensome on their overall well-being. Ultimately, the intentional development of counter-spaces described here should cultivate agency and resistance beyond the classroom. Racial equity is asserted when, as Bañuelos (2006) suggests, counter-spaces of resistance are linked to a "collective claim to space rights within the university" (p. 99). That is, racial equity cannot be limited to considerations of normative standards of retention and attainment but must be realized as a space in which university environment(s) are reflective of the history, knowledge, contributions, and life of racially minoritized students.

Pragmatic Considerations: Inclusive Pedagogy across Multiple Modes of Learning

Inclusive pedagogy can be approached as practices implemented to teach any given curriculum. This curriculum can take the shape of a traditional syllabus and content in a college class as well as pedagogy that expands beyond the classroom. The theoretical foundations and teaching practices associated with inclusive pedagogies can be implemented into engagement with colleagues across campus and inform the development of co-curricular programs that bolster student learning in the classroom.

In this way, the facilitator of the curriculum provides an invitation to all participants to shape the learning experience together, whether it's curricular or co-curricular. There are a myriad of theoretical models of inclusive pedagogy that provide practical nuggets of pedagogical wisdom to help create a frame and recipe for how to go about facilitating implementation or praxis. For instance, Howell and Tuitt (2003) share characteristics of inclusive pedagogy as establishing opportunities for dialogue, engaging in personal narratives, and sharing power. These characteristics and list were extended by Salazar et al. (2010) and then Kiyama et al. (2017) to include collaboration, facilitation of large and small group discussions, read alouds, experiential learning, formative assessments, and beyond. The aforementioned suggestions offer an opportunity for faculty to reflect on how to then operationalize each across content, student characteristics, and multiple learning identities.

Students' voices should be invited to give feedback on content, implementation, and assessment of materials, so that the content can be modified to reflect individual experiences, knowledge, and talents. In a classroom, this may look like allowing students to deviate from mandated content so that they, in consultation with their instructor, can (re)design the content reflecting their cultural histories and knowledge. An anonymous check-in at the midpoint or early in the term can allow for the instructor to co-facilitate dialogue with students concerning what is working, not working, or shifts in the pedagogy or curriculum to be considered. An important consideration with including student voice and feedback is ensuring instructors are engaging in self-reflexivity in the dialogical process. Self-reflexivity is often considered when discussing researchers but must also be considered in classroom settings as well. Self-reflexivity includes considering one's own experiences and biases when engaging with course content and the learning process, and how past experiences shape interpretations of the content being developed (Creswell, 2009, p. 216). In this case, instructors must consider their experiences of receiving student feedback and engaging with student voice. Hence, instructors must ask themselves how past experiences with engaging with student voice and feedback shaped their practice and abilities to be open to feedback. Self-reflexivity must be centered to be attentive to the ways in which student voice and feedback are digested, received, and reflected upon.

As an administrator, this may mean bringing together team members to voice their particular expertise so that tasks are aligned with ability, cultural knowledge, and strengths. While compositional diversity (Museus, 2014) is critical to enriching a learning environment, epistemological diversity must be considered as well when building out inclusive educational spaces with faculty and staff. And, while tapping into the funds of knowledge of faculty and staff is critical, we must consider how labor can be racialized as tokenization and cultural taxation of faculty of color (Tierney & Bensimon, 1996) must be considered when facilitating opportunities for team learning. The facilitation of inclusive learning environments and how to enact these spaces must not solely land on the bodies of faculty of color. Instructors and administrators can create a more inclusive learning environment by soliciting feedback and approaching complex learning objectives or administrative functions with adaptability and a willingness to introspectively interrogate assumptions. Ultimately, this creates a learning community in which we continue to learn and grow from others. This is an empowering practice for students and staff, and a critical step in asserting "the other" as equal. One way in which we create inclusive learning opportunities is to co-teach with students.

Co-teaching and Co-learning: Student Reflection of Inclusive Pedagogies

Accepting "the other" as equal, not only recognizing but genuinely embracing the different forms of knowledge that all participants bring to the classroom, requires high levels of introspection, reflection, and humble willingness to create the necessary conditions for everyone to shine. These efforts run the intentional and calculated risk that in that process, the traditional position of power of the instructor will be relinquished. Good, inclusive teaching, then, cannot be reduced to a series of techniques because it must emerge from the identity and integrity of the teacher; we ultimately teach who we are (Palmer, 1998). We must look inward to get to know ourselves first before we can know who our students are (Palmer, 1998). Looking inside, noticing our strengths but also our shortcomings, requires a healthy dose of courage that is usually inspired by a profound desire and commitment to build a more equitable learning system in higher education. In the reflection that follows, Paula Adamo shares her co-teaching experience with Judy Marquez Kiyama. Adamo and Kiyama co-taught the same Inclusive Pedagogies seminar in spring 2019 that originally inspired this chapter in spring 2018.

Student Reflection: On a warm spring Monday evening, as students trickled into the first class on reshaping educational spaces, we all knew it would be different. A small group of twelve graduate students coming from all different professional backgrounds, races, ethnicities, nationalities, sexual orientations, languages, and religions gathered in a classroom that provided a picture-like background of the Rocky Mountains for an experience that we could tell would be memorable for us all.

The instructor was committed to model what she preached right from the start: a more inclusive way to teach at the higher educational level. The first sign of this commitment was to have a student as a co-instructor in the class, not as a mere assistant to help with mechanical grading but as a partner in the teaching-learning process. A strong message is sent when an instructor, who is perfectly capable to lead the class on her own, still decides to invite a former student to co-teach. There is commitment for a richer class experience for the new wave of students, but there is also generosity toward those coming behind us by helping ease their way into a different field. Equally important, there is the humility and willingness to enter in sustained instructional dialogue, learning from the other's strengths in the process. Additional meetings, and again, a renegotiation of roles in and outside the classroom by giving someone else the power to design part of a class as she sees fit, is a major signal that this class will not be a traditional one. The reshaping of higher education begins from the instructional design.

As students settle nervously in the classroom, the instructor welcomes them one by one, warmly. Some students start chatting with one another, others sit quietly. With the same attentiveness and care we see when a dinner host will not start serving without all the guests at the table, the instructor checks her roster and says softly: "We are all here; we can begin." The tone is welcoming, calm, but confident. The instructor introduces herself and asks in a non-tokenistic tone how everyone is doing, modeling the honesty of her tiredness herself. She then introduces her co-teacher and invites all students do a brief introduction.

After establishing some of the guideposts for the class, she shares that the curriculum as well as the modes of instruction will emerge in an organic manner as a response to the specific needs of students. The class moves on to the first activity: poem writing on our identity. As any good teacher knows, we cannot expect from students what we are not willing to do ourselves, so the main instructor shares a very personal and moving poem on where she is from. The tone is set. This class will require from all participants a lot more than close reading of texts and polished writing, this class will require deep *introspection and honesty. This class will symbolize the ultimate expression of change in higher education.*

Throughout the quarter, all participants—instructor, co-instructor, and students—danced the most delicate choreography. Each participant got a chance to change the rhythm and intensity of music and the instructor simply made sure that we all felt respected and heard and that we could all follow everyone's lead. There was no obligation to dance at all times, we could just move our heads or tap our feet and still feel how the sound waves enter our bodies and change it, forever. The invitation to select our own way of expressing ourselves meant that with some rhythms, one might have felt out of place, uncomfortable, and awkward, but with others, not only with our own selection, we could learn how much we had in common with the rest or how much more we knew without having realized it. The richness of the music selections made everyone learn at least a few new rhythms, music origins, and ways of moving and interacting with the space. It was a beautiful and challenging experience to dance to someone else's rhythm, at least for once, but surely opening the invitation to keep daring to push our own comfort zones. Most of us tried dancing in someone else's dance shoes, minimally for the duration of the song, but surely enhancing this ability and improving the inclination for future instances.

Students chose to share their knowledge and understanding of particular texts in the most varied and imaginable ways. I witnessed a second-language learner become completely fluent when he was able to swim in his territory through mindfulness and meditation. I witnessed another student invite the class to do black-out poetry and his impeccable reading made my eyes water. I witnessed an experienced K–12 teacher share her own interpretation of the concept of funds of knowledge so that her students and families would be able to share with the rest of the class all they know but what many times goes unnoticed in a traditional classroom. All these were examples of a magnificent expression of teaching and learning. It was a magnificent example of how an instructor's courage to let go of the reins of her class because she realizes that all participants, when given the opportunity and clear framework to work with, can become amazing, creative, and efficient leaders. To the untrained eye, one might question when an instructor decides to place herself not at the head of the table but to the side, as one more participant. When she is able to move from the center of the stage to the corner, letting students be in the center could be perceived as an "easier" position to take. The trained eye, however, knows that the reason why this can be done in a successful way is by experience, training, thought, and clear planning on how to provide the circumstances for the student to bloom in the center. The trained eye knows that much thought and an extreme level of attentiveness are taking place to provide that space. The instructor makes room but is always behind the scenes, ready to jump in in case someone needs a gentle, supporting intervention.

In educational spaces that are being reshaped with intellectual and emotional preparation, dedication, love, and courage, students are able to shine because the instructor is not afraid to take the risk to let them take the spotlight. This audacious way of teaching, Parker Palmer (1998) would say, is also an exercise of deep vulnerability that makes us feel a little naked in front of a class, daily. At times, students may even turn off the lights because they know that the only way to show their beautiful neon colors is by using black lights. It takes audacity, expertise, confidence, and humility to recognize that many times is a matter of instructors allowing for the space for neon colors to shine, even when it means that we become almost invisible. THAT is the beauty and power of inclusive teaching: recognizing that not everyone shines under the same type of light and that inclusive pedagogies helps us provide the conditions for a brighter, richer, and more colorful learning experience for all.

Reflective Questions for Educators

The following questions were posed by Kiyama and colleagues (2017) in their chapter on incorporating funds of knowledge as a culturally responsive pedagogy. The questions are intended to move us to a place of transformation, one that adopts "humanizing and dignity-affirming policies, practices, and processes" (TRERP principle 5; Johnson et al., this volume, p. 00). This excerpt is taken from pages 177–178 of their chapter, "Funds of Knowledge as a Culturally Responsive Pedagogy in Higher Education."

1. How is the researcher/instructor located in pedagogical exploration?—This question is adapted from Ladson-Billings (1995) and leads us to consider not only theoretical foundations of culturally responsive pedagogy but culturally responsive methodological practices as well in our attempt to gather information about students' social and cultural contexts.

2. How can (culturally responsive) pedagogy promote the kind of student success that engages larger social structural issues in a critical way? (Ladson-Billings, 1995, p. 469).

3. In attempting to become culturally responsive, what should the role of teacher versus facilitator be? (Freire & Macedo, 2003, p. 189). We would add—what roles do the students take on within the community of learners that is being developed?

4. How do we make sure to create a dialogue as a process of learning and knowing rather than a dialogue as conversation that mechanically focuses on the individual's lived experience? (Freire & Macedo, 2003, p. 193).

5. What do my teaching practices say about my assumptions, values, and beliefs about teaching? What constrains my view of what is possible in teaching? (adapted from Osei-Kofi et al., 2004, p. 61).

Our goal with this chapter was to demonstrate how inclusive pedagogies could be developed with intentional focus on the cultural and collective knowledge of racially minoritized student populations, while also emphasizing a space that allows for creative expression of critical consciousness. As Women of Color we have collectively created that space for one another, in the course that we shared together, in the classroom in which we teach, and in writing this chapter, and accordingly, we close by honoring our positionalities.

Concluding by Honoring Positionality

Culturally responsive pedagogies tend to be frequently associated with the K–12 context. However, as students (and faculty) in higher education we have experienced and benefited from such practices being regularly implemented in the classrooms in which we learn, grow, and develop into educators and practitioners. Racial equity is practiced when we, as Women of Color, have felt validated, heard, and deeply respected in classrooms in which such culturally responsive and holistic practices have been implemented. Simultaneously, we recognize that as instructors and administrators we also hold power in the learning environments—a power imbalance that must be explored especially when issues of race, class, gender, sexuality, income, language, and national origin are interrogated (Higginbotham, 1996; Osei-Kofi et al., 2004). Therefore, we take seriously the call to name our own positionalities, to challenge our own biases and assumptions, as they affect power dynamics in the classroom (Higginbotham, 1996; Osei-Kofi et al., 2004). We embrace and emulate these practices as instructors and administrators of higher education because of positive experiences that have affirmed our cultural identities and lived experiences.

Paula Adamo: Having been a student for the majority of my life, and a college instructor for almost half, I have learned that every class brings the opportunity to transform a strict transaction of content into a moment that might have a life-changing impact on all its participants. Since I was a little girl in my home country of Argentina and later as a woman in the United States, my life has been immensely enriched by the type of teachers that can make this type of magic happen. I now want to dedicate my career to understanding and disseminating the intricacies of this magic.

Liliana Diaz Solodukhin: I enter this work as a mother, partner, and student whose intersecting identities as a working-class, first-generation Latina inform my research and praxis. I strongly believe research should create a positive impact on the lives of people and communities.

Janiece Z. Mackey: I come to this research as a Black cisgender mother, wife, and PhD candidate who is a critical conscious–preneur and praxticioner (Mackey, 2015) centering my teaching, research, and service in critical race praxis.

Adrienne Martinez: I am a first-generation, Latina, working professional and a mother. Throughout my academic journey, I've worked full-time and built a career as a higher education practitioner with a focus on equity, though I still imagine a career path in the classroom.

Judy Marquez Kiyama: I am a first-generation college student, a Mexican American embracing her Chicana activist identity, a working-class kid, a mother, a scholar. These cannot be separated. Each inform my role as an administrator and professor of higher education.

Notes

1. For access to the *(Re)Shaping Educational Spaces with Inclusive Pedagogies* syllabus referenced throughout this chapter, visit: https://portfolio.du.edu/Judy.Kiyama/page/69476 or contact jkiyama@email.arizona.edu.

2. Funds of knowledge are defined as the "historically accumulated and culturally developed bodies of knowledge and skills essential for household or individual functioning and well-being" (Moll et al., 1992, p. 133) and are central to the ways in which people engage with one another and share valuable knowledge.

3. Here Diaz Solodukhin is sharing a specific example from her own collaborative research project with her advisor, Dr. Cecilia Orphan.

References

Bañuelos, L. E. (2006). "Here they go again with the race stuff": Chicana negotiations of the graduate experience. In D. Delgado Bernal, C. A. Elenas, F. E. Godinez, & S. Villenas (Eds.), *Chicana/Latina education in everyday Life: Feminista perspectives on pedagogy and epistemology* (pp. 95–112). State University of New York Press.

Bensimon, E. M. (2007). The underestimated significance of practitioner knowledge in the scholarship on student success. *Review of Higher Education, 30*(4), 441–469. doi:10.1353/rhe.2007.0032.

Bovill, C., Cook-Sather, A., Felten, P., Millard, L., & Moore-Cherry, N. (2016). Addressing potential challenges in co-creating learning and teaching: Overcoming resistance, navigating institutional norms and ensuring inclusivity in student-staff partnerships. *Higher Education, 71*, 195–208.

Brockenbrough, E. (2014). Becoming queerly responsive: Culturally responsive pedagogy for Black and Latino urban queer youth. *Urban Education, 51*(2), 170–196.

Burke, P. J., Crozier, G. & Misiaszek, L. I. (2017). *Changing pedagogical spaces in higher education: Inequality, diversity and misrecognition*. Routledge.

Campbell, K. G. (2004). *Freedom of speech, imagination, and political dissent: Culturally centering the free speech principle* (Order No. 3134429). Available from Dissertations & Theses.

Cress, C. M. (2008). Creating inclusive learning communities: The role of student–faculty relationships in mitigating negative campus climate. *Learning Inquiry, 2*(2), 95–111.

Creswell, J. W. (2009). *Research design: Qualitative, quantitative, and mixed methods approaches* (3rd ed.). Sage.

Diaz Solodukhin, L., & Orphan, C. (2020). Operationalizing funds of knowledge: Examining a reciprocal research relationship between a white faculty member and a Latino student. *Journal of Diversity in Higher Education*. Advance online publication. https://doi.org/10.1037/dhe0000286

Delgado, R., & Stefancic, J. (2001). *Critical race theory: An introduction*. New York University Press.

Freire, P. (2000/1970). *Pedagogy of the oppressed*. 30th anniversary ed. Bloomsbury Press.

Freire, P., & Macedo, D. P. (2003). A dialogue: Culture, language, and race. In A. Howell & F. Tuitt (Eds.), *Race and higher education: Rethinking pedagogy in diverse college classrooms* (pp. 189–214). Harvard Education.

Harper, S. R. (2013). Am I my brother's teacher? Black undergraduates, racial socialization, and peer pedagogies in predominantly white postsecondary contexts. *Review of Research in Education, 37*(1), 183–211.

Higginbotham, E. (1996). Getting all students to listen: Analyzing and coping with student resistance. *American Behavioral Scientist, 40*(2), 203–211.

hooks, b. (1994). *"Theory as liberatory praxis" in teaching to transgress: Education as the practice of freedom.* Routledge.

Howell, A. & Tuitt, F. (2003). *Race and higher education: Rethinking pedagogy in diverse college classrooms.* Harvard Education.

Gaxiola Serrano, T. J., González Ybarra, M., & Delgado Bernal, D. (2019). "Defend yourself with words, with the knowledge that you've gained": An exploration of *conocimiento* among Latina undergraduates in ethnic studies. *Journal of Latinos and Education, 18*(3), 243–257.

González, N., Moll, L., & Amanti, C. (2005). *Funds of knowledge: Theorizing practices in households, communities and classrooms.* Routledge.

Kaldis, B. (2009). The university as microcosm. *Educational Philosophy and Theory, 41*(5), 553–574.

Kiyama, J. M., Rios-Aguilar, C., & Deil-Amen, R. (2017). Funds of knowledge as a culturally responsive pedagogy in higher education. In J. M. Kiyama & C. Rios-Aguilar (Eds.), *Funds of knowledge in higher education: Honoring students' cultural experiences and resources as strengths* (pp. 175–188). Routledge.

Ladson-Billings, G. (1995). Toward a theory of culturally relevant pedagogy. *American Educational Research Journal, 32*(3), 465–491.

Ladson-Billings, G. (1999). Preparing teachers for diverse student populations: A critical race theory perspective. *Review of Research in Education, 24*, 211–247.

Ladson-Billings, G. (2017). The (R)Evolution will not be standardized: Teacher education, hip hop pedagogy, and culturally relevant pedagogy 2.0. In D. Paris & H. S. Alim (Eds.), *Culturally sustaining pedagogies: Teaching & learning for justice in a changing world* (pp. 141–156). Teachers College Press.

Mackey, J. Z. (2015). Counter-stories of my social science academic and career development from a critical "praxticioner" and "conscious-preneur." Master's thesis, University of Colorado Denver.

Martinez-Cosio, M., & Iannacone, R. M. (2007). The tenuous role of institutional agents: Parent liaisons as cultural brokers. *Education and Urban Society, 39*(3), 349–369.

Moll, L. C. (2014). *L.S. Vygotsky and education.* Routledge.

Moll, L. C., Amanti, C., Neff, D., & González, N. (1992). Funds of knowledge for teaching: Using a qualitative approach to connect homes and classrooms. *Theory into Practice, 31*, 132–141.

Muñoz, S., Espino, M. M., & Antrop-González, R. (2014). Creating counter-spaces of resistance and sanctuaries of learning and teaching: An analysis of Freedom University. *Teachers College Record, 116*, 1–32

Museus, S. (2014). The culturally engaging campus environments (CECE) model: A new theory of success among racially diverse college student populations. *Higher Education: Handbook of Theory and Research, 29,* 189–227.

Nola, R., & Irzik, G. (2005). *Philosophy, science, education and culture.* Springer.

Osei-Kofi, N., Richards, S. L., & Smith, D. G. (2004). Inclusion, reflection, and the politics of knowledge: On working toward the realization of inclusive classroom environments. In L. I. Rendón, M. Garcia, & D. Person (Eds.), *Transforming the first-year experience for students of color* (pp. 55–66). University of South Carolina, National Resource Center for the First-Year Experience and Students in Transition.

Palmer, P. J. (1998). *The courage to teach.* Jossey-Bass.

Paris, D., & Winn, W. T. (2014). *Humanizing research: Decolonizing qualitative inquiry with youth and communities.* Sage.

Quaye, S. J., & Chang, S. H. (2012). Fostering cultures of inclusion in the classroom: From marginality to mattering. In S. D. Museus & U. M. Jayakumar (Eds.), *Creating campus cultures: Fostering success among racially diverse student populations* (pp. 88–105). Routledge.

Rendón, L. I. (1994). Validating culturally diverse students: Toward a new model of learning and student development. *Innovative Higher Education, 19*(1), 33–51.

Rendón, L. I., & Muñoz, S. M. (2011). Revisiting validation theory: Theoretical foundations, applications, and extensions. *Enrollment Management Journal, 5*(2) 12–33.

Salazar, M. C., Stone Norton, A., Tuitt, F. A. (2010). Waving promising practices for inclusive excellence into the higher education classroom. In L. B. Nilson & J. E. Miller (Eds.), *To improve the academy: Resources for faculty, instructional, and organizational development* (pp. 208–224). Jossey-Bass.

Sefa Dei, G. J. (2010). *Teaching Africa: Towards a transgressive pedagogy.* Springer.

Solórzano, D. (1997). Images of words that wound: Critical race theory, racial stereotyping and teacher education. *Teacher Education Quarterly, 69*(1/2), 60–73.

Tierney, W. G., & Bensimon, E. M. (1996). *Promotion and tenure: Community socialization in academe.* SUNY Series: Frontiers in Education. State University of New York Press.

Tuck, E., & Yang, K. W. (2014). R-Words: Refusing research. In D. Paris & M. T. Winn (Eds.), *Humanizing research: Decolonizing qualitative inquiry with youth and communities* (pp. 223–248). Sage.

Tuitt, F., Haynes, C., & Stewart, S. (2018). Transforming the classroom at traditionally white institutions to make Black Lives Matter. *To Improve the Academy, 37,* 63–76.

Weiler, K. (2003). Freire and a feminist pedagogy of difference. In A. Howell & F. Tuitt (Eds.), *Race and higher education: Rethinking pedagogy in diverse college classrooms* (pp. 215–242). Harvard Education.

Williams, B. (2016). Radical honesty: Truth telling as pedagogy for working through shame in academic spaces. In F. Tuitt, C. Haynes, & S. Stewart (Eds.), *Race, equity, and the learning environment: The global relevance of critical and inclusive pedagogies in higher education* (pp. 71–82). Stylus.

Vélez-Ibáñez, C., & Greenberg, J. (2005). Formation and transformation of funds of knowledge. In N. González, L. C. Moll, & C. Amanti (Eds.), *Funds of knowledge: Theorizing practices in households, communities, and classrooms* (pp. 47–70). Routledge.

Villalpando, O. (2003). Self-segregation or self-preservation? A critical race theory and Latina/o critical theory analysis of a study of Chicana/o college students. *International Journal of Qualitative Studies in Education, 16*(5), 619–646. doi:10.1080/0951839032000142922

5

Developing Intersectional Consciousness

A De/colonial Approach to Researching Pedagogy in the Higher Education Context

MILDRED BOVEDA

As access to higher education is expanding, faculty and instructors must consider how to engage college and university students with a range of needs and experiences. Today, students who are pursuing postsecondary education are far more diverse than ever before, yet there is a consensus that more can be done to attract and retain racially minoritized students in colleges and universities (e.g., Byrd, 2019). It is critical, moreover, for instructors to have an understanding of the interconnectedness and complexity of sociocultural identities (e.g., race, gender, sexuality, class, citizenship, dis/ability), as no one category of identity captures all aspects of what a student brings to the classroom (e.g., Harris & Patton, 2019).

Intersectionality, as conceptualized by Black feminist theorists, requires examinations of diversity beyond one or two sociocultural markers of identities (Cho et al., 2013; Crenshaw, 1989). Instead, intersectionality provides a lens for examining how systemic oppression against those with multiple minoritized and marginalized identities—that is, ableism, ageism, classism, colonialism, heterosexism, imperialism, nationalism, patriarchy, religious bigotry, and white supremacy—interconnects in complex ways (Collins, 1990, 2000). In this chapter, I revisit research I conducted across three universities that focus, in part, on inclusive pedagogical practices within the higher education context. More specifically, I examine how faculty and students in university-based teacher education programs understood complex and intersecting issues of equity. I describe the conceptualization of the *intersectional competence* construct (Boveda, 2016; Boveda & Aronson, 2019), and a protocol I co-developed for college and university faculty to collaborate to teach with *intersectional consciousness* in mind (Boveda & Weinberg, 2020a; Boveda & Weinberg, 2020b).

In addition to describing constructs and tools that attend to intersectionality within the university-based teacher education programs, I delineate the co-constructed de/colonial ethical considerations I developed for research involving teacher education faculty in the United States. To ensure equity-minded policy and practice recommendations, I offer the potentialities of bringing together Black feminist epistemology with de/colonial research ethics in teacher education, recognizing each centers people who have firsthand insights as knowledge-maker (i.e., those with embodied experiences with systematic oppression such as Black women or individuals with disabilities). In alignment with the translational racial equity research-practice (TRERP) framework proposed by Johnson and colleagues (this volume), the constructs and considerations presented in this chapter initially emerged by engaging with racialized educators and faculty members operating within the context of university-based teacher education. Similarly, as the TRERP framework insists that issues in higher education be framed within their "full context," this chapter describes the tensions that arose as I attempted to center oft-marginalized voices. The de/colonial ethical considerations serve to caution myself and other researchers to not overstate liberatory agendas and as reminders that knowledges generated within westernized universities have created and sustained inequities throughout the world. I conclude, therefore, by describing the broader implications that de/colonial research ethics, intersectional competence, and intersectional consciousness have for institutions of higher education, and how these ideas may inform those engaged in research on pedagogical practices with undergraduate and graduate students.

Faculty of Color in University-Based Teacher Education Programs

Teacher educators in higher education institutions have the dual responsibilities of preparing teachers to work in P–12 settings and meeting the teaching, service, and scholarly demands of their institutions. Their work as pedagogues has implications at the primary, secondary, and higher education levels due to teacher candidates' current and future work with diverse student populations in P–12 schools. The complexities of serving primary, secondary, and tertiary students in the United States can no longer be discussed without also considering the ableist, imperialist white supremacist patriarchy that systematically shapes and structures policies and practices influencing classroom environments (Grech, 2015; hooks, 1994). One underexplored aspect of these environments is *who* researches and teaches in university-based teacher education programs. Discourse around the sociocultural identities of P–12 teachers has focused on statistics such as "80% of teachers are white women," or that the majority of pupils teacher educators are preparing are also white women (Sleeter, 2017). These numbers problematize the demographic divide between educators and P–12 students without sufficiently interrogating the kinds of knowledges and ways of knowing privileged in US schools or the colleges and universities preparing P–12 schoolteachers.

Faculty and students who consider their intersectional identities and the colonial histories of their university-based teacher preparation are better equipped to engage diverse colleagues, students, and families to improve the experiences of all learners. Though underrepresented, faculty of color hold great potential for studying and explaining the inequitable challenges that persist in teacher education as they often are situated in equity-based research communities (e.g., Merryfield, 2000; Ohito, 2019; Suh & Hinton, 2015) and have experienced the marginalizing effects of the white, westernized academy (e.g., Ladson-Billings, 2005). For example, faculty at minority-serving institutions in the United States also contend with colonial and white supremacist forces (Exkano, 2013; García, 2018), even enduring racial microaggressions and racial battle fatigue (e.g., Boveda, 2019b). The field must continue to acknowledge the unique embodied and intersectional understandings teacher educators of color bring to their work within equity-based education and research. This acknowledgment has implications for how knowledge is considered, produced, and disseminated within these communities and beyond.

The limited empirical studies that explicitly examine teacher educators of color focus primarily on their role as instructors and their pedagogical practices (e.g., Busey & Waters, 2016; Dixson & Dingus, 2007; Goodwin, 2004; Hill-Brisbane & Dingus, 2007). It is rare to find articles that emphasize the theoretical underpinnings and onto-epistemic orientations of these faculty and how they inform their practice. One exception is a study that asked teacher educators about their philosophical orientations and beliefs about the purposes of education (Flynn et al., 2013). Flynn and colleagues found that, when compared to white respondents, teacher educators of color tended to have "a postmodern/social reconstructionist or progressive orientation" (p. 62) as evident by their focus on social justice and social and cultural issues. Relatedly, my colleagues and I argued for an intersectional, de/colonial orientation toward curriculum studies (Boveda et al., 2019) and ethical considerations for preparing teachers and leaders for urban contexts (Boveda & Bhattacharya, 2019). In addition to teaching praxis or curriculum considerations, however, university-based teacher educators of color are also engaged in education *research*. In this chapter, I describe intersectional and de/colonial theoretical framings to teacher education research—approaches informed, in part, by my embodied experiences at predominantly white institutions and at a Hispanic-serving institution (Boveda, 2019a, 2019b). As such, I call for a closer examination of the dominant ontologies and epistemologies privileged in teacher education research and practices happening within the westernized academy (Grosfoguel, 2013).

Intersectionality and Teacher Education Research

This chapter contributes to the ongoing discourse of intersectionality in the higher education literature (Harris & Patton, 2019; Haynes et al., 2020), and as intersectionality pertains to pedagogical practices. I draw from intersectionality, Black feminist thought, and transnational feminisms to envisage ways college and university faculty develop understandings about intersecting marginalized identities. I specifically attend to the multiple and interlocking ways schools perpetuate social inequities through a colonial project that centers Eurocentric and patriarchal ways of being and knowing.

INTERSECTIONAL COMPETENCE

The language of intersectionality, introduced by Black feminist scholars (Crenshaw, 1989), provides a way to discuss the complexities involved in simultaneously considering sociocultural identities in the teaching and learning process (Artiles, 2013; Collins & Bilge, 2016). Of primary concern are the effects of multiple *markers of difference* (i.e., minoritized or marginalized categories of age, citizenship, class, dis/ability, ethnicity, gender, linguistic origin, nationality, religion, socioeconomic status, or sexuality). The construct of intersectional competence describes teachers' preparedness to respond to the multiple, intersecting markers of identities in P–12 schools. Each of the eight indicators of the intersectional competence construct, and the literature that informed their derivation, is briefly described as follows.

Studies in special education that utilize intersectionality as a lens informed indicators 1–3 of the intersectional competence construct. These indicators were (1) *the ability to clearly identify sociocultural group categories and markers of difference* (Arms et al., 2008; Artiles, 2013; Waitoller & Kozleski, 2013); (2) *an understanding of the interlocking and simultaneous effects of multiple markers of difference* (e.g., Ferri & Connor, 2008; García & Ortiz, 2013; Natapoff, 2005); and (3) *an understanding of the systems of oppression and marginalization* that occur at the intersection of multiple markers of difference (Artiles et al., 2011; Connor, 2006, 2008; Erevelles & Minear, 2010; Liasidou, 2013; McCall & Skrtic, 2009).

Indicators 4–5 relate to preservice teachers' ability to collaborate to assess and address the needs of diverse learners, including students with disabilities. Derived from studies of collaborative teacher preparation for general and special education preservice teachers, indicators include: (4) *the capacity to co-construct and negotiate professional roles and responsibilities when teaching students with diverse abilities* (Pugach et al., 2014; Blanton et al., 2018); and (5) *the ability to assess how structural forces (i.e., cultural, linguistic, economic) influence the experiences of students with disabilities and their families* (McCall et al., 2014).

Indicators 6–8 relate to preservice teachers' readiness to instruct racially, ethnically, and linguistically diverse students and students with dis/abilities: (6) *an understanding that personal and professional beliefs about the value of diversity are distinct but interrelated; each is susceptible to change* (Pohan & Aguilar, 2001); (7) *a belief of teaching as agency for social change* (Enterline et al., 2008); and (8) *evidence of high expectations for all students* (Liang & Zhang, 2008).

The intersectional competence measure (ICM) assesses preservice teachers' intersectional competence. The items developed to demonstrate these indicators were largely informed by university students who were of minoritized racial, ethnic, and linguistic origins (Boveda & Aronson, 2019). Given how Black feminist theory privileges the experiences of those often relegated to the periphery of dominant research agendas (Collins, 2000), it was important to construct the phrasing of the items based on how people of color and culturally and linguistically diverse preservice teachers understood the construct, which often is shaped by the colonial and imperial function of the westernized academy discussed further later. Moreover, bell hooks's use of the phrase "imperialist white supremacist capitalist patriarchy" is critical and anchors my efforts to embrace complexity as I continue to validate the ICM:

> I wanted to have some language that would actually remind us continually of the interlocking systems of domination that define our reality and not to just have one thing be like, you know, gender is the important issue, race is the important issue, but for me the use of that particular jargonistic phrase was a way, a sort of short cut way of saying all of these things actually are functioning simultaneously at all times in our lives and that if I really want to understand what's happening to me, right now at this moment in my life, as a black female of a certain age group, I won't be able to understand it if I'm only looking through the lens of race. (hooks, 1997)

Intersectional Consciousness Collaboration Protocols

While the ICM is an evaluative tool that assesses educators' intersectional competence, the intersectional consciousness collaboration (ICC) protocols offer guiding questions that help faculty plan for instruction with intersectional consciousness in mind—that is, their understandings of how educational systems are implicated in social inequalities (e.g., Boveda, 2019b). In 2019, with the support of internal grants from Arizona State University at Mary Lou Fulton Teachers College and its provost office, I co-constructed two versions of the ICC protocol with my colleague and STEM teacher educator Andrea Weinberg. One centered the university students' future role as teachers. The second, the ICC for teacher education (ICC-TE), was designed for university faculty collaborations and emphasized how teacher educators plan, instruct, and reflect on the preparation of teachers. The ICC-TE offers scaffolded items for making these pedagogical moves.

The ICC is comprised of six elements. The first element of the protocol focuses on establishing an intersectionally conscious collaboration (e.g., Boveda, 2016). University faculty must begin by exploring their professional and personal identities when attempting to meet the needs of diverse learners. The second concerns curriculum development and pedagogical planning (e.g., Goodnough et al., 2009; Tobin & Roth, 2006). The third element emphasizes collaboration around instruction that centers diverse students (e.g., Pugach et al., 2014; Weinberg et al., 2019). ICC Element 4 focuses on assessment, analysis of student data, and soliciting feedback from students (e.g., Grant & Zwier, 2011). Items prompting reflection and co-generative dialogues are found in the fifth element of the protocol (e.g., Roth et al., 2002; Souto-Manning, 2019). The sixth element focuses on creating plans to sustain productive, ethical, and lateral dynamics in intersectionally conscious partnerships (e.g., Andrews & Tjosvold, 1983; Boveda & Aronson, 2019).

The protocol is designed for faculty members to challenge assumptions and personal biases, collaborate with diverse colleagues, and keep intersectionality in mind when making pedagogical decisions. While the present version of the protocol was found robust for the teacher education context, it can also inform the work of others who teach in higher education. For example, the ICC protocol is in use by physics instructors (Boveda & Weinberg, 2020a). The questions of the ICC encourage faculty to reflect on what they have learned about their educational trajectories that could help them better understand one another or their students (e.g., revelations about gendered or racialized dynamics in their respective academic field, societal forces impacting students' experiences, accommodations needed in instruction to address the needs of students with disabilities). Also, faculty are encouraged to reflect on any disorienting dilemmas and internal or external conflicts experienced while teaching or planning for diverse students. In other words, to facilitate intersectional consciousness and reflect for action, this protocol asks faculty to focus on who might potentially benefit or struggle with the pedagogical and epistemological approaches privileged in colleges and universities. The ICC-TE requires faculty to consider how to engage students with learning activities that are personally, culturally, and professionally relevant.

Focus groups with teacher educators who have reviewed or who are implementing the protocol suggest that the first element requires multiple discussions between collaborators. Teacher educators discussed how retracing their personal histories and professional experiences drew them to university-based teacher education. They were able to identify the tensions and possibilities of intersectional consciousness by spending sustained time identifying pain points in their childhood experiences with oppressive forces like racism, classism, and sexism. For example, a white faculty member from the Southern region of the United States discussed her frustration with bigotry in her family and her tendency to pull away from those she suspects are racists. In return, a teacher educator who self-identifies as multiracial explained to her white colleague that rejecting those who exhibit bigotry is not a privilege she can afford, as it would leave her further marginalized. She explained how her spiritual beliefs helped her cope with white supremacy and patriarchy. Other findings indicated that one conversation about how faculty members experienced or understand intersectionality is insufficient. As the experiences shared by each collaborator increase vulnerability, these conversations must be processed and unpacked, sometimes requiring multiple conversations. They found the items in the first and sixth elements especially useful for this process.

De/colonization and Higher Education

As the developer of these pedagogical tools, it is critical to situate how my embodied experiences inform my research and pedagogical practices. I am a Black woman who was born and educated in the United States. My first learned and spoken language was Spanish, and I have familial ties to the Dominican Republic. I am situated within university-based teacher education, special education, and education policy research communities—all of which are predominantly white spaces.

The distinct contexts where these research studies have taken place matter. First, these constructs were developed in the United States, a country that has been an imperial political, economic, and epistemic force felt around the world, inclusive of the US hegemony in educational research (see Ivanović & Ho, 2019). Further, to contextualize the implications of the development of these tools within and for the university setting, it is critical to understand how institutions of higher education have historically served—and continue to enact—a colonial function. The exploitation of Indigenous people, lands, and resources, and the transatlantic enslavement of Africans precipitated the establishment of institutions of higher education throughout stolen lands (de Sousa Santos, 2015; Wilder, 2014), the westernization of universities around the globe (Grosfoguel, 2013), and the eventual privileging of epistemologies (mostly of white men) from five countries of the Global North: France, Germany, Italy, the United Kingdom, and the United States (de Sousa Santos, 2010; Grosfoguel, 2013). Furthermore, this process happened simultaneously as epistemicides continued through the erasure and devaluation of the knowledge, ways of knowing, languages, and intellectual contributions of people who survived genocides and colonial subjugation. Therefore, in referencing decoloniality while writing in English and working at a US university, it is difficult to fully separate my participation in university-based endeavors from my role as a Black feminist teacher educator who desires to disrupt these hegemonic structures.

Second, I developed the items within different regions across the United States. I began to develop the items within my hometown of Miami, Florida, and continued to validate these constructs with participants from Midwestern and Southwestern universities. I conducted focus groups and interviews within different types of research-intensive universities including public, private, predominantly white, and minority-serving institutions. While participants in Miami were largely from the surrounding region, many had familial ties to the Caribbean, Central and South. In contrast, in the Southwestern and Midwestern contexts, the preservice teachers and teacher educators came from a range of US states; those who self-identified as Latinx or Hispanic all had familial ties to Mexico. I also found that the notion of race/ethnicity and attitudes toward language differences was greatly shaped by the distinct colonial histories of the university and its geographic location. In other words, when thinking about critiquing the imperialist white supremacist capitalist patriarchy present in the US academy, I needed to recognize the multiplicity and diversity of colonial histories that exist within this nation (Boveda & Bhattacharya, 2019). For example, I have reflected when collaborating and conducting research with Indigenous faculty, doctoral students, and preservice teachers in the Southwestern region, as my de/colonial experiences and marginalizing histories are distinct yet interconnected with theirs.

Third, as scholars such as George Dei (2000) and Shalini Puri (2004) explain in their critiques of white supremacy, colonialism, and imperialism in the Americas, "invocations of blackness or refusals of

'Westernization' . . . by themselves have been no guarantee of progressive racial politics, far less progressive gender or sexual politics" (Dei, 2000, p. 51). Demonizing all western knowledge or romanticizing all precolonial, Black, and Indigenous ways of being is, ironically, as essentialist and reductive as the binaried and dualistic ways privileged in the westernized university (Grosfoguel, 2013).

Therefore, as I consider my transnational histories and analyze my experiences across the US academy, I align with Black feminist and transnational scholars who recognize that neither colonization nor decolonization ever existed separate from each other.

Even with my positionality as a Black woman/Afro-Latina with familial ties to the Global South, as a US-based scholar publishing primarily in English I contend with the privileges I have as a representative of these institutions. That is, I recognize that my work as a university-based teacher educator is related to a westernized university system that has historically advanced the oppression of Indigenous, Black, Brown, and disabled bodies (Grech, 2015), and the indoctrination of western and patriarchal superiority in knowledge-making (Grosfoguel, 2013).

De/colonial Ethical Guidelines for the Practice and Research of University-Based Instruction

There are several overlapping aspects between the foundational elements of the intersectional competence construct for preservice teachers, intersectional consciousness for university-based teacher educators, and the de/colonial approaches I espouse. These intersections include the co-construction of roles and responsibilities and the recognition of how complex embodied experiences are avenues for social change. Furthermore, given that the goals of these tools are to heighten intersectional consciousness to shift away from marginalizing educational practices, they are clearly in conversation with the emphasis of transformational change in this volume.

The following points are considerations for de/colonial ethical approaches in educational research for those who would like to research university-based teacher education and higher education pedagogical praxis (adopted from Boveda & Bhattacharya, 2019). These ethical guidelines are applicable for those designing courses that (a) address minoritized communities that the instructor(s) are not a part of, and (b) have minoritized students who have matriculated into the course. They are presented as questions to encourage higher education instructors, researchers, and scholars to consider how addressing intersecting systems of oppression can happen without further centering westernized, essentialist, or other oppressive ways of being and knowing.

MOVING BEYOND ESSENTIALIZING

- When referencing marginalized communities, is there an understanding of how the specific histories of the communities were established? If so, who created and upheld the knowledge?
- If faculty claim to be representatives of marginalized communities, do they explain or allude to any privileged positions they embody that more vulnerable community members do not?
- If faculty are not representative of a minoritized group discussed, is there evidence of due diligence to locate cultural differences between the faculty member and said group? If conducting research, does the researcher continuously interrogate her interpretations?

AVOIDING EPISTEMICIDE

- Is there evidence that the authorities/elders from the community were consulted? Are faculty aware of which insiders' voices are privileged and why?
- Is there evidence the college/university representatives were invited or welcomed into the community about which they speak?
- If there are critiques or expansions to previous analyses about the community, by community members, are the merits of those findings acknowledged?

DISRUPTING DEHUMANIZING EPISTEMOLOGY

- Are the people of minoritized communities chastised for interpretations of their lived experiences that conflict with the consensus of the academy?

- Are people's suffering and the conditions that sustain and proliferate their suffering understood in terms of their context or is it framed from a deficit perspective?
- When engaging in or evaluating research, are methods of inquiry situated in ways that honor the de/colonial histories of the participants of the study?
- In classroom readings, are minoritized community members seen as more than data providers from whom to extract information? What would a dignified and ethical relationship with participants look like within the study's context?

ENGAGING AND INTERROGATING CO-GENERATIVE EPISTEMOLOGY

- Are the ways knowledge construction occurs in minoritized and racialized communities honored and interrogated for colonial influences and antiracist desires of resistance?
- Are decisions being made regarding what would remain as sacred insider communal knowledge and what can be shared with the world at large?
- In what ways are sources outside of westernized academic discourses centered and integrated into inquiry? Into curriculum and pedagogy? Are they integrated as an afterthought, or as the leading onto-epistemic orientations?

Implications for Research of Pedagogical Practice in Institutions of Higher Education

In the United States, quality university-based teacher education research and practice is predicated on the work of instructors who prepare teachers with the realities of P–12 schooling in mind. I offer two pedagogical tools and a set of ethical considerations that I co-constructed and developed to evaluate the effectiveness and integrity of equity work in university-based teacher education (i.e., the ICM, the ICC protocol, the guiding questions for de/colonial research ethics). I described the approaches I took to study the pedagogical practices of teacher educators and preservice teachers and their understandings of how schools—including institutions of higher education—are implicated and entangled in interlocking, systemic oppression. In my research, I center the experiences of people of color in alignment with Black feminist orientations and de/colonial research ethics. It is true that institutions of higher education are now becoming more accessible across the world. Beyond knowing and understanding the sociocultural identities of students, I argue, pedagogues and researchers must also consider their own sociocultural identities when planning for how to address diversity within the higher education context and to prepare professionals for the greater diversity that exists outside the university context.

This chapter has implications for research in higher education, including researchers of the pedagogical practices of college and university faculty, the unique experiences faculty of color bring to university teaching and research, and collaborative teaching in higher education. This chapter offers multiple tools (i.e., ICM and ICC-TE) and de/colonial considerations because, as underscored in the principles of TRERP (Johnson et al., this volume), transformational change requires multifocal strategies and reforms. Furthermore, the chapter emphasizes equity in ways that directly tackles complexity by keeping social-historical and sociocultural considerations at the forefront, while maintaining a critical eye on the role that knowledge production within the westernized academy plays in sustaining inequities around the world. Institutions of higher education addressing diversity, equity, and inclusion must contend with the historical and systematic exclusion of minoritized people from *accessing* universities and *defining* dominant research agendas. Centering the scholarly activities of faculty of color is critical to diversifying whose epistemologies are deemed viable in higher education research and pedagogy.

References

Andrews, I. R., & Tjosvold, D. (1983). Conflict management under different levels of conflict intensity. *Journal of Occupational Behaviour, 4,* 223–228.

Arms, E., Bickett, J., & Graf, V. (2008). Gender bias and imbalance: Girls in US special education programmes. *Gender and Education, 20*(4), 349–359.

Artiles, A. J. (2013). Untangling the racialization of disabilities. *Du Bois Review: Social Science Research on Race, 10*(2), 329–347.

Artiles, A., Kozleski, E., & Waitoller, F. (Eds.). (2011). *Inclusive education: Examining equity on five continents.* Harvard University Press.

Blanton, L. P., Pugach, M. C., & Boveda, M. (2018). Interrogating the intersections between general and special education in the history of teacher education reform. *Journal of Teacher Education, 69*(4), 354–366.

Boveda, M. (2016). *Beyond special and general education as identity markers: The development and validation of an instrument to measure preservice teachers' understanding of the effects of intersecting sociocultural identities* (2998). FIU Electronic Theses and Dissertations. http://digitalcommons.fiu.edu/etd/2998

Boveda, M. (2019a). An Afro-Latina's navigation of the academy: Tracings of audacious departures, re-entries, and intersectional consciousness. *Feminist Formations, 31*, 103–123.

Boveda, M. (2019b). Intersectional competence within diverse Latinx communities: Conceptualizing differences at a Hispanic serving institution. In N. D. Hartlep & D. Ball (Eds.), *Racial battle fatigue in faculty: Perspectives and lessons from higher education* (pp. 101–114). Routledge.

Boveda, M., & Aronson, B. A. (2019). The privileging of the special education professional identity: Exploring preservice teachers of color understanding of multiple, intersecting sociocultural markers. *Remedial and Special Education, 40*(4), 248–260.

Boveda, M., & Bhattacharya, K. (2019). Love as de/colonial onto-epistemology: A post-oppositional approach to contextualized educational research ethics. *Urban Review.* https://doi.org/10.1007/s11256-018-00493-z

Boveda, M., & Weinberg, A. (2020a). Facilitating intersectionally conscious collaborations in physics education. *Physics Teacher, 58*, 480–483.

Boveda, M., & Weinberg, A. E. (2020b). Intersectionally conscious collaboration protocol: Teacher educators version1.figshare. Online resource. doi.org/10.6084/m9.figshare.13252085.v4

Busey, C. L., & Waters, S. (2016). Who are we? The demographic and professional identity of social studies teacher educators. *Journal of Social Studies Research, 40*(1), 71–83.

Byrd, D. (2019). The diversity distraction: A critical comparative analysis of discourse in higher education scholarship. *Review of Higher Education, 42*, 135–172.

Collins, P. H. (1990). *Black feminist thought: Knowledge, consciousness, and the politics of empowerment.* Routledge.

Collins, P. H. (2000). *Black feminist thought: Knowledge, consciousness, and the politics of empowerment* (2nd ed.). Routledge.

Collins, P. H., & Bilge, S. (2016). *Intersectionality.* John Wiley & Sons.

Connor, D. (2006). Michael's story: "I get into so much trouble just by walking": Narrative knowing and life at the intersections of learning disability, race and class. *Equity & Excellence in Education, 39*(2), 154–165.

Connor, D. (2008). *Urban narratives: Portraits in progress—Life at the intersection of learning disability, race, & social class.* Peter Lang.

Cho, S., Crenshaw, K. W., & McCall, L. (2013). Toward a field of intersectionality studies: Theory, applications, and praxis. *Signs: Journal of Women in Culture and Society, 38*(4), 785–810. https://doi.org/10.1086/669608

Crenshaw, K. (1989). Demarginalizing the intersection of race and sex: A Black feminist critique of antidiscrimination doctrine, feminist theory and antiracist politics. *University of Chicago Legal Files*, 139–167.

Dei, G. (2000). Rethinking the role of indigenous knowledges in the academy. *International Journal of Inclusive Education*, 4(2), 111–132.

de Sousa Santos, B. (2010) *Epistemologias del sur*. Siglo XXI.

de Sousa Santos, B. (2015). *Epistemologies of the South: Justice against epistemicide*. Routledge.

Dixson, A. D., & Dingus, J. E. (2007). Tyranny of the majority: Re-enfranchisement of African-American teacher educators teaching for democracy. *International Journal of Qualitative Studies in Education*, 20(6), 639–654.

Enterline, S., Cochran-Smith, M., Ludlow, L. H., & Mitescu, E. (2008). Learning to teach for social justice: Measuring change in the beliefs of teacher candidates. *New Educator*, 4(4), 267–290.

Erevelles, N., & Minear, A. (2010). Unspeakable offenses: Untangling race and disability in discourses of intersectionality. *Journal of Literary & Cultural Disability Studies*, 4(2), 127–145.

Exkano, J. (2013). Toward an African cosmology: Reframing how we think about historically Black colleges and universities. *Journal of Black Studies*, 44(1), 63–80.

Ferri, B. A., & Connor, D. J. (2010). 'I was the special ed. girl': Urban working-class young women of colour. *Gender and Education*, 22(1), 105–121.

Flynn, J. E., Kemp, A. T., & Page, C. S. (2013). Promoting philosophical diversity and exploring racial differences in beliefs about the purposes of education: What it means for African-American learners. *Journal of the Texas Alliance of Black School Educators*, 5(1), 53–71.

García, G. A. (2018). Decolonizing Hispanic-serving institutions: A framework for organizing. *Journal of Hispanic Higher Education*, 17(2), 132–147.

García, S. B., & Ortiz, A. A. (2013). Intersectionality as a framework for transformative research in special education. *Multiple Voices for Ethnically Diverse Exceptional Learners*, 13(2), 32–47.

Goodnough, K., Osmond, P., Dibbon, D., Glassman, M., & Stevens, K. (2009). Exploring a triad model of student teaching: Pre-service teacher and cooperating teacher perceptions. *Teaching and Teacher Education*, 25(2), 285–296.

Goodwin, A. L. (2004). Exploring the perspectives of teacher educators of color: What do they bring to teacher education? *Issues in Teacher Education*, 13(2), 7–24.

Grant, C. A., & Zwier, E. (2011). Intersectionality and student outcomes: Sharpening the struggle against racism, sexism, classism, ableism, heterosexism, nationalism, and linguistic, religious, and geographical discrimination in teaching and learning. *Multicultural Perspectives*, 13(4), 181–188.

Grech, S. (2015). Decolonising 21 Eurocentric disability studies: Why colonialism matters in the disability and global South debate. *Social Identities*, *21*(1), 6–21.

Grosfoguel, R. (2013). The structure of knowledge in westernized universities: Epistemic racism/sexism and the four genocides/epistemicides of the long 16th century. *Human Architecture: Journal of the Sociology of Self-Knowledge*, *11*(1), 73–90.

Harris, J. C., & Patton, L. D. (2019). Un/doing intersectionality through higher education research. *Journal of Higher Education*, *90*(3), 347–372.

Haynes, C., Joseph, N. M., Patton, L. D., Stewart, S., & Allen, E. L. (2020). Toward an understanding of intersectionality methodology: A 30-year literature synthesis of Black women's experiences in higher education. *Review of Educational Research*, *90*(6), 751–787.

Hill-Brisbane, D. A., & Dingus, J. E. (2007). Black women teacher educators: Creating enduring Afriographies as leaders and change makers. *Advancing Women in Leadership*, *22*. https://doi.org/10.18738/awl.v22i0.260

hooks, b. (1994). *Teaching to transgress*. Routledge.

hooks, b. (1997). bell hooks: Cultural criticism and transformation. Media Education Foundation. https://www.mediaed.org/transcripts/Bell-Hooks-Transcript.pdf

Ivanović, L., & Ho, Y. S. (2019). Highly cited articles in the education and educational research category in the social science citation index: A bibliometric analysis. *Educational Review*, *71*(3), 277–286.

Ladson-Billings, G. J. (2005). Is the team all right? Diversity and teacher education. *Journal of Teacher Education*, *56*(3), 229–234.

Liang, X., & Zhang, G. (2009). Indicators to evaluate pre-service teachers' cultural competence. *Evaluation & Research in Education*, *22*(1), 17–31.

Liasidou, A. (2013). Intersectional understandings of disability and implications for a social justice reform agenda in education policy and practice. *Disability & Society*, *28*(3), 299–312.

McCall, Z., McHatton, P. A., & Shealey, M. W. (2014). Special education teacher candidate assessment: A review. *Teacher Education and Special Education*, *37*(1), 51–70.

McCall, Z., & Skrtic, T. (2009). Intersectional needs politics: A policy frame for the wicked problem of disproportionality. *Multiple Voices for Ethnically Diverse Exceptional Learners*, *11*(2), 3–23.

Merryfield, M. M. (2000). Why aren't teachers being prepared to teach for diversity, equity, and global interconnectedness? A study of lived experiences in the making of multicultural and global educators. *Teaching and teacher education*, *16*(4), 429–443.

Natapoff, A. (1995). Anatomy of a debate: Intersectionality and equality for deaf children from non-English speaking homes. *Journal of Law and Education*, *24*(2), 271–278.

Ohito, E. O. (2019). Mapping women's knowledges of antiracist teaching in the United States: A feminist phenomenological study of three antiracist women teacher educators. *Teaching and Teacher Education, 86*. 102892.

Pohan, C. A., & Aguilar, T. E. (2001). Measuring educators' beliefs about diversity in personal and professional contexts. *American Educational Research Journal, 38*(1), 159–182.

Pugach, M. C., Blanton, L. P., & Boveda, M. (2014). Working together: Research on the preparation of general education and special education teachers for inclusion and collaboration. In P. D. Sindelar, E. D. McCray, M. T. Brownell, & B. Lignugaris/Kraft (Eds.), *Handbook for research on special education teacher preparation* (pp. 143–160). Routledge.

Puri, S. (2004). *The Caribbean postcolonial: Social equality, post/nationalism, and cultural hybridity*. Palgrave.

Roth, W., Tobin, K., Zimmermann, A., Bryant, N., & Davis, C. (2002). Lessons on and from the dihybrid cross: An activity-theoretical study of learning in coteaching. *Journal of Research in Science Teaching, 39*(3), 253–282. doi:10.1002/tea.10018

Sleeter, C. E. (2017). Critical race theory and the whiteness of teacher education. *Urban Education, 52*(2), 155–169.

Souto-Manning, M. (2019). Toward praxically-just transformations: Interrupting racism in teacher education. *Journal of Education for Teaching, 45*(1), 97–113.

Suh, Y., & Hinton, K. (2015). Mirroring ourselves: Teacher educators of color reading multicultural texts. *Issues in Teacher Education, 24*(2), 23–42.

Tobin, K., & Roth, W. M. (2006). *Teaching to learn: A view from the field*. Vol. 4. Sense.

Waitoller, F. R., & Kozleski, E. B. (2013). Working in boundary practices: Identity development and learning in partnerships for inclusive education. *Teaching and Teacher Education, 31*, 35–45.

Weinberg, A. E., Sebald, A., Stevenson, C. A., & Wakefield, W. (2020). Toward conceptual clarity: A scoping review of coteaching in teacher education. *Teacher Educator, 55*(2), 190–213.

Wilder, C. S. (2014). *Ebony and ivy: Race, slavery, and the troubled history of America's universities*. Bloomsbury.

6

From the Theater to Higher Education

Using Movies to Facilitate Intergroup Racial Dialogues

ERICKA ROLAND

> The gut punch of the movie is ultimately meant to say that racism is a human problem and the "woke" people know not to call themselves "woke."
>
> —Jordan Peele, director of *Get Out*

Movies such as *CRASH* (2004), *Dear White People* (2014), and *Get Out* (2017) have played a role in portraying racism in America. As a form of popular culture, these films invite diverse audiences to make meaning of such interactions within historical and contemporary contexts. The preceding quote by Jordan Peele, director of *Get Out* (2017), highlights how his movie is used as a tool to provoke dialogue from the audience long after the film has ended. Movies on racism are not made and watched in a vacuum; therefore, a particular movie in the right learning environment can challenge our worldview on race, racism, and other interlocking systems of oppression.

Higher education institutions have a history of being sites of racist practices and policies while also being a space to think and engage with the possibilities of racial equity (Patton, 2016). Consequently, scholars argue that racial dialogues in higher education are essential to uncovering everyday discrimination, healing racial injustices, and fostering humanizing race relations or racial equity (Miller & Donner, 2000; Ramasubramanian et al., 2017; Sue, 2013, 2016). Racial equity is a standard of justice, including addressing the root causes of racism and eliminating policies, practices, attitudes, and cultural messages that reinforce differential outcomes by race. In short, racial dialogues should work to promote racial equity. Higher education has sought to facilitate racial dialogues in and out of the classroom using, for example, intergroup dialogues and guest speakers, to engage students on race and racism (Zúñiga et al., 2007). Much has been written about facilitation approaches to racial dialogue; however, there is an opportunity for higher education practitioners to use movies as a tool to facilitate these conversations.

The purpose of this chapter is to contribute to the discourse on ways to facilitate racial dialogues with racially and ethnically diverse participants in higher education. In this chapter, I discuss the importance of talking about race and racism as it connects to how we learn about ourselves and others. I also outline intergroup dialogues as a way racial dialogue has been facilitated in higher education. Next, I briefly review the literature on movies as an educational strategy to encourage adult development around race consciousness. Then, guided by this review and principles from the Johnson and colleagues (this volume) translational racial equity research-practice (TRERP) framework, I delineate the use of movies as a facilitation tool in racial dialogue across seven steps. I argue that the central aim of facilitating racial dialogues using movies is to create an educative process for participants to engage before, during, and after the dialogues. My goal in this chapter is not to propose an exhaustive framework but to generate fresh thinking about ways higher education faculty and staff might facilitate racial dialogues with cross-racial groups.

Race and Racism Dialogues

Given the social, historical, and political context of race in the United States and higher education, dialogue on racism in and out of college classrooms—undergraduate and graduate—remains limited. Educational spaces are socially constructed by individuals or collective attributes (ethnicity, class, race, sexuality, and others) that influence facilitation of and engagement in racial dialogues. Thus, such dialogues often provoke intense emotions that cause white individuals to experience discomfort and People of Color to fear being tokenized, resulting in a potential clash of racial realities (Merriweather et al., 2018; Quaye, 2012; Sue, 2016). While negative experiences with racial dialogues may cause increased antagonism among students, misunderstandings, and barriers in learning, these conversations can also challenge preconceived notions about race and racism and create shared meaning with others from different perspectives. Successful engagement in racial dialogues can expand racial consciousness, in which participants develop the ability to analyze racism, increase racial literacy, and dispel stereotypes and misinformation about other groups (Gurin et al., 2002; Sue 2013). Dialogues include such topics as race, racism, whiteness, and white privilege (Sue, 2016; Sue et al., 2010). Scholars insist that engaging in open dialogue on race and racism matters as it allows us to examine the core of the United States' democracy and the potential to heal racial and ethnic divides (Sue, 2016; West, 2001).

Burbules and Bruce (2001) describe dialogue as a process with moments of resistance and negotiations by participants whose ways of knowing and being are continually being reconstructed. As such, racial dialogues involve a collective effort focusing more on the process than the outcome. Racial dialogues can challenge participants to increase compassion for others, broaden their horizons, engage in a greater sense of connectedness with others, and appreciate people of all colors, ethnicities, and cultures (Metcalfe & Game, 2008; Sue, 2016). The space and mode of facilitating are essential to racial dialogue. Gutierrez and colleagues (1995) offer the concept of a "third space" that is developed when participants and facilitators create space for authentic interactions in the dialogue, even in times of group tension or conflict. It is impossible to remove risk from racial dialogues; however, Arao and Clemens (2013) introduce the concept of "brave space" that encourages participants to remain engaged when faced with challenges. Participants are immersed in a mode of engagement that allows for discomfort to be part of the learning process. Cross-racial dialogues are more apt to be generative when participants are respectful and responsive, which requires the facilitator to be mindful of the where and how of dialogues. To engage students in racial dialogues with varying degrees of experience and comfort, facilitators must have knowledge and skills to guide such dialogue.

The facilitator's role in racial dialogues is to navigate the environment, emotions, and various interactions alongside students for a productive conversation on racism. Quaye (2012) found that postsecondary educators preparing for racial dialogues: (a) thought about one's role as a facilitator, (b) established ground rules for discussion, (c) managed students' comfort levels and readiness to participate in the dialogues, and (d) found ways to build groups that were racially/ethnically diverse. Torosyan and Cook-Sather (2018) added that both participants and facilitators should co-create opportunities in racial dialogues for development of racial consciousness; organize intentional steps to build trust and emotional sensitivity, and draw out diverse perspectives; and adopt an attitude, stance, tone, or approach for radical listening, reciprocal learning, and the acknowledgment of competing contributions to the dialogue. To accomplish transformative facilitation in racial dialogue, educators can use various pedagogical approaches including readings, writing, lectures, role-playing, reflection, multimedia, and intergroup dialogue (Gurin et al., 2015; Murray-Johnson, 2018; Pawlowski, 2018; Quaye, 2014).

Intergroup Dialogue in Higher Education

Universities nationwide engage students in intergroup dialogue (IGD) to bring together people from different social identities in a structured and facilitated environment (Zúñiga et al., 2007). The use of IGD helps students explore their own and others' social identities, status, and the role of social structures in relationships of privilege and inequity. Nagda and colleagues (2009) noted that IGD provides students with the opportunity to develop empathy, motivation, and skills to communicate across differences toward social justice. At the center of IGD are distinctive communication processes with goals to foster learning environments for all participants in the dialogue. A four-staged critical-dialogic model outlines the communication process that includes engaging self, appreciating differences, critical reflection, and alliance building. Gurin et al. (2015) noted, "Critical processes depict communication where participants apply critical analysis, seeking to understand self and group dynamics in the context of broader social systems; it does not mean that participants are critical of one another" (p. 48). Although researchers report the positive effects of IGD, Frantell and colleagues (2019) posit that there are some significant gaps. Little research has been done to understand how different racial groups (i.e., Students of Color or white students) contribute to the educative process. For example, in a cross-racial IGD, it may become the responsibility of Students of Color to teach and share their experiences with racism and whiteness with white students for the latter to understand racial oppressions.

Critical scholars explored the tensions of bringing white students into consciousness around white privilege and racism while also engaging Students of Color in race consciousness within classrooms (Blackwell, 2010; Evans-Winters & Hines, 2019). These scholars have noted that Students of Color become representatives of their own or all racial ethnic minority groups or as culture experts and educators. Therefore, the experiences of Students of Color are decentered and only used for the racial consciousness development for white students.

Consequently, there are assumptions that Students of Color have already reached racial consciousness or that they benefit from witnessing white peers race consciousness–raising (Blackwell, 2010). If racially minoritized students are burdened in IGDs to foster racial equity for white students, racial inequity is reinforced. Facilitators must negotiate dynamics between students with different racial identities within dialogues that promote racial equity. Ultimately, racial dialogues with a diverse group require a shared experience that considers various racial consciousness levels.

Movies as a Facilitation Tool

Movies as a pedagogical tool for transformative learning have been used across multiple academic disciplines in higher education to teach on topics such as racism, equity, and social change (Champoux, 1999; Jarvis & Burr, 2011; Tisdell, 2008; Wilson et al., 2017). The use of movies in racial dialogues invites participants to make meaning of race relations by identifying power dynamics that manifest into racism while providing an intentional opportunity for participants to understand their racial positionality by reproducing culture norms. Thus, movies in racial dialogue give a starting point for reflection and in-depth discussion (Champoux, 1999; Jarvis & Burr, 2011; Tisdell, 2008; Wilson et al., 2016). Put differently, characters, narratives, metaphor, satire, aesthetics, and symbolism in movies can serve as case studies and experiential exercises for students to dialogue on race, class, gender, sexuality, and other power relations in society. Marshall (2003) confirmed that the pedagogical impact of movies as a shared experience could help break down barriers and build trust to encourage students to take risks in open dialogues around difficult subjects. Perhaps movies as a pedagogical tool allow for a unique way for engaging racial dialogues that promote racial equity and create space for race consciousness-raising of all students.

Tisdell (2008) described drawing from popular cultures, such as movies, as critical pedagogy can create opportunities for students to critique and develop solutions to social inequities. Undergirded by critical pedagogy and critical literacy, scholars have pointed to critical race media literacy to develop analytical skills to read various forms of media (Alvermann et al., 2018; Tisdell, 2008). Critical pedagogy as a teaching philosophy is grounded in inviting students to question and challenge uneven power relations and to undermine oppression in society and learning experiences with a goal toward equity (Giroux, 2011; hooks, 1994). As critical pedagogy fosters critical awareness, critical literacy focuses on skill and knowledge development to read, interpret, and produce certain cultural texts and artifacts (movies, books, news media) (Kellner & Share, 2007). Together critical pedagogy and critical literacy with media (movies) involves teaching approaches that cultivate skills in analyzing media codes, stereotypes, dominant values, ideologies, and competencies to interpret the multiple meanings and messages generated by media texts (Alvermann et al., 2018; Kellner & Share, 2007; Tisdell, 2008). Yosso (2002) added that critical media literacy in pedagogy helps students develop awareness of themselves concerning power structures and oppression in society.

To explicitly deal with racism using critical media literacy, Yosso (2002) and Agosto et al. (2016) draw from critical race theory (CRT) to examine racial oppression through media. Critical race media literacy as a pedagogical tool examines how People of Color are racialized to develop critical consciousness throughout various media platforms. In a qualitative study of the use of media footage involving race and racism in a professional development session, Agosto et al. (2016) found grounding their pedagogical approach in critical race media literacy provided space for critical discussion in connection to everyday educational practices. Critical media race literacy includes "reading" and challenging white privilege and white supremacy through media texts, images, and discourses. In doing so, movies are a way to understand culture formation of privilege and oppression and serve as a vehicle for counternarratives that challenge systemic inequities (Giroux, 1996; Guy, 2007).

The translational racial equity research-practice (TRERP) framework introduced in this volume helps bridge theories such as critical pedagogy and critical race media literacy to practice. Using movies as a facilitation tool allows for the complex and mutually constitutive relationship of research, everyday life, and practice for racial equity. Thus, enacting principles of TRERP, in the context of using movies in racial dialogues, invites the collaboration between researcher, practitioners, and community members to promote transformational change in various spaces. The process of engaging in facilitation practices that are equity focused can be inspired beyond formal higher education institutions, environments, and policies to frame and represent the full context of race and racism. Practitioners engaging in racial dialogues can use principles of the TRERP framework as a tool for reflection, asking questions such as: (a) Who is being centered in this dialogue? (b) Who is being asked to educate? And why? (c) What narratives are being constructed that reinforce racism and white supremacy? (d) How is the dialogue engaging with other interlocking systems of oppressions that influence how racism is manifested in various material and institutional conditions?

Guide to Facilitating Racial Dialogue Using Movies

I offer the following steps to facilitate such dialogue in various higher education spaces rooted in critical pedagogy, critical race media literacy, and TRERP. These steps include: (1) selection of movie, (2) facilitator reflection, (3) movie delivery, (4) probing questioning and leading the dialogue, (5) supplemental activities, (6) conflict and resistance, and (7) postdialogue reflections. Throughout the steps, there is an intentional focus on racial equity that informs the facilitation decisions. Put differently, teaching and learning on racial equity must focus on the process rather than be limited to the dialogue outcomes. The process centering allows for opportunities for racial consciousness development for facilitators and participants, thus encouraging a collective development of racial consciousness to learn and enact racial equity from various perspectives and experiences. To provide an example of how such steps might be applied, I weave the movie *Dear White People* through the steps.

SELECTION OF MOVIE

First, facilitators need to select an appropriate movie to ground racial dialogues. The movie should explicitly center racism—this can be determined by the movie's summary, trailer, director interviews, and reviews.

For example, the movie *Dear White People* focuses on racial tension at an Ivy League college after a party involving white students in Blackface and Students of Color responding to the incident. The movie's premise is to engage the audience in thinking about and exploring racism in a so-called postracial America. Additionally, facilitators should avoid movies with a white gaze that create tropes and storylines from the perspectives of whiteness (i.e., *The Help*). A white gaze in movies makes white people the "savior" or "solution" to racism while erasing the experiences of People of Color. Instead, facilitators should select a movie that centers People of Color stories and a worldview that destabilizes the dominant gaze as standard reality. hooks (1994) offered the term "oppositional gaze" to explain the practice of analyzing media representation of People of Color, especially Black women. The movie selection can become part of racial dialogues to understand whiteness as a cultural construction and the meaning of centering People of Color. The movie selected can also open dialogue around critical spectatorship that focuses on the development of critical race media literacy (CRML) that extends the conversation beyond dialogues to ways of being and knowing in everyday experiences.

When selecting a movie, I suggest using a film that connects to the audience or learning environment. For example, *Dear White People* would be appropriate for the preparation of student affairs professionals as the movie centers on out-of-classroom experiences on a college campus. Also, this movie is currently available on multiple streaming platforms and was extended into a series on Netflix, which participants can access before and after dialogues. No movies are off-limits, no matter the year of release. For instance, I have used the movie *Higher Learning* (1995) in a graduate course on popular culture and higher education to connect how films have long highlighted racism on college campuses. It is important to note the selection of movies is not limited to the Black experience in the United States but can include other racial and ethnic groups who experience racism in our society.

FACILITATOR REFLECTION

Movies often reflect the times or provide flashbacks or forward to issues. Thus, these movies can evoke an emotional, physical, and intellectual reaction that may restrict the facilitation of racial dialogue. Consequently, facilitators should watch the movie and reflect on their response in connection to facilitating. For example, *The Hate You Give* includes multiple scenes of violence that highlight Black death by police officers and community members. Due to the link to recent events and reflecting, a facilitator may decide not to show this movie if they feel their reaction would restrict their ability to facilitate. I am not suggesting facilitators be neutral in these dialogues. However, they should be mindful of how they might influence the interactions. In addition to being aware of their feelings about the selected film, facilitators should reflect on their social identities (i.e., race, gender, sexual orientation) and how they interact with other identities that may influence dialogues. Facilitators should reflect on their privileges and oppressions, as well. Such reflection should concern the movie, participants, and the conversation environment.

The facilitator plays a crucial role in racial dialogues and needs to have knowledge and skills to guide these dialogues with students who likely will have varying degrees of previous experience and comfort with participating in racial exchanges (Quaye, 2014). Facilitators should reflect on their knowledge around racism and skill sets to lead such dialogue that may result in resistance and conflict. Although the movies serve as a co-facilitator, there should be a reflection on co-facilitating with other individuals who may provide participants with different perspectives. Through reflection, facilitators can engage in race consciousness development to impact how they facilitate racial dialogues.

MOVIE DELIVERY

Facilitators need to consider the modes of viewing the movie. They may show the whole movie or clips, either before or during the dialogue. Participants viewing the movie or clips before a public viewing may provide more processing time. Also, providing participants with various of ways to engage with the movie welcomes different ways to learn and process. Considerations of how participants can view the movie should include the transcriptions and other resources to meet their accessibility needs. The facilitator should give thought to how participants have access to the movie (i.e., library, Netflix) and provide the movie for all regardless of platform. These pedagogical choices create the shared experiences that students will rely on during the dialogue.

Using the movie *Dear White People*, four key clips can be selected that include the following scenes. First, the "Bringing Black Back" clip about two Black student leaders campaigning for the leadership role in the Black House (dorm). This scene highlights intergroup differences among Black students in a historically white institution's quest for racial equity. The "Who Am I?" scene is the second clip that highlights racial identity development and performance of the main character Sam, who is biracial and feels stuck between two different cultural expressions. The third clip is the "Dining Hall Dispute" where the Black and white students have a discussion on race relations in the United States (i.e., President Obama, affirmative action). The "Blackface Party" scene is the fourth clip that shows the party with white students in Blackface, interracial gay interactions, and code-switching of Black students in predominately white environments. These scenes provide opportunities to examine racism and other -isms (sexism, heterosexism) that challenge goals of racial equity. The selection of four key clips provides the premise of the movie regardless of student familiarity. While showing the movie or clips during the dialogue, the facilitator should include the closed captions. Finally, facilitators may consider having clips prepared during the presentation to highlight moments in the film where participants can dive deeper or simply refresh their memory.

PROBING QUESTIONING AND LEADING THE DIALOGUE

Facilitators should prepare for racial dialogues by setting goals appropriate for the participants, space, time, and context (e.g., course curriculum, leadership training). For example, goals in a graduate course on educational leadership with students who have not discussed race, racism, and whiteness may entail gaining the language of these topics and understanding the multiple ways they manifest. The facilitator should also prepare probing questions that push participants beyond their comfort areas without creating a dangerous environment. No facilitator can predict how the dialogue will unfold, but having questions that ask participants to use the movie to make meaning of the racism will be helpful.

Probing questioning is a technique that supports meaning-making as it promotes the development of deep-level reasoning that leads to improved comprehension and learning (Craig et al., 2006). As a method, probing questioning helps the facilitator know when to push and pull back, allowing space for participants to process the dialogue. In a racial dialogue on the movie *Dear White People*, for example, possible probing questions for the graduate course on leadership might be: (1) What are the characters' racial identities, and how do they engage with others?

(2) How are race and racism portrayed in the clips? And (3) How does Samantha White challenge racism through leadership? These questions guide students through dialogue by building on various concepts of race, racism, and social change. In the preceding questions, it is evident that it is the responsibility of facilitators to address critical topics as they lead the dialogue, which includes assisting participants in understanding and analyzing racial power relations and their role in such power relations and racial equity. Facilitators must be explicit about drawing participants' attention to racial power relations throughout the phases of dialogue. Racial power relations refer to the political and social manifestation of privilege and oppression, both historically and in the current context (Miles, 2004). For example, in *Dear White People*, the Blackface party scene provides an opportunity to engage in dialogue around the socialization of race and racism that influences decision-making and everyday interactions. Within this domain, facilitators should ask probing questions related to concepts such as race, racism, whiteness, and other social identities that are present in the movie.

Facilitators should invite participants in racial dialogues to situate themselves in the constructed system of race and racism. Racial dialogues can offer participants the opportunity to examine and make meaning of their own and others' racial identity and group membership. The use of movies in these dialogues will draw one's attention to the characters and storylines; therefore, facilitators need specific probing questions that reflect on their personal values, attitudes, identities, and practices that are both complicit with and resistant to racial privilege and oppression. Questions are designed more to get participants to connect the movie to everyday life and less about the aesthetics or critique of the movie. Participants should be making meaning of the movie, not just being spectators. During the facilitation, the movie serves as a co-facilitator; therefore, referring back to the movie with questions provides reference points for students with differing perspectives and experiences.

Also, facilitators should ask probing questions that refer to racial equity practices or how students can use racial dialogue to inspire radical action around racial privilege and oppression. Engaging in dialogue on racism is the beginning of challenging racism and part of the action. There also must be a consideration regarding the implementation of racial equity practices that deconstruct racism and reconstruct antiracist practices, policies, and relationships. For example—using the movie *Dear White People* there should be probing questions related to the enactment of racial equity on college campuses and student lives. Participants can provide social changes they would implement in each *Dear White People* clip and how such a goal for racial equity connects to everyday life. Facilitators must give a call to action within these racial dialogues and encourage participants to apply such dialogue in practice.

SUPPLEMENTAL ACTIVITIES

Facilitators should consider activities that help participants generate dialogue. Such actions could include scene mapping, small group discussions, concentric circles, role-playing, media gallery, and much more. Scene mapping is a worksheet used to assist participants to focus on specific interactions within the movie. For instance—using the four clips from *Dear White People*, the facilitator could provide a worksheet that guides participants to identify the various ways racism is portrayed in the clips. The use of scene mapping should occur while participants are viewing the movie or clips.

Small group discussions invite all participants into the dialogue and provide space for everyone to talk. Some prompts for small group discussions using *Dear White People* may include: (1) What scenes stood out to you? (2) How was racism depicted in the clips? (3) How do nonverbal interactions play into racism? Participants can speak to their neighbors for small group discussions; however, the use of concentric circles can provide participants with the opportunity to share with a wide range of participants. Concentric circles are structured with participants sitting in two concentric circles facing each other and respond to the prompts from above. After each prompt, one of the circles moves to the left or right, so each participant now faces a new partner with whom they discuss a new prompt. Small group discussion and concentric circles can help participants build community by getting to know each other and encouraging deeper discussions in the larger group. During these activities, the facilitator should be moving around the space, engaging with the small groups, and being a pace keeper to allow all participants to engage the prompts.

When transitioning into a larger group dialogue, role-playing can help participants make deeper meaning of the movie scenes. Participants should reenact scenes and act out things that are missing, exaggerate certain points, and address issues in the scene. For instance, using the fourth clip from *Dear White People*, participants can be asked to role-play a scene and change the racial incident response from different perspectives. Such an activity allows more perspective on the dialogue and prompts the understanding of positionality in relation to racism and whiteness. In movies that focus on racism and less on racial equity, the role-playing activity can invite participants to think about ways racial equity can be enacted on a college campus and student life through practices and policy. The last activity I would suggest is a media gallery walk before or during dialogue. For example, a silent media gallery includes pictures from the various scenes from *Dear White People* and comments from the director and characters that may evoke thoughts and feelings around the movie that could be a catalyst for dialogue. The media gallery could also include social media posts (e.g., Twitter and blogs), making meaning of the movie from various perspectives, which could disrupt the barrier between real world and entertainment.

CONFLICT AND RESISTANCE

Conflict and resistance are common in racial dialogues as participants work through tensions from their feelings and experiences of racism. I suggest using movies in racial dialogue as a starting place for an ongoing dialogue; therefore, facilitators can direct participants back to the movie when conflict and resistance arise. Watching the movie, either separately or collectively, creates a shared experience for all participants regardless of experience or knowledge around race and racism. For instance, a Person of Color may use the movie to illustrate their experiences with racism, while a white participant may use the movie to understand racism. This approach tries to alleviate the tension around personal connection by focusing on the movie; however, conflict and resistance cannot be avoided. It is important to note that movies are a starting point for participants to grapple with concepts of race, racism, and whiteness. As the dialogue progresses, facilitators should consider ways to engage participants more deeply in self-reflection and race consciousness development.

POSTDIALOGUE REFLECTIONS

In the literature and practice, racial dialogues are often limited to preparation and what occurs during the interactions. Brookfield (2010) highlights the need for students to continuously engage in critical reflection for personal and institutional transformation. The use of movies as a pedagogical tool in racial dialogues offers participants opportunities to be critical spectators by inviting them to reflect on the dialogue and other media forms. For example, after a dialogue using the movie *Dear White People*, students may be asked to think about how they can address racism in higher education or how they can pay attention to other media platforms (e.g., news and social media) with similar narratives around racism on college campuses. The facilitator can provide additional resources (e.g., readings, podcasts, and other movies/TV) for students to continue thinking through race and racism. For instance, *Dear White People* was made into a Netflix series. Students could use critical race media literacy to understand how the series deals with racism or how the series moves away for racial equity. Finally, the facilitator can challenge participants to engage others in racial dialogues using the movie in face-to-face and social media interactions. The postdialogue activities' goal is to engage participants in ongoing reflection and discussion to evoke transformative learning using popular culture.

Conclusion

The use of movies as a facilitation tool in racial dialogues provides a shared experience that can provoke emotional reactions, foster critical self-reflection, and stimulate animated discussions. Racial dialogues can be challenging to facilitate and participate in; therefore, innovative pedagogical approaches may help navigate feelings of discomfort, anger, and anxiety. Based on the proposed steps, the incorporation of movies in racial dialogues is not a static process by which facilitators merely follow the aforementioned steps. Instead, facilitators need a commitment to using movies as a critical form of guiding racial dialogues that pay close attention to the rapidly shifting cultural landscape and the ever-evolving needs, interests, and desires of individuals in higher education. Using movies as a basis for personal and pedagogical reflection in racial dialogues is neither a perfect approach nor a simple undertaking. Sometimes empowering, sometimes tricky—but always powerful—movies in racial dialogues in higher education can promote racial equity on campus and beyond.

References

Agosto, V., Karanxha, Z., & Cobb-Roberts, D. (2016). Critical (race) media literacy in the curriculum of faculty development: The retreat to teachable moments. In N. Croom & T. Marsh (Eds.), *Envisioning critical race praxis in higher education through counter-storytelling* (pp. 107–120). Information Age.

Alvermann, D. E., Moon, J. S., Hagwood, M. C., & Hagood, M. C. (2018). *Popular culture in the classroom: Teaching and researching critical media literacy*. Routledge.

Arao, B., & Clemens, K. (2013). From safe spaces to brave spaces: A new way to frame dialogue around diversity and social justice. In L. M. Landreman (Ed.), *The art of effective facilitation: Reflections from social justice educators* (pp. 135–150). Stylus.

Bell, B. P., Gallner, K., Parris, T., Simien, J., Thompson, T., Williams, T. J., Roadside Attractions (Firm), . . . Lions Gate Films. (2015). *Dear white people*. Lions Gate.

Blackwell, D. M. (2010). Sidelines and separate spaces: Making education anti-racist for students of color. *Race Ethnicity and Education, 13*(4), 473–494.

Brookfield, S. (2010). Critical reflection as an adult learning process. In N. Lyons (Ed.) *Handbook of reflection and reflective inquiry*, 215–236.Springer.

Burbules, N. C., & Bruce, B. C. (2001). Theory and research on teaching as dialogue. In V. Richardson (Ed.), *Handbook of research on teaching* (4th ed., pp. 1102–1121). American Education Research Association.

Champoux, J. E. (1999). Film as a teaching resource. *Journal of Management Inquiry, 8*(2), 206–217.

Craig, S. D., Sullins, J., Witherspoon, A., & Gholson, B. (2006). The deep-level reasoning questions effect: The role of dialogue and deep-level reasoning questions during vicarious learning. *Cognition and Instruction, 24*, 565–591.

Evans-Winters, V. E., & Hines, D. E. (2019). Unmasking white fragility: How whiteness and white student resistance impact anti-racist education. *Whiteness and Education*, 1–16. https://doi.org/10.1080/23793406.2019.1675182

Frantell, K. A., Miles, J. R., & Ruwe, A. M. (2019). Intergroup dialogue: A review of recent empirical research and its implications for research and practice. *Small Group Research*. 1046496419835923.

Gurin, P., Dey, E. L., Hurtado, S., & Gurin, G. (2002). Diversity and higher education: Theory and impact on student outcomes. *Harvard Educational Review, 72*(3), 330–366.

Gurin, P., Sorensen, N., Lopez, G. E., & Nagda, B. R. A. (2015). Intergroup dialogue: Race still matters. In *Race and social problems* (pp. 39–60). Springer.

Gutierrez, K., Rymes, B., & Larson, J. (1995). Script, counterscript, and underlife in the classroom: James Brown versus *Brown v. Board of Education*. *Harvard Educational Review, 65*(3), 445–472.

Giroux, H. A. (1996). Democratic education and popular culture. *International Journal of Social Education*, *11*(1), 59–69.

Giroux, H. A. (2011). *On critical pedagogy*. Continuum.

Guy, T. C. (2007). Learning who we (and they) are: Popular culture as pedagogy. *New Directions for Adult and Continuing Education*, *2007*(115), 15–23.

hooks, b. (1994). *Teaching to transgress: Education as the practice of freedom*. Routledge.

Jarvis, C., & Burr, V. (2011). The transformative potential of popular television: The case of *Buffy the Vampire Slayer*. *Journal of Transformative Education*, *9*(3), 165–182.

Kellner, D., & Share, J. (2007). Critical media literacy, democracy, and the reconstruction of education. In D. Macedo & S. R. Steinberg (Eds.), *Media literacy: A reader* (pp. 3–23). Peter Lang.

Marshall, E. O. (2003). Making the most of a good story: Effective use of film as a teaching resource for ethics. *Teaching Theology & Religion*, *6*(2), 93–98.

Merriweather, L. R., Guy, T. C., & Manglitz, E. (2018). Creating the conditions for racial dialogue. In *Teaching race: How to help students unmask and challenge racism* (pp. 131–150). Jossey-Bass.

Metcalfe, A., & Game, A. (2008). Significance and dialogue in learning and teaching. *Educational Theory*, *58*(3), 343–356.

Miles, R. (2004). *Racism*. Routledge.

Miller, J., & Donner, S. (2000). More than just talk: The use of racial dialogues to combat racism. *Social Work with Groups*, *23*(1), 31–53.

Murray-Johnson, K. (2018). (En)gauging self: Toward a practical framework for race talk. *Adult Learning*, 1–11. doi:1045159518805890

Murray-Johnson, K., & Ross-Gordon, J. M. (2018). "Everything is about balance": Graduate education faculty and the navigation of difficult discourses on race. *Adult Education Quarterly*, *68*(2), 137–156.

Nagda, B. A., Gurin, P., Sorensen, N., & Zúñiga, X. (2009). Evaluating intergroup dialogue: Engaging diversity for personal and social responsibility. *Diversity & Democracy*, *12*(1), 4–6.

Patton, L. D. (2016). Disrupting postsecondary prose: Toward a critical race theory of higher education. *Urban Education*, *51*(3), 315–342.

Pawlowski, L. (2018). Creating a brave space classroom through writing. In S. Brookfield (Ed.), *Teaching race: How to help students unmask and challenge racism* (pp. 63–86). John Wiley & Sons.

Quaye, S. J. (2012). Think before you teach: Preparing for dialogues about racial realities. *Journal of College Student Development*, *53*(4), 542–562.

Quaye, S. J. (2014). Facilitating dialogues about racial realities. *Teachers College Record*, *116*(8), 1–42.

Ramasubramanian, S., Sousa, A. N., & Gonlin, V. (2017). Facilitated difficult dialogues on racism: A goal-based approach. *Journal of Applied Communication Research*, *45*(5), 537–556.

Sue, D. W. (2013). Race talk: The psychology of racial dialogues. *American Psychologist, 68*(8), 663–672.

Sue, D. W. (2016). *Race talk and the conspiracy of silence: Understanding and facilitating difficult dialogues on race.* John Wiley & Sons.

Sue, D. W., Rivera, D. P., Capodilupo, C. M., Lin, A. I., & Torino, G. C. (2010). Racial dialogues and white trainee fears: Implications for education and training. *Cultural Diversity and Ethnic Minority Psychology, 16*(2), 206.

Tisdell, E. J. (2008). Critical media literacy and transformative learning: Drawing on pop culture and entertainment media in teaching for diversity in adult higher education. *Journal of Transformative Education, 6*(1), 48–67.

Torosyan, R., & Cook-Sather, A. (2018). Balancing direction and response: Four dimensions of transformative facilitation in educational development. *To Improve the Academy, 37*(2), 188–206.

West, C. (2001). *Race matters.* Beacon Press.

Wilson, D. A., Raish, V., & Carr-Chellman, A. (2017). Film use to promote understanding in change and diffusion of innovation. *Systemic Practice and Action Research, 30*(3), 277–293.

Yosso, T. J. (2002). Critical race media literacy: Challenging deficit discourse about Chicanas/os. *Journal of Popular Film and Television, 30*(1), 52–62.

Zúñiga, X., Nagda, B. R. A., Chesler, M., & Cytron-Walker, A. (2007). Intergroup dialogue in higher education: Meaningful learning about social justice. *ASHE Higher Education Report, 32*(4), 1–128.

Zúñiga, X., Nagda, B. R. A., & Sevig, T. D. (2002). Intergroup dialogues: An educational model for cultivating engagement across differences. *Equity & Excellence in Education, 35*(1), 7–17.

PART III
STUDENT AND CAMPUS LIFE

7

Reimagining Institutionalized Support for Undocumented and DACA College Students

A Critical Approach

SUSANA M. MUÑOZ AND STEPHEN SANTA-RAMIREZ

> Institutions of higher education make undocumented students feel undesired and dismissed when their issues and concerns are afterthoughts; these feelings can lead to attrition. The questions for higher education to grapple with are, how can colleges and universities take a humane stance on supporting undocumented students? Can institutions of higher education truly practice and celebrate equity and diversity if undocumented students are excluded from the conversation due to a lack of institutional support?
>
> —Susana M. Muñoz, *Identity, Social Activism, and the Pursuit of Higher Education*

We recall a point in time where many colleges and universities were essentially afraid to come out in support of undocumented[1] and Deferred Action for Childhood Arrivals (DACA) college students.[2] Today, approximately 450,000 undocumented or DACA-eligible college students are enrolled in US colleges and universities (Redden, 2020), yet institutional support for these student communities varies across college campuses.

Unfortunately, the notion of support is not universal for undocumented and DACA students. Even when support does exist, it does not guarantee student success within higher education, due in part to the national political climate. The Trump administration's employment of hostile rhetoric toward Black and Brown undocumented (im)migrant bodies—including threats of mass deportation, efforts to undermine equal protection for (im)migrant communities (O'Connor & Figueroa, 2017), and the rescinding of former president Barack Obama's 2012 Executive Order of the DACA program—has resulted in undocumented Latinx students experiencing an uptick of racism and discrimination on college campuses across the nation (Herrera & Obregon, 2018; Muñoz & Vigil, 2018).

As a response to this racial equity issue, this chapter interrogates notions of support for undocumented and DACA students by providing case study examples from two institutions, Colorado State University and Arizona State University. First, we present literature on undocumented college students in conversation with institutional support and campus climates. Next, we offer our two case studies of institutional and student-led initiatives, resources, and support for undocumented and DACA students, followed by a critical analysis to interrogate institutional practices using Gonzales and colleagues' (2018) four frames (labor, intersectional, reparative, and epistemic) to examine organization practice and change. Finally, we conclude with recommendations for transformational change that senior-level administrators and institutional policymakers can consider.

Undocumented and DACA College Students

According to the U.S. Census Bureau's 2014–2018 American Community Survey data, more than 11 million undocumented individuals live in the United States (Migration Policy Institute, 2021). Of those, approximately 675,000 are minors (Passel & Cohn, 2018). Although these individuals' racial and ethnic backgrounds are diverse, most arrive to the United States from Mexico and other Latin American countries. The majority of the undocumented and DACA collegians across the nation—including the two states our case studies are pulled from—reflect the overall population in liminal legal statuses (Hernandez & Ortiz, 2016). Each year nearly 100,000 undocumented students graduate from US high schools. Yet, while undocumented (im)migrants have the right to access K–12 public education due to the ruling in the 1982 *Plyer v.*

Doe (1982) case, access to postsecondary education continues to be a challenge. While 19 states have passed bills granting in-state tuition for undocumented and/or DACA students (NCSL, 2019)—which addresses access to some extent—these students continue to face challenges and barriers navigating their college experiences due to a lack of substantive and institutionalized support systems (Muñoz & Vigil, 2018).

The emboldened, anti-(im)migration rhetoric in the United States has also exacerbated how undocumented students negotiate institutional agents and spaces. Research has found negative repercussions of the "Trump effect" (heightened, emboldened racism) in K–12 schools and higher education (Muñoz et al., 2018) through a record number of anti-(im)migrant and anti-Muslim incidents (Soria, 2018; Southern Poverty Law Center, 2016). Given the turbulent political climate, where racist nativism microaggressions and legal violence (Muñoz & Vigil, 2018) continue to infiltrate undocumented and DACA college students' academic trajectories, in what ways are colleges and universities institutionalizing support for undocumented students?

INSTITUTIONAL SUPPORT

Institutional support for undocumented and DACA college students looks and feels vastly different across state and institutional contexts. Researchers have considered college and university agents, peer support networks, and support programs essential to undocumented students' holistic success and how colleges and universities can create inclusive educational experiences (Pérez et al., 2011). Institutional agents can be transformative educators as they attempt to leverage this privilege and their positions to disrupt social inequities for organizational and transformational change (Chen & Rhoads, 2016; Kezar, 2014; Stanton-Salazar, 2011).

Southern (2016) conducted a study employing Kezar's (2007) phases for agenda institutionalizing (mobilization, implementation, institutionalization) to understand how institutionalized support for undocumented and DACA students becomes standard practice in higher education. Southern (2016) found that student and ally activism, personal commitments and professional values, institutional missions, and on-and-off campus partnerships were catalysts for institutionalized support. This scholar also noted that the phases of institutionalization start as a sporadic action. These sporadic actions lead to more formalized structures and policies, which lead to changed behavior and actions (Southern, 2016). While some examples of institutionalized support for undocumented and DACA college students include the formation of physical support resource centers and full-time staff (Cisneros & Reyna Rivarola, 2020; Southern, 2016), this does not challenge the systemic oppressive structures and culture of whiteness and anti-(im)migration sentiments among individuals who also occupy these learning spaces.

Valenzuela et al. (2015) developed an institutional undocu-competence (IUC) framework to gauge institutional capacity and how well community colleges serve their undocumented and DACA college students. This framework calls for visible support, including an establishment of an office "of equal standing with other student resource offices" (p. 94), training about their needs and the state and national policies impacting these collegians, coalition building with community partnerships, establishing a campus-wide task force to share progress, dissemination of imperative information regarding financial aid and other resources, and honor student–led activism and initiatives. These essential competencies are central to creating more structures and policies to institutionalize holistic support for undocumented and DACA collegians. The question that institutional agents must ask is whether these institutionalized support efforts create climates of equity and justice.

CAMPUS CLIMATE

Campus racial climate can be referred to as the overall racial environment of the college or university that could potentially foster poor academic performance and high stop out rates for students who are Black, Indigenous, and People of Color (BIPOC; Solórzano et al., 2000; Yosso et al., 2009). General campus climate studies (Hurtado et al., 2012; Milem et al., 2005) address historical influence, compositional diversity of climate, psychological and behavioral climate, and organizational/structural climate as components of the racial climate on college campuses. Considering that the vast majority of undocumented and DACA college students in the United States are Latinx from Mexico and Central America (Cebulko, 2013; Hernandez & Ortiz, 2016), the following highlights existing literature on campus climate studies centering the experiences of Latinx students specifically, as well as other BIPOC collegians who are marginalized on campuses across the United States.

One of the earliest published studies on campus climate is from Hurtado (1992), who described the ongoing racial issues that occurred on college campuses in the 1980s—mostly at non-Native colleges and universities[3] (NNCUs)—and how similar problems continue to be present toward collegians who are BIPOC in the ivory tower today. As a result of hostile racist and anti-(im)migrant sentiments on and off college campuses, students have engaged in advocacy and activism efforts on their respective campuses (e.g., Black Lives Matter movement and protests against the Trump administration's decision to rescind DACA).

In promotional advertisements, many NNCUs position their institutions as welcoming and inclusive for all students; however, some Latinxs and other BIPOC collegians do not feel that is an accurate representation of their collegiate experience (Santa-Ramirez et al., 2020; Yosso et al., 2009). Many of these collegians report feeling marginalized, alienated, isolated, unsupported, and unwelcomed by their white peers and faculty members (Love, 2009; Harper & Hurtado, 2007; Hurtado & Carter, 1997; Yosso et al., 2009). One challenge to noninclusive campus climates is the pervasiveness of whiteness in physical spaces, academic curriculum, policies, practices, and campus events and activities (Harper & Hurtado, 2007), which inhibits Latinx students' sense of belonging (Hurtado & Ponjuan, 2005; Strayhorn, 2018), including those who are also undocumented.

As a result of campus climate studies, Hurtado and Carter (1997) offer the concept of sense of belonging, which "captures the individual's view of whether he or she [sic] feels included in the college community" (p. 327). Scholarship on college student experience and sense of belonging suggests a salient relationship between belonging (i.e., social and academic integration on campus) and student retention and graduation (Tovar et al., 2009; Hausmann et al., 2007). Scholars also found that Latinx students have a greater sense of belonging and report more favorable perspectives about campus when exposed to racial and ethnic registered student organizations and academic courses where their cultural backgrounds are celebrated (Hurtado & Carter, 1997; Harper & Hurtado, 2007; Hurtado & Ponjuan, 2005; Montelongo et al., 2015; Santa-Ramirez, 2018). Further, BIPOC students often create their own social and academic counterspaces representing their school and home (Santa-Ramirez et al., 2020; Yosso et al., 2009) to shelter from the psychological-emotional harms of microaggressions (Harper & Hurtado, 2007) experienced regularly.

When there is a greater presence of faculty, staff, and BIPOC students with shared backgrounds, in addition to support services and programs catering to those from historically marginalized identity groups, BIPOC collegians often report less hostile campus environments (Museus, 2014; Santa-Ramirez, 2018). Although we acknowledge that it may be counterproductive for these collegians to cultivate a sense of belonging within an endemically racist society, which includes higher education institutions (Stokes, 2021), for colleges and universities, it is crucial to analyze undocumented students' belongingness further. It is important to learn with whom, in what contexts, and where these students may be finding or creating physical and virtual spaces where they can be their authentic selves (Means & Pyne, 2017; Vaccaro & Newman, 2016), in addition to the counterspaces that are validating their intersecting identities and experiences (Nunez, 2011). Further, all members of a campus community must be included in policy decision-making processes and educational conversations, which include those student communities that are often left out (e.g., undocumented and DACA, trans*,[4] Native and Indigenous students) and rendered "invisible" (Brayboy, 2004).

How We Arrived at This Work

For over a decade, I, Susana, have been working with and for undocumented and DACA students on examining issues of college persistence, identity development, social activism, and campus climate. I show up as a ciswoman and identify as a white-passing Chicana (im)migrant. While my (im)migrant identity and whiteness were left unexamined in my doctoral coursework, the work that I have engaged with and for undocumented and DACA students has led me to unpack the privileges associated with my arrival to the United States in the late 1970s under my mother's fiancée visa. Other than my mother being unable to attend her sister's funeral in Mexico during the four-year wait for our citizenship status because my stepfather had citizenship in the United States, I recall no struggle. My (im)migrant experience is in stark contrast to what most, if not all, undocumented and DACA students endure today.

As a white-passing Chicana, I navigate most spaces with the benefits that my white skin affords. It is only when individuals are aware of my surname that I get that all too familiar question, "Where are you from?" When individuals learn that I'm originally from Mexico, their flummoxed facial expressions are indicative that my language, skin, professional stature, and educational accolades do not fit into their dominant notions (stereotypes and biases) of a Mexican (im)migrant. My hyperconsciousness of my privileges, along with being in community with undocumented and DACA college students, informs my purpose, research, and teaching. I hold a deep understanding that the liberation of undocumented (im)migrants and other minoritized peoples around the globe is tied to my liberation.

I, Stephen, resided and worked in Arizona between 2016 and 2020 (during the "Trump era"). Over the last several years, I have worked in collaboration with and alongside undocumented and DACA students, mostly in Michigan, Texas, and Arizona. My current community commitment is to further explore Latinx undocumented and DACA students' everyday college experiences during turbulent and contested sociopolitical times—more specifically, how different policies positively or negatively affect these collegians' on-and-off campus involvements, belonging, and advocacy and activism efforts. Before relocating to Arizona, I was part of the senior student affairs leadership team at a Hispanic-serving institution in Texas, leading diversity, social justice, and inclusion campus initiatives.

For about a decade of my life, my (then) stepfather was undocumented from Brazil. Living in a mixed-status family and working with diverse undocumented and DACA students at different universities over the years, I began engaging in this work more extensively because of my personal and professional experiences and passions for equity, and racial and social justice. I recognized the need not to lump all Latinx students together when working alongside these collegians; collectively, these communities do not represent a homogeneous group. These populations' identities and collegiate experiences are diverse in many ways. Latinx undocumented and DACA students vastly differ from their US-born/citizen peers due to their liminal legal statuses and the effects of anti-(im)migrant laws, policies, and climates. Further, although we share analogous identities and experiences being first-generation students, Latinx, and from high financial need families, as I engage alongside these students who typically fit within these categories, I recognize that I can be considered an outsider to many within these communities. I was born on US soil, identifying as Puerto Rican, who would be automatically granted US citizenship. Thus, reciprocity is critically vital to me. I actively build trust and rapport with the undocumented and DACA student community as an active and collaborative co-conspirator and friend who is overall interested in educational equity and human rights for all.

Guiding Critical Organizational Framework

We use Leslie Gonzales and colleagues' (2018) framing of organizational theories in our case studies analysis. These scholars propose new ways to reimagine organizational theory using four frames to examine organizations: labor, intersectional, reparative, and epistemic. *Labor justice* unveils the disproportionate labor (emotional and physical), which often falls on women's shoulders and those who are BIPOC. It also examines the structural conditions and environments of those who are producing outcomes for the organization. By allowing for multiple voices to be present in the leadership decision-making, the organization attempts to dismantle the power structures and hierarchies that often uphold whiteness. *Intersectional justice* examines the myriad of injustices one endures simultaneously (i.e., racism, classism, sexism, transphobia). It unveils how diversity efforts and rhetoric are merely cosmetic shifts "rather than interrogat[ing] and dismantle[ing] the depths of racism, sexism, heteronormativity, and other isms" (p. 530). It is also imperative that the leader takes the position of the learner and is willing to acknowledge their own shortcomings. *Reparative justice* highlights how colleges and universities use tools of colonization to sustain whiteness and white supremacy. It requires institutions to rewrite their historical foundation in unsanitized and critical ways. Reparative justice also centers Indigenous knowledge and leadership as the guiding compass for how institutions hold themselves accountable. *Epistemic injustices* unveil how colleges and universities construct limited notions of whose knowledge and which knowers are deemed worthy by higher education. This form of justice questions how the organizational culture, a collective of norms, practices, and values, account for "who and what constitutes as legitimate and valuable" (p. 544). In the following section, we present two case studies and then apply the frames mentioned earlier to formulate a critical organizational analysis.

CASE STUDY: COLORADO STATE UNIVERSITY (CSU)

Studies have highlighted racial campus climate issues for undocumented and DACA students in Colorado (Ishiwata & Muñoz, 2018; Muñoz & Vigil, 2018; Muñoz et al., 2018). The Ishiwata and Muñoz article specifically highlights Colorado State University's institutional efforts and response to creating more humane spaces at CSU for undocumented and DACA students. Between 2006 and 2008, Colorado passed laws that required undocumented (im)migrants to show proof of lawful presence, and Colorado passed an in-state tuition ban for undocumented students. After five attempts to pass an in-state tuition policy, the Colorado ASSET (Advancing Students for a Stronger Economy Tomorrow) bill passed in 2013. To qualify, students must have attended a Colorado high school for at least three consecutive years, attained a GED or high school diploma, and enrolled in a college or university within 12 months after earning a diploma or GED.

CSU, situated on the Ute, Arapaho, and Cheyenne peoples' original land, is a public land grant university located in Fort Collins, with approximately 33,000 undergraduate students and 20 percent of the total population identifying as "minority." The university currently enrolls over 200 students that fall within the broad category of being undocumented (ASSET only, DACA only, ASSET & DACA, undocumented without ASSET or DACA). In 2016, the assistant vice president of student affairs spearheaded the ASSET Implementation Team consisting of 11 student services offices, such as financial aid, enrollment management, mental health counselors, student case managers, career services, legal advisors, and one faculty member. CSU has been engaged in 26 campus initiatives (see appendix) over the last five years. More recently, the Career Center Initiative has more intentionally engaged with providing undocumented and DACA students with more tailored services. They have conducted workshops on how undocumented graduates can work after graduation; created inclusive fellowships; and provided one-on-one advising, legal services assistance for business documentation, resources for starting a business, and mentoring services between students and industry.

A point of pride for CSU is the 2017–2018 retention rates for ASSET students (96%), which have consistently wavered above the average for all CSU students (86%). Despite the national turmoil with the rescinding of DACA by the Trump administration in 2018, the DREAMERS United student organization, alongside university and off-campus support systems, built institutional capacity of support largely due to student activism. As faculty members, I, Susana, and my colleague Eric Ishiwata were able to use our faculty tenured/tenure-track positions to (1) [amplify] Dreamers' voices and efforts through coaching, power-sharing, and behind the scenes organizing, (2) [steer] the university's stakeholder taskforce away from quick-fix solutions, and (3) [connect] the DACA repeal to broader patterns and structures of on-campus ethno-racial antagonisms (Ishiwata & Muñoz, 2018, p. 573)

While CSU is proud of the work accomplished to create institutionalized support, we acknowledge that "quick-fix" solutions do not absolve CSU from addressing the deeper systemic issues that have plagued the campus. These issues include systemic racism, which has emerged in recent years through incidents such as vandalism found at a mosque near campus, the construction of a cardboard "border wall" on the school's plaza, white supremacist signage found posted on campus, a noose hung outside an African American student's room in a residence hall, the invitation of Charlie Kirk (a white conservative activist) on campus that led to conflict between students and neo-Nazi groups, and the racial profiling of two Native Americans on a campus tour resulting in a parent calling campus police because they "looked like they didn't belong" (Ishiwata & Muñoz, 2018). More recently, a photo of white students in Blackface, and the potential attendance of border patrol at CSU's career fair, have undoubtedly added to the hostile campus climate.

CASE STUDY: ARIZONA STATE UNIVERSITY (ASU)

Historically, the state of Arizona, which borders Mexico, has an extensive history of enacting multiple forms of toxic anti-(im)migration discourses and, more specifically, anti-Latinx/Mexican policies and laws that have continuously relegated undocumented and DACA students to the margins. The exclusionary and discriminatory laws and policies in Arizona targeting undocumented and DACA (im)migrants continue to be an up-and-down roller coaster ride. Dougherty et al. (2010) even compared the racial and ethnic hostile climate toward Latinx and non-white (im)migrants to "what Mississippi was during the civil rights movement and in the '60s, that's what Arizona is to the undocumented community" (p. 161).

In recent years, the state enacted House Bill 2281, which banned ethnic studies (i.e., academic programs that promote Mexican American and Indigenous history) in K–12 public schools. In 2010, Senate Bill 1070, also known as the "show me your papers" policy, was also employed, granting Arizona government officials (e.g., police officers) legal permission to "stop-and-frisk" and legally racially profile anyone who appears "suspicious." For six years before the policy's demise, BIPOC individuals they thought may be undocumented (im)migrants were direct targets due to bias and stereotypes. From 2015 to 2018, students with DACA were granted access to in-state resident tuition (ISRT), but the policy was repealed in 2018 through a state resident voter-protected statute, Proposition 300. Enacted in 2006, Proposition 300 was voted on by state residents to exclude undocumented (im)migrants from applying to state-funded services, which also included ineligibility for ISRT and financial aid that is funded or subsidized by state monies (Cisneros & Lopez, 2016; Dorador, 2019; Muñoz, 2015; Olivas, 2009).

In 2018, the Arizona Supreme Court and Board of Regents ruled that students with DACA were no longer eligible for ISRT. This ruling resulted in the largest community college system in Arizona experiencing an enrollment decrease of nearly 40 percent of undocumented and DACA students (Leingang, 2018). ASU only had a 6 percent increase in freshman undocumented and DACA student enrollment compared to a 38 percent increase in the year prior (Leingang, 2018). Regardless of the vast challenges and barriers undocumented and DACA students face in Arizona, the following case highlights some of Arizona State University's resources to these collegians enrolled at the institution.

Arizona State University's main campus in Tempe sits on two American Indian tribes' ancestral homelands: the Akimel O'odham (Pima) and Pee Posh (Maricopa) peoples. There are currently approximately 2,000 DACA students enrolled in one of the three public state universities (ASU, University of Arizona, and Northern Arizona University) or within the Maricopa Community College System (Dorador, 2019). At ASU, there are an array of resources and services catering to approximately 300 currently enrolled undocumented and DACA students. One of these resources is a dedicated department, DREAMzone, which presently houses one professional staff member and a few undergraduate and graduate team members. DREAMzone acts as a social and academic resource for the undocumented, DACA, and students with mixed (im)migration status and family communities at ASU.

Similar to LGBT+ Safe Zone Ally Training commonly offered at different postsecondary institutions around the country, DREAMzone provides training to educate further and bring awareness to the university community (students, faculty, and staff) on the laws and policies that affect undocumented and DACA students' access and persistence in college, in addition to how to best support these students' attainment of their personal and academic goals (Cisneros & Lopez, 2016). The DREAMzone staff actively work with other ASU departments, colleges, and community organizations to provide resources and support for undocumented and DACA students to persist in college and toward graduation. For example, DREAMzone partners with the university's counseling services to offer biweekly Support Circles, exclusively for students who identify as either undocumented, DACA beneficiaries, or from mixed-status families. A university counselor facilitates these support circles. They are intended to be a *brave* place for students to authentically, openly, and honestly reflect and speak about their feelings and lived experiences—past and present. Further, ASU offers counseling sessions free of charge to their undocumented and DACA collegians—a waived fee for these communities. Lastly, different departments and student organizations have collaborated to offer an annual one-day weekend workshop for prospective undocumented and DACA students and their families. This free workshop is hosted each spring semester on a Saturday. It consists of an admission workshop facilitated in English and Spanish, scholarships and financial resources and information, current undocumented and DACA student testimonios, and lunch.

Besides institutional-level resources and support services, there is also a registered student organization on campus, Undocumented Students for Education Equity (USEE), that meets as a general assembly biweekly. This organization focuses on advocacy efforts and social support for undocumented, DACA recipients, and the broader BIPOC (im)migrant community. USEE was formed by a few DACA student leaders shortly after the 2016 US presidential election results were announced, as a way to best advocate for educational equity concerns faced by these communities in Arizona and around the country writ large. Since the enactment of USEE, these student advocates have proposed and received a university-sponsored grant to commence a peer-mentoring program, Dreamer to Dreamer—an initiative for and by undocumented and DACA students at ASU. Moreover, USEE members have partnered with DREAMzone and El Concilio (an umbrella organization for diverse Latinx-based student organizations) to host an annual benefit dinner to raise funds for the organization's development of the We Rise Scholarship. Through these students' advocacy efforts, 18 current and incoming undocumented and DACAmented students have been awarded with monetary scholarships.

Although ASU does not currently offer ISRT or free legal services to their undocumented and DACA students and families like some institutions across the country (e.g., University of California, Berkeley), in August 2019, the Arizona Board of Regents passed the "Non-Resident Tuition Rate for Arizona High School Graduates" (Gómez, 2019, p. 1) policy. Among the three state colleges, undocumented students, regardless of (im)migration status, now have access to tuition at a rate of 150 percent. This means that these collegians who graduated from an Arizona public high school are eligible to enroll at one of the three public state universities at a tuition rate between in-state and out-of-state, which equates to an annual tuition reduction of as much as $12,700 (Gómez, 2019). Within the first month of the policy revision (August–September 2019), approximately 30 undocumented students without DACA at ASU have benefited from this policy change and had their tuition reduced (Gómez, 2019).

Although ASU has implemented various resources to support their undocumented and DACA students, similar to CSU, there have been occasions where support does not always translate into humanizing actions and behaviors toward these collegians. For example, during the spring 2019 semester, many undocumented and DACA students and allies protested on ASU's Tempe campus against border patrol agents' invitation by administrators to recruit students at a job fair. This protest occurred in the spring, shortly after university administrators invited border patrol agents to campus at the University of Arizona (U of A). The U of A incident received national attention after some student advocates were arrested and threatened to be legally charged for their activism efforts against border patrol presence on campus. ASU, not learning from U of A's actions, shortly after had these agents actively on campus recruiting. Following the incident at ASU, USEE student leaders were made aware that border patrol agents were previously invited to recruit on campus at the job fairs, even after the college's leadership team issued multiple university-wide institutional statements indicating their support of a safe and inclusive community for undocumented and DACA students amid the anti-(im)migrant federal and state-level laws and policies.

Critical Analysis of CSU and ASU

Race and racism are integral components of our society, deep-seated into our everyday practices. This includes our higher education institutions, which continue to marginalize and oppress various racialized and minoritized communities (Delgado & Stefancic, 2010). As a result of racist nativist and anti-(im)migrant federal and state-level laws and policies, both universities highlighted in this chapter have been and continue to be affected. For example, as previously mentioned, in 2006, Arizona passed Proposition 300, which excludes all public higher education systems from providing DACA and undocumented students in-state tuition and state financial aid. Although CSU and ASU have made progressive strides to support their undocumented and DACA students in diverse ways, there is ample room for improvement.

Gonzales and colleagues' (2018) *labor justice* illuminates how the emotional and physical labor of creating humane and just spaces for undocumented and DACA students is racialized. This stands true for what BIPOC faculty, staff, and undocumented and DACA students regularly endure at ASU and CSU. Although both universities provide institutional-level resources that largely benefit these communities (e.g., ASU's 150% tuition rate eligibility versus the out-of-state student rate), a vast majority of the support services and initiatives have been implemented by undocumented and DACA student leaders and activists themselves (i.e., peer mentoring program). From a justice standpoint, there is a difference between institutions employing student-centered/directed programming initiatives and BIPOC students being forced to advocate for their existence and dignity by requesting more institutionalized forms of resources and support. Students should be central to the conversations regarding their definition of institutionalized support and success. However, their time and labor are not free. On the other hand, college leaders and administrators should be privy to how much time BIPOC undocumented and DACA students spend cultivating humane spaces for themselves. When institutions calculate grade point averages for institutional scholarships and funding, how do they account for the additional emotional labor placed on undocumented and DACA students to sustain their wellness and human dignity?

Gonzalez and colleagues' (2018) *intersectional justice* examines the myriad of "isms" that uphold systemic oppression. At both CSU and ASU, many of the undocumented and DACA students are faced by and are often targets of hostile, racist nativist campus climates (e.g., border patrol agents invited to recruit at ASU, and a border wall display in the center of campus at CSU). Even when resources and support for undocumented and DACA students are present, how much of these practices are "band-aid" approaches? Resource centers, task forces, financial aid, and student organizations cannot rid campuses of racism and other systems of oppression. As an attempt to address racist nativism in more systemic and structural ways, senior-level institutional agents and policymakers need to unpack their positionality and notion of whiteness within their leadership styles and values. Undocumented and DACA students are often placed in positions where they have to be the "teachers" of their lived experiences to their professors and other administrators. We have witnessed many of these collegians getting asked to share their (im)migrant narratives over and over again and being exploited for this added labor, often enforcing their revisiting traumatic and painful memories. To better learn about their experiences, policy effects, and how to best support and not exploit them, a DREAMzone-like training should be a requirement for all campus individuals, including the president, cabinet members, college and university legal teams, faculty, staff, and students.

Reparation justice works to highlight how whiteness and white supremacy are enacted in institutional policies and practices. One question to ponder is: How is the history of undocumented and DACA students preserved and nurtured by college campuses? How and what we document regarding the history of minoritized populations in higher education has a longitudinal influence on how they (re)envision themselves in these *spaces*. Wilder (2014) posits that American colonial universities were founded on the backs of enslaved Black people and by stealing Indigenous children and land. All higher education institutions must come to terms with their violent and white supremacist histories by presenting the multiple truths of how land, water, and other environmental resources were obtained. The text on a popular shirt worn by many Chicanxs, "We didn't cross the border, the border crossed us," exemplifies how the original peoples of the West and Southwest United States were considered part of Mexico. Yet, government entities' mistrust (higher education) stems from white settlers' broken policies and treaties to Indigenous Peoples. Undoing hundreds of years of systemic racism requires institutions to acknowledge their role in the settler-colonial process.

Having a limited understanding of whose knowledge and which knowers are deemed worthy by higher education creates *epistemic injustices*. Take the example of border patrol being present on campus for career fairs. Colleges and universities may deem this event as "no big deal" and will rest on the laurels of "we have to treat all employers the same," or "the First Amendment protects all forms of speech." What is left unexamined are the sociopolitical issues the presence of border patrol have on Black and Brown (im)migrant bodies. Even when undocumented and DACA students advocate against this indignation, their community and familial knowledge is often met with empathy but with no real action. Operating under the auspices of higher education policies and laws that fail to interrogate race misguides colleges and universities to claim race neutrality, which in turn reproduces whiteness. Principles of community or values of diversity and inclusion will only take institutions so far without the intentional interrogations of race and racism.

Concluding Thoughts and Recommendations

To be clear, our purpose is not to minimize the progress and diligent work of staff members, advocates, and undocumented and DACA students themselves who are fighting for transformational change at CSU, ASU, and other higher education institutions. However, if we are genuinely interested in the critical institutionalization of support for these collegians, we must interrogate how higher education spaces are suppressing the work. Fish swimming upstream against the water currents are often seen in a holding pattern. This is how we see current institutionalized practices at many colleges and universities across the United States. Racial and (im)migrant justice occurs when higher education institutions truly embody a "learner" attitude and transform to fit the needs of undocumented, DACA, and other minoritized students. Not simply when it benefits the interest of the institution. Congruent with this book's overall concept of translational racial equity research-practice (TRERP; see the introduction) along with our guiding framework centering labor, intersectional and reparative justices, and epistemic injustices, we pose the following recommendations for senior-level administrators and policymakers to consider as they institutionalize support for undocumented and DACA students:

- Coordinate university-wide efforts to fundraise money for these collegians. Funding can be used for DACA renewals (currently $495 biannually), an emergency crisis fund, and private scholarships. For example, at CSU, a discretionary fund was created, and a targeted email was sent out to specific people on campus asking for donations toward this cause.

- Create a university task force, including currently enrolled undocumented and DACA students and alumni, across campus representation such as legal services, admissions, retention, and financial aid with a direct reporting line to the university president's cabinet. The task force can address issues experienced by the undocumented and DACA student communities by developing strategic plans for more inclusive policies, practices, and services for the holistic success (through college and postgraduation careers) of this population of students.

- Campus leadership should consider community partnerships with nonprofit entities and legal experts to expand their knowledge of (im)migrants' resources and support.

- Understanding racial equity and anti-(im)migration rhetoric should be considered during student orientations and onboarding faculty and staff. One way this can be addressed is by implementing some form of a DREAMzone training that highlights the local and state context for this population.

- Create and promote virtual, physical, and other supportive spaces (e.g., Undocumented/DREAM Center, university website).

- Provide free legal aid support for both students and their families.

- Institutional "Work-Study" programs to alleviate the stressors of students having to find off-campus employment opportunities. Undocumented and DACA students are not eligible to work for federally funded Work-Study programs.

- Stop exploiting these collegians by not offering compensation when they are asked by institutions to share their (im)migrant stories, which often triggers traumatic events and feelings. Storytelling is sacred and should be treated as such. Undocumented and DACA students should be monetarily paid for their labor and contributions to the broader campus community.

- Value the expertise and lived experiences of undocumented and DACA students and how their knowledge and labor are highly needed in higher education but not intentionally sought. College and university leaders should be actively, strategically, and intentionally recruiting and hiring undocumented and DACA student alum as full-time employees, consultants, and featured speakers. As exemplified throughout this chapter, these collegians have many skills and competencies to contribute to the larger campus community, including working directly with and for undocumented and DACA students.

- All campuses should be sanctuary spaces for BIPOC undocumented and DACA collegians. University leadership must enact policies explicitly banning Immigration and Customs Enforcement (ICE) and border patrol officers from entering campus grounds. Further, university leadership should have detailed conversations with such organizations on how their presence, even at campus job fairs, continues to inflict trauma and stress on their BIPOC undocumented and DACA student body.

Considering the ongoing anti-Black and Brown (im)migrant sociopolitical climate and long-lasting effects of the Trump administration, authentic advocacy and an ethic of love and care is needed from all institutional agents. Campus leaders should understand that undocumented and DACA students are just trying to survive each day without fears of deportation, their DACA statuses taken away, racist nativist rhetoric, dangerous and untrusting campus climates, and additional exclusionary laws and policies. A transformation rooted in racial justice and humanization allows the fish to swim with the current, thus allowing them to reach their destination without pained struggles.

Notes

1. As defined by the National Immigration Law Center, an undocumented student is a foreign national who: (1) entered the United States without inspection or with fraudulent documents, or (2) entered legally as a non(im)migrant but then violated the terms of their status and remained in the United States without authorization.

2. Fought for by undocumented (im)migrant communities, Deferred Action for Childhood Arrivals (DACA) is a program enacted in 2012 as an Executive Order under the Obama administration. Eligible recipients of this program are protected from deportation in addition to work authorization for a renewal period of two years. DACA provides beneficiaries with lawful presence but not lawful status. DACA(mented) students and other individuals are beneficiaries of the DACA program.

3. Following the workings of Tachine and colleagues (2017), we chose to use NNCU instead of the commonly referenced term "historically white institution" to center the existence and history of Native communities.

4. The asterisk is utilized after trans to depict the multiple identities and categorical statuses for those who identify as trans* (Nicolazzo, 2016).

References

Brayboy, B. (2004). Hiding in the ivy: American Indian students and visibility in elite educational settings. *Harvard Educational Review, 74*(2), 125–152.

Cebulko, K. B. (2013). *Documented, undocumented, and something else: The incorporation of children of Brazilian immigrants.* LFB Scholarly.

Cisneros, J., & Lopez, A. (2016). DREAMzone: Educating counselors and human service professionals working with undocumented students. *Journal for Social Action in Counseling and Psychology, 8*(2), 32–48.

Cisneros, J., & Reyna Rivarola, A. R. R. (2020). Undocumented student resource centers. *Journal of College Student Development, 61*(5), 658–662.

Chen, A. C., & Rhoads, R. A. (2016). Undocumented student allies and transformative resistance: An ethnographic case study. *Review of Higher Education, 39*(4), 515–542.

Delgado, R., & Stefancic, J. (2010). *Critical race theory: An introduction* (2nd ed.). New York University Press.

Dorador, R. (2019). A path forward for Arizona: Amending the in-state tuition policy to include undocumented students. *Harvard Journal of Hispanic Policy, 31*, 1–8.

Dougherty, K. J., Nienhusser, H. K., & Vega, B. E. (2010). Undocumented immigrants and state higher education policy: The politics of in-state tuition eligibility in Texas and Arizona. *Review of Higher Education, 34*(1), 123–173.

Gómez, L. (2019). ASU: 30 students have benefited from reduced tuition covering undocumented (im)migrants. *AZ Mirror.* https://www.azmirror.com/blog/asu-30-students-have-benefited-from-reduced-tuition-covering-undocumented-(im)migrants/

Gonzales, L. D., Kanhai, D., & Hall, K. (2018). Reimagining organizational theory for the critical study of higher education. In M. B. Paulsen (Ed.), *Higher education: Handbook of theory and research* (pp. 505–559). Springer.

Harper, S. R., & Hurtado, S. (2007). Nine themes in campus racial climates and implications for institutional transformation. In S. R. Harper & L. D. Patton (Eds.), *Responding to the realities of race on campus* (pp. 7–24). New Directions for Student Services, No. 120. Jossey-Bass.

Hausmann, L. R. M., Schofield, J. W., & Woods, R. L. (2007). Sense of belonging as a predictor of intentions to persist among African American and white first-year college students. *Research in Higher Education, 48*(7), 803–839.

Hernandez, S., & Ortiz, A. M. (2016). Latinx college students. In M. J. Cuyjet, C. Linder, M. F. Howard-Hamilton, & D. L. Cooper (Eds.), *Multiculturalism on campus: Theory, models, and practices for understanding diversity and creating inclusion* (pp. 83–111). Stylus.

Herrera, L. J. P., & Obregon, N. (2018). Challenges facing Latinx ESOL students in the Trump era: Stories told through testimonios. *Journal of Latinos and Education*, 1–9.

Hurtado, S. (1992). The campus racial climate. *Journal of Higher Education*, 63(5), 539–569.

Hurtado, S., Alvarez, C. L., Guillermo-Wann, C., Cuellar, M., & Arellano, L. (2012). A model for diverse learning environments. In *Higher education: Handbook of theory and research* (pp. 41–122). Springer.

Hurtado, S., & Carter, D. F. (1997). Effects of college transition and perceptions of the campus racial climate on college students' sense of belonging. *Sociology of Education*, 70(4), 324–345.

Hurtado, S., & Ponjuan, L. (2005). Latino educational outcomes and the campus climate. *Journal of Hispanic Higher Education*, 4, 235–251.

Ishiwata, E., & Muñoz, S. M. (2018). "They tried to bury us": Scholar advocacy in the wake of the DACA rescission. *New Political Science*, 40(3), 558–580.

Kezar, A. J. (2007). Tools for a time and place: Phased leadership strategies to institutionalize a diversity agenda. *Review of Higher Education*, 30(4), 413–439.

Kezar, A. (2014). *How colleges change: Understanding, leading, and enacting change*. Routledge.

Leingang, R. (2018, September 24). Big drop in 'dreamers' enrolled at Maricopa Community Colleges after tuition ruling. AZ Central. https://www.azcentral.com/story/news/politics/arizona-education/2018/09/24/arizona-tuition-ruling-big-drop-dreamers-community-colleges/1374502002/

Love, D. (2009). Student retention through the lens of campus climate, racial stereotypes, and faculty relationships. *Journal of Diversity Management*, 4(3), 21–26.

Means, D. R., & Pyne, K. B. (2017). Finding my way: Perceptions of institutional support and belonging in low-income, first-generation, first-year college students. *Journal of College Student Development*, 58(6), 907–924. doi:10.1353/csd.2017.0071

Migration Policy Institute. (2021). Unauthorized immigrant population profiles. https://www.migrationpolicy.org/programs/us-immigration-policy-program-data-hub/unauthorized-immigrant-population-profiles?gclid=Cj0KCQiA9P__BRC0ARIsAEZ6irg_E80YVCeFf69Bwq0QW7pq0IXI2_asuqmgmc4WhkONip5oXlb7QK8aAvw1EALw_wcB

Milem, J. F., Chang, M. J., & Antonio, A. L. (2005). *Making diversity work on campus: A research-based perspective*. Association American Colleges and Universities.

Montelongo, R., Alatorre, H., Hernandez, A., Palencia, J., Plaza, R., Sanchez, D., & Santa-Ramirez, S. (2015). Latina/o students and involvement: Outcomes associated with Latina/o student organizations. In D. Mitchell Jr., K. Soria, E. Daniele, & J. Gipson (Eds.), *Student involvement and academic outcomes: Implications for diverse college student populations* (pp. 93–106). Peter Lang.

Muñoz, S. M. (2015). *Identity, social activism, and the pursuit of higher education: The journey stories of undocumented and unafraid community activists*. Peter Lang.

Muñoz, S. M., & Vigil, D. (2018). Interrogating racist nativist microaggressions and campus climate: How undocumented and DACA college students experience institutional legal violence in Colorado. *Journal of Diversity in Higher Education, 11*(4), 451.

Muñoz, S. M., Vigil, D., Jach, E. M, & Rodriguez-Gutierrez, M. M. (2018). Unpacking resilience and trauma: Examining the "Trump effect" in higher education for undocumented Latinx college students. *Association of Mexican American Educators Journal, 12*(3), 33–52. doi:10.24974/amae.12.3.405

Museus, S. D. (2014). The culturally engaging campus environments (CECE) model: A new theory of success among racially diverse college student populations. In Michael B. Paulsen (Ed.), *Higher education: Handbook of theory and research* (pp. 189–227). Springer.

National Conference of State Legislatures (NCSL). (September 2019). Undocumented student tuition: Overview. https://www.ncsl.org/research/education/undocumented-student-tuition-overview.aspx

Nicolazzo, Z. (2016). *Trans* in college: Transgender students' strategies for navigating campus life and the institutional politics of inclusion*. Stylus.

Nunez, A. M. (2011). Counterspaces and connections in college transitions: First-generation Latino students' perspectives on Chicano studies. *Journal of College Student Development, 52*(6), 639–655. doi:10.1353/csd.2011.0077

O'Connor, B. H., & Figueroa, A. (2017). A time to keep silence and a time to speak. *Anthropology & Education Quarterly, 48*(4), 411–419.

Olivas, M. A. (2009). Undocumented college students, taxation, and financial aid: A technical note. *Review of Higher Education, 32*(3), 407–416.

Passel, J., & Cohn, D. (2018, November). Most unauthorized immigrants live with family members. Pew Research Center. https://www.pewresearch.org/hispanic/2018/11/27/most-unauthorized-immigrants-live-with-family-members/

Pérez, W., Muñoz, S., Alcantar, C., & Guarneros, N. (2011). Educators supporting Dreamers: Becoming an undocumented student ally. In J. Landsman & C. W. Lewis (Eds.), *White teachers/diverse classrooms: Creating inclusive schools, building on students' diversity, and providing true educational equity* (pp. 299–313). Stylus.

Redden, E. (2020, April). Report finds growth in undocumented student population. *Inside Higher Ed*. https://www.insidehighered.com/news/2020/04/17/report-estimates-more-450000-undocumented-immigrants-are-enrolled-higher-ed

Santa-Ramirez, S. (2018). "Mi familia": Counterstories of first-generation Latina/x students navigating a racially hostile campus climate. In K. Soria (Ed.),

Evaluating campus climate at U.S. research universities: Opportunities for diversity and inclusion (pp. 151–168). Springer.

Santa-Ramirez, S., Wells, T., Sandoval, J., & Koro, M. (2020). Working through the experiences of first-generation students of color, university mission, intersectionality, and post-subjectivity. *International Journal of Qualitative Studies in Education*, 1–16. https://doi.org/10.1080/09518398.2020.1783012

Solórzano, D. G., Ceja, M., & Yosso, T. J. (2000). Critical race theory, racial microaggressions, and campus racial climate: The experiences of African American college students. *Journal of Negro Education*, 69(1), 60–73.

Soria, K. M. (2018). *Evaluating campus climate at US research universities*. Springer.

Southern, K. G. (2016). Institutionalizing support services for undocumented students at four-year colleges and universities. *Journal of Student Affairs Research and Practice*, 53(3), 305–318.

Southern Poverty Law Center. (2016, November 28). *The Trump effect: The impact of the 2016 presidential election on our nation's schools*. https://www.splcenter.org/20161128/trump-effect-impact-2016-presidential-election-our-nations-schools

Stanton-Salazar, R. D. (2011). A social capital framework for the study of institutional agents and their role in the empowerment of low-status students and youth. *Youth & Society*, 43(3), 1066–1109.

Strayhorn, T. L. (2018). *College students' sense of belonging: A key to educational success for all students*. Routledge.

Stokes, S. (2021). A sense of belonging within the imaginative constraints of racial realism: A critical race analysis of Latinx students' racialized experiences during the Trump presidency. *International Journal of Qualitative Studies in Education*. Advanced online publication. doi: 10.1080/09518398.2021.1956632

Tachine, A., Cabrera, N., & Yellow Bird, E. (2017). Home away from home: Native American students' sense of belonging during their first year in college. *Journal of Higher Education*, 88(5), 785–807.

Tovar, E., Simon, M. A., & Lee, H. B. (2009). Development and validation of the college mattering inventory with diverse urban college students. *Measurement and Evaluation in Counseling and Development*, 42(3), 154–178.

Vaccaro, A., & Newman, B. M. (2016). Development of sense of belonging for privileged and minoritized students: An emergent model. *Journal of College Student Development*, 57, 925–942. doi:10.1353/csd.2016.0091

Valenzuela, J. I., Pérez, W., Perez, I., Montiel, G. I., & Chaparro, G. (2015). Undocumented students at the community college: Creating institutional capacity. *New Directions for Community Colleges*, 2015(172), 87–96.

Wilder, C. S. (2014). *Ebony and ivy: Race, slavery, and the troubled history of America's universities*. Bloomsbury.

Yosso, T. J., Smith, W. A., Ceja, M., & Solórzano, D. G. (2009). Critical race theory, racial microaggressions, and campus racial climate for Latina/o undergraduates. *Harvard Educational Review*, 79(4), 659–690.

Appendix

List of CSU Initiatives (Ishiwata & Muñoz, 2018, pp. 570–572)

1. Established a DACA repeal task force with monthly meetings organized around a common agenda of service provision to CSU's undocumented students, with the Office of Student Affairs serving as the backbone organization.

2. Positioned counseling services staff in the trusted spaces of the cultural/advocacy offices to support impacted students, even prior to the September 5, 2017, rescission.

3. Hired an additional mental health clinician for the cultural resource centers with specific competencies around impacted students' needs and backgrounds.

4. Established a weekly group therapy session specifically for Dreamers, facilitated by a professional with specific competencies on the emotional needs of our students.

5. Provided guidance for academic advisors and Career Center counselors on how to build trusting relationships with and best serve undocumented students.

6. Leveraged civic, public, and private-sector relationships to connect impacted students with internships, employment, and structured pathways to graduate school and law programs.

7. Coordinated with the offices of Colorado's congressional delegation to monitor our students' DACA reapplication processes.

8. Signed on to lobbying efforts led by the Association of Public and Land Grant Universities and the American Council on Education.

9. Established a student crisis fund through collaborative university fundraising efforts that reimbursed students' legal costs related to the DACA repeal.

10. Partnered with off-campus 501(c)(3) organizations to create a more flexible, application-based student fund to cover one-time emergency requests.

11. Coordinated with the Financial Aid and President's Offices to find creative solutions for supporting impacted students with graduate school tuition.

12. Adjusted allocations for supplemental student health coverage to accommodate the higher costs for women's health care.

13. Launched a "one-stop" webpage—a virtual front desk—designed to help impacted students navigate Dreamer-specific information and resources.

14. Arranged for monthly campus visits by local immigration attorneys who offer one-on-one consultations, which are included as part of students' fees.

15. Held "know your rights" information sessions to prepare students for potential interactions with law enforcement and ICE agents.

16. Facilitated conversations between students and the Colorado State University and Fort Collins Police Departments to clarify that local agencies do not act as extensions of DHS or ICE and, if changes were to occur, students would receive advance notice.

17. Conducted a media relations workshop to prepare students for interview requests from print, radio, and television journalists.

18. Organized professional development workshops (DREAMzone trainings) and wrote articles to assist faculty and staff building respectful relationships with undocumented students.

19. Issued university-wide notices clarifying that CSU employees hold no role in reporting or inquiring about students' immigration statuses.

20. Reviewed university information systems to safeguard students' personal information.

Reimagining Institutionalized Support

21. Reached out to nonstudent members of the CSU community who were equally impacted by recent immigration policies.
22. Provided hands-on faculty advising for the Dreamers United student organization's weekly meetings.
23. Collaborated with Dreamers United to sponsor a campus-wide speaking event for Jose Antonio Vargas, an Emmy-nominated filmmaker, Pulitzer Prize–winning journalist, and undocumented activist.
24. Addressed food security concerns by connecting students to existing campus resources and created a volunteer meal provision program that supplied home-cooked dinners to the weekly Dreamers United meetings.
25. Facilitated ongoing dialogues between impacted students and CSU's president Tony Frank.
26. Established contingency Individualized Education Plans that would allow for degree completion in the event that currently enrolled students are no longer in the country.

8

Rethinking Postsecondary Education Access and Success to Advance Racial Equity for Rural Black Students

DARRIS R. MEANS, AARON T. GEORGE, AND JENAY WILLIS

The 2016 US presidential election results placed a national spotlight on rural communities in the United States, as elected officials, researchers, and the media pointed to the urban-rural economic and social divide to explain the election of Donald Trump over Hillary Clinton (Brownstein, 2016; Means, 2018b; Pappano, 2017; Shearer, 2016). This newfound national attention on rural communities has led to a series of notable stories on rural students and their postsecondary education access and success (Means, 2018b), including articles in the *New York Times* ("Colleges Discover the Rural Student" by Laura Pappano), *The Atlantic* ("The Rural Higher-Education Crisis" by Jon Marcus and Matt Krupnick), *The Hechinger Report* ("Some Colleges Extend Scholarships and Other Help to Rural High School Grads" by Jon Marcus), and the *Wall Street Journal* ("For Colleges, a Rural Reckoning" by Douglas Belkin). These news articles, along with a growing body of research and scholarship, have brought light to the structural challenges rural students face along their pathways to postsecondary education, which have led rural students to be less likely than their nonrural peers to: (a) enroll in postsecondary education immediately after high school, if at all; (b) be continuously enrolled in postsecondary education; and (c) attain a postsecondary education degree (Byun et al., 2015; Byun et al., 2012b; Hu, 2003; Koricich et al., 2018). These inequities have been amplified during the COVID-19 pandemic with concerns about current and growing declines in postsecondary education enrollment for rural students and enrollment at colleges and universities that serve rural geographical regions (Marcus, 2020). The gaps in educational outcomes for rural students are undergirded by educational, social, economic, health, infrastructure, and political challenges in rural communities, including loss of industry and economic bases, school consolidation and school budget constraints, closure of hospitals, and lack of access to broadband internet (Cain, 2021; Frakt, 2018; Johnson & Zoellner, 2016; McNamee et al., 2020; Sage & Sherman, 2014; Tieken, 2014; Williams & Grooms, 2016).

The national conversation on rural communities, families, and students that emerged during the 2016 presidential election and since that time, at worst, portrayed rural people and students as *all* white, and, at best, have only briefly acknowledged rural People of Color as an afterthought (Genovese, 2019; Means, 2018b). This monolithic portrayal of rural communities also ignores the racial and ethnic diversity across rural communities in the United States (Cain, 2021; Genovese, 2019; Greenough & Nelson, 2015; hooks, 2009; Means, 2018b). For instance, of the 8.9 million public students attending schools in rural communities in the United States (19% of the US public school population), approximately 1 in 4 are Students of Color (Showalter et al., 2017).

Given the significant population of rural Students of Color, their college-going and collegiate experiences must be considered by college and university leaders seeking to promote postsecondary education access and success for rural students. Additionally, while the term People of Color can be useful to express solidarity across racially minoritized groups (Adams, 2018; Liddell, 2018), postsecondary education researchers and leaders should attempt to dissect the college-going and collegiate experiences across racially minoritized groups. In this chapter, we specifically focus on how higher education leaders and policymakers can promote racial equity for rural Black students. One in 10 rural students identify as Black and 14 percent of Black elementary and secondary students in the United States attend rural schools (NCES, 2010, 2013). Researchers have found postsecondary education access and success challenges at the intersection of race and geographical locale for rural Black students (Chambers, 2021; Flowers, 2021; Harris & Worthen, 2003; Irvin et al., 2012; Strayhorn, 2009). For example, Irvin and colleagues (2012) found that rural Black students perceived there to be more educational barriers for pursuing postsecondary education than their rural white peers. In addition, 29 percent of rural white adults who are 25 and older have an associate's degree or higher compared to 17 percent of rural Black adults (U.S. Department of Agriculture, 2017). These postsecondary education access and success challenges at the intersection of race and geographical locale must be acknowledged and addressed by postsecondary education leaders and policymakers in order to better promote racial equity for rural Black students.

In this chapter, we first offer a statement about our positionalities, followed by a literature review on postsecondary education access and success for rural students, specifically rural Black students. We then describe the conceptual framework for the chapter, which includes community cultural wealth (Yosso, 2005), critical race theory (Delgado & Stefancic, 2001), and translational racial equity research-practice (TRERP; Johnson et al., this volume). Taken together, findings from our literature review along with our conceptual framework and previous study findings from the first author, Darris Means, and colleagues inform the set of recommendations we present in the following section for postsecondary education leaders and policymakers to enhance racial equity for rural Black students. We organize recommendations into two categories: (1) rethinking postsecondary education access and (2) rethinking postsecondary education success. Our focus on rural Black students is not to deny or minimize the racial inequities in higher education for other racially minoritized student populations. Instead, our aims are to provide rich, specific context for how higher education can better promote racial equity and justice for rural Black students and to problematize one-size-fits-all approaches to promote racial equity across racially minoritized student populations. In addition, we believe it is critical for college and university leaders and policymakers to remember that rural Black students also reflect diversity in social class, gender identity, sexuality, religion/spirituality, and other social identities.

Centering Ourselves in Racial Equity

As the authors of the chapter, we approach this work from a critical paradigm (Guba & Lincoln, 1998), centering the lived experiences of rural Black people from an asset-based perspective and critiquing and addressing structural inequities for rural Black people. We each are committed to racial equity and justice in higher education. We each bring our positionalities, subjectivities, and interests to this work; thus, we center ourselves in this chapter so readers have additional context for how this work is positioned through our lenses and life experiences.

Darris is a Black queer man from South Carolina who was a first-generation college student and raised in a low-income family. He has worked in higher education for fourteen years, promoting equity and justice in practice and scholarship for a number of student populations, including those who are racially minoritized, poor and working class, first generation, queer, and/or rural. For the past eight years, his scholarship and research have primarily focused on postsecondary education access and success for rural Black and Latinx students. Aaron is a Mexican American queer man from the West Coast of the United States. He also identifies as a first-generation college student who was raised in a working-class family. For the past eleven years, Aaron has worked as a student affairs professional across the United States in a number of areas, including housing and residence life, fraternity/sorority life, student conduct, and gender and LGBTQ initiatives. Jenay identifies as a Southern Black woman who is a native of a rural community in Georgia. Drawing on her rural Southern roots, her research agenda focuses on college accessibility and transition for rural Black students.

Postsecondary Education Access and Success for Rural Students

Defining *rural* does not equate to a one-size-fits-all approach (Ardoin, 2018; Cain, 2021; Hawley et al., 2016) and is often defined "by what it is not" (Greenough & Nelson, 2015, p. 323). Greenough and Nelson (2015) elaborated that the "Census Bureau has detailed criteria for population counts and densities in identifying urban places (generally 2,500 people or more in a densely settled area), but rural is simply left as an endlessly diverse collection of residual 'not urban' places" (p. 323). Researchers have also challenged narrow definitions of rural to highlight how connectedness to place can define *rural* for some people (Howley et al., 2005; Tieken, 2014). For example, Howley and colleagues (2005) argued that the "*rural* in rural is not most significantly the boundary around it, but the meanings inherent in rural lives, wherever lived" (p. 1).

Across the various definitions of rural, postsecondary education access and success for rural students have received more attention from the general public since the 2016 US presidential election (Belkin, 2017; Marcus, 2018; Marcus & Krupnick, 2017; Pappano, 2017). Existing rural research on postsecondary education access and success is largely inclusive of comparing across geographical contexts (rural, suburban, and urban), finding that rural students are often disadvantaged as relates to postsecondary education access and success (Byun et al., 2012b; Byun et al., 2015; Hu, 2003; Irvin et al., 2012; Lee et al., 2017; Snyder et al., 2009). For example, the rate at which rural students go on to enroll in postsecondary education and graduate is much lower than that of urban and suburban students (Byun et al., 2012b; Byun et al., 2015). Researchers have found that socioeconomic status and access to resources may be major contributors to the gap in postsecondary education enrollment and graduation for rural students (Byun et al., 2015; Koricich, 2014; Koricich et al., 2018).

Current research and national attention on postsecondary education access and success for rural students has primarily focused on white students (e.g., Means, 2018b). However, there is a growing body of research directing attention to factors that influence postsecondary education access and success for rural Black students (e.g., Cain, 2021; Chambers, 2021; Chambers & Crumb, 2021; Flowers, 2021; Gafford, 2021; Irvin et al., 2012; Means, 2019; Means et al., 2016; Strayhorn, 2009). In the next two sections, we provide literature on postsecondary education access for rural Black students and postsecondary education success for rural Black students.

RURAL BLACK STUDENTS AND POSTSECONDARY EDUCATION ACCESS

Researchers have examined how the intersection of race and geographical locale may influence postsecondary education access for rural Black students (Chambers, 2021; Flowers, 2021; Gafford, 2021; Irvin et al., 2012; Means, 2019; Means et al., 2016; Strayhorn, 2009). Rural Black students have high aspirations for pursuing postsecondary education (Chambers, 2021; Gafford, 2021), but Strayhorn (2009) found that rural Black men in high school have lower college aspirations than their urban and suburban peers, particularly their suburban peers, regardless of socioeconomic status and academic achievement. Researchers have found that accessibility to postsecondary education for rural Black students centers around the availability of resources and knowledge of the college-going process (Farmer et al., 2006; Gafford, 2021; Hines et al., 2021; Means, 2019; Means et al., 2016). For instance, Farmer and colleagues (2006) examined adults' perceptions of successful outcomes for rural Black high school students, and they found that there was a lack of local programs and services for rural Black youth to learn about postsecondary education. Chambers (2021) also found that math performance is a factor related to postsecondary education enrollment, finding "Black rural students with higher mathematics performance are more likely to be enrolled/persist in four-year institutions" (Discussion, para. 3). More recent research has found postsecondary education access and aspirations differences within rural Black student populations (Gafford, 2021). For example, Gafford (2021) found that young, rural African American women at one high school were more likely to aspire to attend college compared to young, rural African American men.

While researchers have acknowledged postsecondary education access challenges for rural Black students, researchers have also described the tight-knit communities available in rural contexts, which is viewed as a strength for supporting rural youth (Johnson & Zoellner, 2016; Tieken, 2014), including rural Black youth (Farmer et al., 2006). The notion of tight-knit communities reflects the critical role of social networks, including families, and individual assets for promoting postsecondary education access for rural Black students (e.g., Allen, 2013; Farmer et al., 2006; Flowers, 2021; Griffin et al., 2011; Means, 2019; Means et al., 2016). For example, Allen (2013) found that rural, Black, second-generation college students relied on support from their parents to access and succeed in postsecondary education. Beyond familial and school networks, researchers have found that college access programs and religious organizations or religious leaders were critical sources of support for rural Black students as they pursued postsecondary education (Combs et al., 2021; Farmer et al., 2006; Griffin et al., 2011; Means, 2019; Means et al., 2016).

RURAL BLACK STUDENTS AND POSTSECONDARY EDUCATION SUCCESS

Most higher education research on rural Black students focuses on postsecondary access, limiting the understanding of the postsecondary education experiences of rural Black students. However, several researchers have discussed the transition, college experiences, and postsecondary education outcomes of rural Black students in higher education over the past decade (Chambers, 2021; Flowers, 2021; Guyton, 2011). Rural Black students described challenging academic transitions, including lack of knowledge about how to receive academic support (Flowers, 2021; Guyton, 2011). Flowers (2021) found that rural Black students in their study had positive interactions with peers, faculty, and staff, but Guyton (2011) found that a few rural Black students experienced racial microaggressions from faculty and staff. While only a few students in Guyton's (2011) study experienced racial microaggressions, other researchers have described historically white college and university campuses as being challenging learning environments for Black students due to overt and subtle racism (e.g., George Mwangi et al., 2018; Hotchkins & Dancy, 2017).

Researchers have also examined college attainment rates by race and ethnicity in rural contexts (Byun et al., 2012a; U.S. Department of Agriculture, 2017). For example, while Byun and colleagues (2012a) did not find a difference between rural white, Asian, and Black students' likelihood of earning a bachelor's degree, the U.S. Department of Agriculture (2017) reported 20 percent of white people living in rural areas had a bachelor's degree or higher compared to only 10 percent of Black people living in rural areas. In addition, rural Black students have high postsecondary education aspirations (Chambers, 2021; Gafford, 2021), but a significant number of rural Black students do not enroll or remain in postsecondary education despite their aspirations (Chambers, 2021). While postsecondary education attainment disparities between Students of Color and white students lead to inequalities (Bowen et al., 2009), Snyder and colleagues (2009) reported that 20 percent of rural Black adults between the ages of 20 and 24 who were not in school but had an associate's degree or higher were not in the labor force compared to only 7 percent of rural white adults. This finding led Snyder and colleagues (2009) to the possible explanation that "higher educational attainment does not eliminate the discrimination against racial and ethnic minority groups in rural labor markets" (p. 11).

Conceptual Framework

Our recommendations are grounded in critical race theory (CRT; Delgado & Stefancic, 2001), community cultural wealth (Yosso, 2005), and translational racial equity research-practice (TRERP; Johnson et al., this volume). These theoretical frameworks and approaches enhance insights and recommendations for advancing racial equity for rural Black students in postsecondary education. Critical race theory and community cultural wealth provide us with lenses to understand how racism influences inequities in education and the assets and resources rural Black students use to pursue postsecondary education despite systemic challenges, and TRERP provides context for how to translate research to promote racial justice and equity in practice and policy.

The tenets of CRT posit that racism is ordinary in every facet of daily life as a means of doing business as usual and that this function of society advances the interests of both upper- and middle-class white people, such that challenging these notions is not a societal priority (Delgado & Stefancic, 2017). That the social construction of whiteness is permanent and pervasive throughout society leads to the importance of centering narratives, counternarratives, and storytelling by People of Color. For example, in looking at rural communities, CRT would argue that white peoples' narratives would be considered the normal experience, necessitating the fact that Black or other People of Color's stories need to be heard, if the goal is to understand the full implications of what it means to be from a rural community. By centering CRT in community cultural wealth, researchers can "examine and challenge the ways race and racism implicitly and explicitly impact . . . social structures, practices and discourses" and center the lived experiences of Students of Color (Yosso, 2005, p. 70).

In studying the educational experiences of Students of Color, some researchers have used the concept of cultural capital to "assert that some communities are culturally wealthy while others are culturally poor" and to focus on the deficits of Students of Color (Yosso, 2005, p. 76). In the resistance to the deficit perspective, Yosso (2005) proposed community cultural wealth as the "knowledge, skills, abilities and contacts possessed and utilized by Communities of Color to survive and resist macro and micro-forms of oppression" (p. 77). Yosso (2005) describes six forms of capital. First is aspirational capital, which refers to the resiliency to "maintain hopes and dreams for the future" despite challenges (p. 77), such as when rural Black students aspire to postsecondary education despite perceived barriers. Linguistic capital is the ability to communicate experiences "in more than one language and/or style" (p. 78). Familial capital examines the cultural capital that is passed through family and kinship networks, such as the support that is available through a community's church or place of strong community bonds. Social capital is the ability to employ social contacts and community resources for "instrumental and emotional support" (p. 79). Navigational capital is the navigating of institutions "not created with Communities of Color in mind" (p. 80). This could include Black college students supporting each other and sharing information about which classes, offices, and spaces on campus are safe and supportive. Finally, is resistant capital, which is the knowledge and ability gained through opposing inequalities.

TRERP as a concept "refers to the process in which practitioner-informed science discoveries that center race, racism, and other interlocking systems of oppressions are translated into institutional practice and policy interventions that aim to improve the material conditions of racially/ethnically minoritized people" (Johnson et al., this volume, p. 00). Johnson and colleagues propose five considerations to use research to promote racial equity in practice: (1) racial equity research should support the disruption and transformation of inequitable structures in education; (2) racial equity research should consider historical and structural context; (3) practitioners, especially racially minoritized practitioners, are important collaborators to support the translation of research into practice; (4) educators "must anticipate and account for the ways in which white supremacy and other interlocking systems of oppression operate to mitigate and undermine organizational change" (p. 00); and (5) college and university leaders must consider changes to structures and policies to promote racial equity. We center the propositions of TRERP to offer recommendations for how college and university leaders and policymakers can promote racial equity in postsecondary education access and postsecondary education success for rural Black students.

Recommendations for Promoting Racial Equity for Rural Black Students

Darris has spent the past eight years studying postsecondary education access and postsecondary success for rural Black students (Means, 2018a, 2018b, 2019; Means et al., 2016). He has completed qualitative research that has included participants who are middle school students, high school students, college students, middle and high school staff, college staff, and community leaders. Drawing upon research from Darris and his colleagues, our conceptual framework, and previous literature, we offer two areas of recommendation for how higher education leaders and educators can rethink approaches and strategies to enhance racial equity for rural Black students: (1) rethinking postsecondary education access and (2) rethinking postsecondary education success.

RETHINKING POSTSECONDARY EDUCATION ACCESS TO PROMOTE RACIAL EQUITY IN HIGHER EDUCATION FOR RURAL BLACK STUDENTS

A student's access to postsecondary education is influenced by multiple contexts: (a) individual (e.g., a student's social and cultural capital), (b) school and community, (c) postsecondary education institutions, and (d) macro influences (e.g., policy, historical and current context for how interlocking forms of oppression have shaped social and economic conditions); (Johnson et al., this volume; Perna, 2006). Across solo and collaborative studies (Means, 2018a, 2018b, 2019; Means et al., 2016), Darris has found consistent themes within multiple contexts that should be considered to help college and university leaders and policymakers rethink postsecondary education access for the purposes of enhancing racial equity for rural Black students: (a) reconceptualize recruitment and outreach efforts, (b) challenge and rethink admission standards, and (c) address college cost concerns.

Reconceptualize Recruitment and Outreach Efforts

For college and university leaders to rethink postsecondary education access to better promote racial equity for rural Black students, they must rethink their recruitment and outreach efforts. Jaquette and Salazar (2018) found that colleges and universities tend to do recruitment visits at primarily white, affluent high schools and communities. An extension of Jaquette and Salazar's (2018) work leads to another question: Are all colleges and universities doing any type of recruitment and outreach to rural communities and, specifically, rural communities with a significant population of racially minoritized students? Given that 90 percent of Black people who reside in rural communities and small towns are in the US South (Housing Assistance Council, 2012), this is a particularly important question for colleges and universities located in this region. College and university leaders should, if they have not already, expand their recruitment and outreach efforts to rural schools, especially rural communities with a significant population of racially minoritized students.

College and university leaders should rethink their understanding of the social networks that rural Black students rely on to support their pathways to postsecondary education. While rural Black students rely on school staff, including teachers and school counselors, to support postsecondary education aspirations and access, rural Black middle school and high school students also discussed other forms of social capital that were critical in supporting their postsecondary education aspirations and access: peers; community-based youth organizations; college access programs; local churches; and family members, including parents, siblings, grandparents, uncles, and aunts (Flowers, 2021; Gafford, 2021; Means, 2019; Means et al., 2016; Yosso, 2005).

College and university leaders must think about ways they are reaching out to local religious communities, community-based youth organizations, and college access programs to provide information about their specific colleges and universities. For example, in addition to secondary schools, college and university admission professionals could partner with a community-based youth organization and religious organizations in a rural community to share information about their institution. College and university admission professionals also have an opportunity to share general resources to support students as they consider postsecondary education options, including certificate programs, associate's degrees, and bachelor's degrees. At the same time, college and university leaders who are designing and/or leading recruitment and marketing efforts should be careful not to rely on deficit-oriented programs, philosophies, and values (e.g., viewing rural Black students and their families as at fault for postsecondary education challenges).

Challenge and Rethink Admission Standards

Means and colleagues (2016) found that rural Black high school students had concerns about the lack of academically rigorous courses at their high school that could prepare them for postsecondary education. Schools with a significant population of racially minoritized students and poor and working-class students often have fewer academic resources and opportunities, reflecting systemic educational inequities in the United States (e.g., Hochschild, 2003; Lee, 2004). While admission officers can consider other measures for college admissions, the disparities across high schools related to academic resources and opportunities do not disappear for students, and higher education institutions continue to rely on standardized tests that have historically and currently been connected to racial and class bias (e.g., Bowen et al., 2009; Park, 2018; Soares, 2007).

College and university leaders may continue to rely on standardized tests for multiple reasons, including the pressure of college rankings that use student standardized test scores as a factor and what they perceive as the value of using standardized test scores in addition to other measures and factors to make college admission decisions (Epstein, 2009). Regardless of college and university leaders' use of standardized test scores as a part of the college admission process, college and university leaders have the opportunity to expand on other measures of success. For example, college and university leaders who still maintain the importance of standardized tests or who cannot eliminate the use of standardized testing without approval from state governing boards can still rethink how much weight will be placed on standardized tests in college admission decisions. In addition, college and university leaders can assess how middle- and upper-class students and white students may be privileged in the college admission process and consider forms of capital in the college admission decision process that may have been traditionally overlooked by colleges and universities (e.g., community organizing and advocacy to address issues related to racism, students who were not engaged in school organizations because they needed to work during their time in high school to support their family).

Address College Cost Concerns

Across studies, rural Black middle school and high school students have a significant concern about college costs and how they will pay for postsecondary education, which has been found to be a significant barrier to postsecondary educational enrollment (Means, 2019; Means et al., 2016). While additional information about financial aid and scholarships could be provided to students and families, the concern related to college costs reflects a systemic challenge that requires individual colleges and universities, states, and the federal government to rethink college costs and financial aid to promote equity and justice in the United States, especially for Black students and families who are often disproportionately affected by student loan debt (e.g., Goldrick-Rab, 2016). However, postsecondary education has become increasingly tied to a private good versus a public good that can have an impact at local, state, and national levels.

Leaders and policymakers within these three systems—colleges and universities, states, and the federal government—must work together to determine how to address college cost concerns and how college costs can undermine racial and class equity in the United States. For college and university leaders, this begins with rethinking the hidden costs of higher education that may prevent students from being able to enroll and persist in postsecondary education (e.g., fees associated with certain courses, enrollment fees, housing application fees). For college and university leaders to rethink postsecondary education access for rural Black students, they must also advocate for and work alongside state and federal policymakers to reduce postsecondary education costs, reduce reliance on student loans, and provide more financial investment in postsecondary education.

RETHINKING POSTSECONDARY EDUCATION SUCCESS TO PROMOTE RACIAL EQUITY IN HIGHER EDUCATION FOR RURAL BLACK STUDENTS

A student's enrollment in postsecondary education is an accomplishment that should not be undermined. However, college and university leaders must rethink postsecondary education success to promote racial equity in higher education for rural Black students. This is particularly important given the college attainment disparities in a rural context for Black people compared to white people (Harris & Worthen, 2003; U.S. Department of Agriculture, 2017). Across solo and collaborative studies (Means, 2019; Means et al., 2016), Darris has found two areas that should be considered to help colleges and university leaders and policymakers rethink postsecondary education success: (1) implementation of asset-based, equity-centered programs and policies and (2) support for postsecondary education institutions that enroll a significant population of racially minoritized and poor and working-class students.

Implementation of Asset-Based, Equity-Centered Programs and Policies

Researchers have discussed how Black students find their historically white institutions to be hostile and unwelcoming learning environments (e.g., George Mwangi et al., 2018; Hotchkins & Dancy, 2017), which leads to important questions for college and university leaders: Do Black students feel seen and heard in supportive ways at your institution? How about rural Black students? We argue that college and university leaders should consider how these student populations, especially racially minoritized rural students, are supported at postsecondary education institutions.

We offer two recommendations for college and universities leaders to rethink postsecondary education success for rural Black students. First, college and university leaders need to consider the intersection of identities for both Black students and rural students; these populations are not monolithic student populations. Thus, professionals charged with designing programs and services to support Black students and rural students should consider the intersecting identities of these student populations. In addition, the programs and services should be asset-based, acknowledging the forms of capital that students bring with them to postsecondary education (Yosso, 2005). For example, college and university leaders developing and implementing programs and services for racially minoritized students, including rural Black students, could build upon students' aspirational capital to support their academic and career goals or their familial capital to understand how their relationships with family and community play a role in their academic and career goals.

Second, college and university leaders must examine organizational structures that may promote and/or hinder postsecondary education success for rural Black students, including the mission and goals of the institution, the resources (e.g., financial, people, and physical spaces), the campus culture, and decision-making processes and structures (Chesler & Crowfoot, 1989; Chesler et al., 2005; Johnson et al., this volume). Additionally, college and university leaders need to consider the ways in which white supremacy and other forms of oppression are reflected in institutional policy processes and hinder postsecondary education success for rural Black students. For example, are the mission and goals (e.g., strategic plans) inclusive of racially diverse and geographically diverse student populations? Do rural racially minoritized students feel a part of the campus? With each major institutional decision, are racially minoritized students and rural students disproportionately affected by the decisions? Finally, given documented educational inequities in rural schools and communities (e.g., Cain, 2021) and the systemic and historical underfunding of schools in predominantly Black neighborhoods and communities (e.g., Anderson, 2017), college and university leaders, student affairs professionals, and faculty should develop and implement accessible academic support resources to promote postsecondary education success for rural Black students and all students, while recognizing the strengths and assets students bring to higher education. However, college and university leaders can fail to support student success if they promote asset-based programs without addressing structural barriers that may hinder degree persistence for rural racially minoritized student populations, including rural Black students.

Support for Postsecondary Education Institutions That Enroll a Significant Population of Racially Minoritized and Poor and Working-Class Students

College and university leaders and policymakers must rethink the support needed for colleges and universities that serve and enroll a significant population of racially minoritized students and poor and working-class students in order to advance racial equity for rural Black students. During the 2015–2016 academic year, Darris led a qualitative case study on college student retention of rural Black students at a technical college in the US South. The technical college selected for the study was a branch campus located in a rural county with a population of 18,000 people; approximately 63 percent of county residents are white, and approximately 34 percent of county residents are Black or African American. Seventeen percent of the residents in the county are living below the poverty line. The branch campus offers diploma programs, certificate programs, and continuing education courses, and it participates in dual enrollment, primarily serving the county in which it was located. As a part of the qualitative case study, Darris interviewed five staff members at the branch campus of the technical college, including the branch campus director and instructors, to learn about their perceptions of how they support rural Black students as they pursue degree programs at the technical college. The perspectives of the practitioners in this study are critical to understand how to better promote racial equity for rural Black students (Johnson et al., this volume). Based on the study, two key areas emerged for how to advance racial equity for rural Black students in higher education: (1) staffing support and (2) student support.

Across interviews with staff members, they described how they had multiple responsibilities on their branch campuses due to limited staff. For example, the branch campus director shared the following:

> I wear a lot of hats. So I'm everything from recruitment, public relations, instructor, as you know I'm an adjunct instructor. I volunteer in the community. I work with testing services, so I'm often the person testing, particularly in the high schools to see if students are eligible for dual enrollment classes. I

> also offer career counseling as I can, working with the main campus and just working within the community and the people I know in the community. Tutoring. So I'll offer my services to help with tutoring . . . And, gosh, anything that comes my way, I guess.

While the student population would fluctuate and would sometimes only be up to 150 students at a time, there were only two full-time staff members at the branch campus, which was a decrease in number of full-time positions that were once available there. The branch campus included high school students in dual enrollment courses, students who had recently completed high school, and students who may have been out of school for some time. In addition, based on the information shared by staff, they were serving a student population with a significant number of poor and working-class students. Simply put, more support was needed to adequately support the needs of students. In addition to the multiple roles and responsibilities of a small full-time and part-time staff, participants discussed the difficulty of recruiting and adequately paying instructors to teach in the rural community in order to increase course offerings at the branch campus.

Not only did staff hold multiple responsibilities at the rural branch campus, they also described how students often held multiple roles and responsibilities that had to be considered in order to support their degree persistence. Students at the branch campus were often working and taking care of their families. The compounded difficulty of recruiting instructors and the multiple responsibilities of current staff often meant limited flexible course offerings for students who had to negotiate work and family responsibilities. While there were more course and degree offerings at the main campus of the technical college, it was approximately 40 miles away from the rural branch campus, leaving students, especially students with transportation issues, with limited options for completing their degrees or making decisions not to continue their degrees.

For college and university leaders and policymakers to advance racial equity for rural Black students in higher education, they must rethink funding for rural colleges and universities, especially rural colleges and universities that serve a significant population of racially minoritized students and poor and working-class students. For example, could college and university leaders and policymakers think of funding formulas that better support colleges and university campuses, including branch campuses, that disproportionately serve traditionally underserved student populations? In addition, college and university leaders and policymakers must rethink who is a college student. Based on the interviews with staff members at this one branch campus, a significant population were working adults with families, which requires a consideration for more diverse course and degree offerings and flexible course deliveries (e.g., online, hybrid) at rural colleges and universities that disproportionately serve traditionally underserved student populations.

Conclusion

In this chapter, we offered recommendations for college and university leaders and policymakers to rethink racial equity in higher education for rural Black students. We focused on two areas of recommendations: (1) rethinking postsecondary education access and (2) rethinking postsecondary education success. For college and university leaders and policymakers to rethink postsecondary education access to advance racial equity for rural Black students, we call them to disrupt how whiteness and middle- and upper-class standards are privileged in college admission standards and to better collaborate with the key social networks of rural Black students to expand recruitment and marketing strategies. We also call college and university leaders and policymakers to address college affordability issues that go beyond providing more financial aid and scholarship information to students.

For college and university leaders to rethink postsecondary education success and to advance racial equity for rural Black students, we call them to consider the nuanced, intersecting social identities of rural students and Black students, not to assume a monolithic postsecondary education experience, and to consider how organizational mechanisms at colleges and universities may be hindering and/or supporting postsecondary education success for rural Black students. In addition, we call college and university leaders and policymakers to rethink how to better support postsecondary education institutions that disproportionately serve traditionally underserved student populations in higher education, including racially minoritized students populations, poor and working-class students, and rural students. We hope our call to rethink postsecondary education access and success for rural Black students leads to practices and policies that better reflect and address the needs of rural Black students.

References

Adams, J. (2018, October 17). Why we need to stop saying 'People of Color' when we mean 'Black people.' *Medium*. https://medium.com/@journo-joshua/we-should-stopsaying-people-of-color-when-we-mean-black-people-29c2b18e6267

Allen, C. J. (2013). *The parental investment of first-generation African American rural college graduates in cultivating college student success* (Order No. 1697492753). ProQuest Dissertations & Theses A&I.

Anderson, C. (2017). *White rage: The unspoken truth of our racial divide*. Bloomsbury.

Ardoin, S. (2018). *College aspirations and access in working-class communities: The mixed signals, challenges, and new language first-generation students encounter*. Lexington Books.

Belkin, D. (2017, December 1). For colleges, a rural reckoning. *Wall Street Journal*. https://www.wsj.com/articles/for-colleges-a-rural-reckoning-1512159888

Bowen, W. G., Chingos, M. M., & McPherson, M. S. (2009). *Crossing the finish line: Completing college at America's public universities*. Princeton University Press.

Brownstein, R. (2016, November 17). How the election revealed the divide between city and country. *The Atlantic*. https://www.theatlantic.com/politics/archive/2016/11/clinton-trump-city-country-divide/507902/

Byun, S., Irvin, M. J., & Meece, J. L. (2015). Rural-nonrural differences in college attendance patterns. *Peabody Journal of Education*, 90(2), 263–279.

Byun, S., Irvin, M. J., & Meece, J. L. (2012a). Predictors of bachelor's degree completion among rural students at four-year institutions. *Review of Higher Education*, 35(3), 463–484.

Byun, S., Meece, J. L., & Irvin, M. J. (2012b). Rural-nonrural disparities in postsecondary educational attainment revisited. *American Educational Research Journal*, 49(3), 412–437.

Cain, E. J. (2021). African American rural students: Exploring the intersection of place and race. In C. R. Chambers & L. Crumb (Eds.), *African American rural education: College transitions and postsecondary experiences* [Kindle]. Emerald.

Chambers, C. R. (2021). Rural pathways to higher education: The role of mathematics achievement and self-efficacy for Black students. In C. R. Chambers & L. Crumb (Eds.), *African American rural education: College transitions and postsecondary experiences* [Kindle]. Emerald.

Chambers, C. R., & Crumb, L. (2021). *African American rural education: College transitions and postsecondary experiences* [Kindle]. Emerald.

Chesler, M. A., & Crowfoot, J. (1989). *Racism in higher education: An organizational analysis*. Center for Research on Social Organizations, University of Michigan.

Chesler, M. A., Lewis, A., & Crowfoot, J. (2005). *Challenging racism in higher education: Promoting justice.* Rowman & Littlefield.

Combs, J., Boettcher, M. L., Lange, A., & Hanks, S. (2021). Rural, Black, and distant: Building relationships to foster higher education access. In C. R. Chambers & L. Crumb (Eds.), *African American rural education: College transitions and postsecondary experiences* [Kindle]. Emerald.

Delgado, R., & Stefancic, J. (2001). *Critical race theory: An introduction.* New York University Press.

Epstein, J. P. (2009, Summer). Behind the SAT-optional movement: Context and controversy. *Journal of College Admission*, 9–19.

Farmer, T. W., Dadisman, K., Latendresse, S. J., Thompson, J., Irvin, M. J., & Zhang, L. (2006). Educating out and giving back: Adults' conceptions of successful outcomes of African American high school students from impoverished rural communities. *Journal of Research in Rural Education, 21*(10), 1–12.

Flowers, J. H. (2021). The privileged rural: The college experiences of rural African Americans. In C. R. Chambers & L. Crumb (Eds.), *African American rural education: College transitions and postsecondary experiences* [Kindle]. Emerald.

Frakt, A. (2018, October 29). A sense of alarm as rural hospitals keep closing. *New York Times.* https://www.nytimes.com/2018/10/29/upshot/a-sense-of-alarm-as-rural-hospitals-keep-closing.html

Gafford, C. M. (2021). Passport with no access: The habitus and cultural capital influences of rural, African American, and low socioeconomic status students' college aspirations. In C. R. Chambers & L. Crumb (Eds.), *African American rural education: College transitions and postsecondary experiences* [Kindle]. Emerald.

Genovese, H. (2019, January 16). People of Color living in America's rural spaces face constant erasure. *Teen Vogue.* https://www.teenvogue.com/story/people-of-color-in-americas-rural-spaces-face-erasure

George Mwangi, C. A., Thelamour, B., Ezeofor, I., & Carpenter, A. (2018). "Black elephant in the room": Black students contextualizing campus racial climate within US racial climate. *Journal of College Student Development, 59*(4), 456–474.

Goldrick-Rab, S. (2016). *Paying the price: College costs, financial aid, and the betrayal of the American dream.* University of Chicago Press.

Greenough, R., & Nelson, S. R. (2015). Recognizing the variety of rural schools. *Peabody Journal of Education, 90*(2), 322–332. doi:10.1080/0161956X.2015.1022393

Griffin, D., Hutchins, B. C., & Meece, J. L. (2011). Where do rural high school students go to find information about their futures? *Journal of Counseling & Development, 89*(2), 172–181.

Guba, E. G., & Lincoln, Y. S. (1998). Competing paradigms in qualitative research. In N. K. Denzin & Y. S. Lincoln, *The landscape of qualitative research: Theories and issues* (pp. 195–220). Sage.

Guyton, C. (2011). *Exploring the lived experiences of rural African American millennials at predominantly white institutions* (Doctoral dissertation). Indiana State University, Terre Haute, Indiana.

Harris, R. P., & Worthen, D. (2003). African Americans in rural America. In D. L. Brown & L. E. Swanson (Eds.), *Challenges for rural America in the twenty-first century* (pp. 32–42). Pennsylvania State University Press.

Hawley, L. R., Koziol, N. A., Bovaird, J. A., McCormick, C. M., Welch, G. W., Arthur, A. M., & Bash, K. (2016). Defining and describing rural: Implications for rural special education research and policy. *Rural Special Education Quarterly, 35*(3), 3–11.

Hines, E. M., Moore III, J. L., Mayes, R. D., Harris, P. C., Singleton II, P., Hines, C. M., Harried, C. J., & Wathen, B-J. (2021). Black males in rural contexts: Challenges and opportunities. In C. R. Chambers & L. Crumb (Eds.), *African American rural education: College transitions and postsecondary experiences* [Kindle]. Emerald.

Hochschild, J. L. (2003). Social class in public schools. *Journal of Social Issues, 59*(4), 821–840.

hooks, b. (2009). *Belonging: A culture of place*. Routledge.

Hotchkins, B. K., & Dancy, T. E. (2017). A house is not a home: Black students' responses to racism in university residential halls. *Journal of College & University Student Housing, 43*(3), 42–53.

Housing Assistance Council. (2012, April). *Race & ethnicity in rural America*. http://www.ruralhome.org/storage/research_notes/rrn-race-and-ethnicity-web.pdf

Howley, C. B., Theobald, P., & Howley, A. (2005). What rural education research is of most worth? A reply to Arnold, Newman, Gaddy, and Dean. *Journal of Research in Rural Education, 20*(18), 1–6.

Hu, S. (2003). Educational aspirations and postsecondary access and choice: Students in urban, suburban, and rural schools compared. *Education Policy Analysis Archives, 11*(14). https://doi.org/10.14507/epaa.v11n14.2003

Irvin, M. J., Byun, S., Meece, J. L., Farmer, T. W., & Hutchins, B. C. (2012). Educational barriers of rural youth: Relation of individual and contextual difference variables. *Journal of Career Assessment, 20*(1), 71–87.

Jaquette, O., & Salazar, K. (2018). Colleges recruit at richer, whiter high schools. *New York Times.* https://www.nytimes.com/interactive/2018/04/13/opinion/college-recruitment-rich-white.html

Johnson, J. D., & Zoellner, B. P. (2016). School funding and rural districts. In S. M. Williams & A. A. Grooms (Eds.), *Educational opportunity in rural contexts: The politics of place* (pp. 3–20). Information Age.

Koricich, A. (2014, April). *The effects of rurality on college access and choice*. Paper presented at the American Educational Research Association (AERA) Annual Conference, Philadelphia, Pennsylvania.

Koricich, A., Chen, X., & Hughes, R. P. (2018). Understanding the effects of rurality and socioeconomic status on college attendance and institutional choice in the United States. *Review of Higher Education, 41*(2), 281–305.

Lee, J. (2004). Multiple facets of inequity in racial and ethnic achievement gaps. *Peabody Journal of Education, 79*(2), 51–73.

Lee, J., Weis, L., Liu, K., & Kang, C. (2017). Which type of high school maximizes students' college match? Unequal pathways to postsecondary destinations for students from varying high school settings. *Journal of Higher Education, 88*(4), 529–560.

Liddell, D. L. (2018). JCSD supplemental style guide for bias-free writing. *Journal of College Student Development, 59*(1), 1–2.

Marcus, J. (2018, December 12). Some colleges extend scholarships and other help to rural high school grads. *The Hechinger Report*. https://hechingerreport.org/some-colleges-extend-scholarships-and-other-help-to-rural-high-school-grads/

Marcus, J. (2020, December 18). Number of rural students planning on going to college plummets. *The Hechinger Report*. https://hechingerreport.org/number-of-rural-students-planning-on-going-to-college-plummets/

Marcus, J., & Krupnick, M. (2017, September 27). The rural higher-education crisis. *The Atlantic*. https://www.theatlantic.com/education/archive/2017/09/the-rural-higher-education-crisis/541188/

McNamee, T., Willis, J., Ganss, K. M., Ardoin, S., & Sansone, V. A. (2020, May 4). Don't forget about rural higher education students: Addressing digital inequities during COVID-19. *Diverse Issues in Higher Education*. https://diverseeducation.com/article/176117/

Means, D. R. (2018a). *Anti-deficit achievement approach: Rural Black students' access to postsecondary education*. Paper presented at the National Forum to Advance Rural Education, Denver, Colorado.

Means, D. R. (2018b). Supporting the pathways to postsecondary education for rural students: Challenges, opportunities, and strategies for moving forward. National Association for College Admission Counseling. https://www.nacacnet.org/globalassets/documents/publications/research/supporting-thepathways-to-postsecondary-education-for-rural-students.pdf

Means, D. R. (2019). Crucial support, vital aspirations: The college and career aspirations of rural Black and Latinx middle school students in a community- and youth-based leadership program. *Journal of Research in Rural Education, 35*(1), 1–14.

Means, D. R., Clayton, A. B., Conzelmann, J. G., Baynes, P., & Umbach, P. D. (2016). Bounded aspirations: Rural, African American high school students and college access. *Review of Higher Education, 39*(4), 543–569.

National Center for Education Statistics (NCES). (2010). *Status and trends in the education of racial and ethnic minorities.* https://nces.ed.gov/pubs2010/2010015/indicator2_7.asp

National Center for Education Statistics (NCES). (2013). *The status of rural education.* http://nces.ed.gov/programs/coe/pdf/coe_tla.pdf

Pappano, L. (2017, January 31). Colleges discover the rural student. *New York Times.* https://www.nytimes.com/2017/01/31/education/edlife/colleges-discover-rural-student.html

Park, J. J. (2018). *Race on campus: Debunking myths with data.* Harvard Education Press.

Perna, L. W. (2006). Studying college access and choice: A proposed conceptual model. In J. C. Smart (Ed.), *Higher education: Handbook of theory and research* (pp. 99–157). Springer Netherlands.

Sage, R., & Sherman, J. (2014). "There are no jobs here": Opportunity structures, moral judgement, and educational trajectories in the rural Northwest. In C. B. Howley, A. Howley, & J. D. Johnson (Eds.), *Dynamics of social class, race, and place in rural education* [chapter 4, Kindle]. Information Age.

Shearer, C. (2016, November 11). The small town–big city split that elected Donald Trump. *The Avenue.* Brookings Institution. https://www.brookings.edu/blog/the-avenue/2016/11/11/the-small-town-big-city-split-that-elected-donald-trump/

Showalter, D., Klein, R., Johnson, J., & Hartman, S. L. (2017). Why rural matters 2015–16: Understanding the changing landscape. A Report of the Rural School and Community Trust Policy Program. *Rural School and Community Trust.*

Snyder, A., McLaughlin, D., & Coleman-Jensen, A. (2009). *The new, longer road to adulthood: Schooling, work, and idleness among rural youth.* Carsey Institute.

Soares, J. A. (2007). *The power of privilege: Yale and America's elite colleges.* Stanford University Press.

Strayhorn, T. L. (2009). Different folks, different hopes: The educational aspirations of black males in urban, suburban, and rural high schools. *Urban Education, 44*(6), 710–731.

Tieken, M. C. (2014). *Why rural schools matter.* University of North Carolina Press.

U.S. Department of Agriculture. (2017). *Rural education at a glance, 2017 edition.* United States Department of Agriculture.

Williams, S. M., & Grooms, A. A. (2016). The politics of place. In S. M. Williams & A. A. Grooms (Eds.), *Educational opportunity in rural contexts: The politics of place* (pp. vii–xii). Information Age.

Yosso, T. J. (2005). Whose culture has capital? A critical race theory discussion of community cultural wealth. *Race Ethnicity and Education, 8*(1), 69–91.

9

Beyond "Woke Play"

Challenging Performative Allyship in Student Affairs' "Diversity, Equity, and Inclusion" Programming

ALI WATTS

"Equity" is having a moment in higher education. The term has been growing in prevalence over the past two decades in both academic scholarship and institutional policy (Anderson, 2012; Bensimon, 2018; Ching, 2017), and increasingly appears as a key theme in education association conferences and student affairs training modules. At a surface level, this feels like forward movement—a growing awareness of (and willingness to publicly acknowledge/address) the necessity of investing in initiatives and strategies that critique the status quo for the purposes of advancing racial justice and addressing the persistent and dramatic educational inequities between white and racially minoritized students.

Despite this growth of equity-minded rhetoric, however, we must remain conscious of the arguments of scholars like Roderick Ferguson (2012), who claim that universities are adept at "absorbing" nominally antiracist discourses—espousing values of diversity, equity, and inclusion in official institutional statements—without working to disrupt persistent and long-standing inequities of power, opportunities, and resources. Theorist Sara Ahmed (2012) refers to this contradiction as the "non-performativity of anti-racism," wherein rhetorical gestures toward social consciousness (e.g., acknowledging privilege, naming racist histories, making land acknowledgments) are used as "proof" of antiracist action, without requiring the follow-up that would actually enact change. Nonperformative "woke" practices result in situations where institutions and individuals can celebrate (and reap social, economic, and reputational benefits from) the appearance of commitments to racial equity, while absolving themselves from any responsibility for doing the difficult work of bringing about organizational change toward dismantling long-standing systems of anti-Blackness and white supremacy in higher education generally and student affairs more particularly. This disconnect between rhetoric and embodied action highlights the importance of embracing the translational racial equity research-practice (TRERP) approach that informs this text (Johnson et al., this volume). Failure to recognize the mutually constitutive and deeply entangled nature of research-practice risks normalizing a culture where institutional stakeholders know how to "say the right words" but fall short of the action necessary for transformative changes in the material conditions for Black, Indigenous, People of Color (BIPOC) within the academy.

The racial equity gap that this chapter seeks to engage, therefore, is the distance between the neoliberal performance of "woke" social consciousness and authentic commitments to change and organizational transformation. My concern is rooted in worries that the institutionalization of equity discourses and projects risks transforming them from tools of radical critique to mere performative gestures—a signaling of social consciousness and *espoused* valuing of concepts like diversity, inclusion, and multiculturalism, without any real drive for action or change behind it. In keeping with the TRERP framework, I also worry about how often these gestures are decontextualized—presented as broad statements of understanding of social issues and inequities, rather than deep investigations of personal, local, and institutional complicity and responsibility for change. I liken this empty performative equity rhetoric to a form of "woke play" where practitioners "say all the right things" and follow the proper checklists of behavior in order to be seen or read as socially conscious, "good" individuals, without actually engaging in serious critique or work toward dismantling systems of oppression.

There is an urgent call for troubling of these so-called ally politics, particularly as they are deployed by individuals who benefit socially, monetarily, politically, or otherwise from their involvement in social movements without taking on any of the risks or responsibilities that come with the work (Ahmed, 2012; Grzanka et al., 2015). Freelon and colleagues (2017) refer to this surface-level activism as "performative wokeness"—an approach that allows self-styled allies to feel good about their contributions (and to appease constituents calling for change) without necessarily engaging in deep learning about the issue being addressed, or considering how their own identities and/or histories may be complicit in the power inequities and systems of oppression being challenged (DiAngelo, 2018). These critics argue that the concept of a "woke liberal" is inherently dangerous in the post-Obama era because it sets up an opportunity for dominant culture individuals (whites and those who engage in Whiteness)[1] to position themselves as exceptions to the rule of racism and racist oppression, as "good whites" who should never be lumped in with the "bad."

The purpose of this chapter, therefore, is to explore the dangers of woke play within the specific context of student affairs departments and graduate preparatory programs. This discussion is particularly relevant for student affairs practitioners because the field espouses a commitment to racial equity work—even including "Social Justice and Inclusion" as a core competency for its practitioners (ACPA & NASPA, 2015, 2016)—and is charged with enacting much of the student development–focused rhetoric of the institution. The chapter begins with a brief anecdote from my own days as a student affairs practitioner in order to both situate my positionality and begin exploring both overt and subtle forms of woke play. Next, I broaden the discussion to review literature related to higher education and student affairs (HESA) graduate programs and the various ways that emerging professionals are socialized to approach issues related to diversity, equity, inclusion, and social justice. I argue that the "culture of nice" (Alemán, 2009; Castagno, 2019; Villarreal et al., 2019) in higher education, and student affairs in particular, encourages practitioners to engage in diluted, gentle, and performative forms of racial solidarity that ultimately serve the hegemonic (anti-Black and settler colonial) status quo rather than promoting institutional transformation. Next, I engage in a discussion with the ACPA's "Strategic Imperative for Racial Justice and Decolonization" to address opportunities for moving beyond woke play to a more critical, reflexive, and productive enactment of racial equity values. The chapter then concludes with a series of recommendations or reflective prompts for those engaging in research-practice to consider as they develop equity-minded programs, advocate for/with students from both majoritized and minoritized communities, and consider their position within their institutional settings.

Performative Wokeness and Positionality: An Anecdote

In the fall of 2015, I sat in the back of a large lecture hall and listened as a colleague from the career services office described the employment benefits of engaging in community activism and organizing to a sea of (almost exclusively white) first-year law students. She argued that large law firms of all kinds were eager to appear socially conscious in the current political moment and were attracted to job candidates who demonstrated a level of nonthreatening "wokeness" about a range of different social and political issues. In particular, she suggested that students might consider getting involved in the #BlackLivesMatter demonstrations being organized at that time to commemorate the one-year anniversary of the state-sanctioned murders of Michael Brown in Ferguson and Eric Garner in Baltimore. "Don't get arrested, of course—You don't want to be too extreme," I recall the advisor admonishing, to a rumble of chuckles and flashing grins. "But being there—maybe organizing a cross-cultural dialogue or a forum with police—that would likely play well with employers right now."

One of the student workers from my office came up to me after the talk and asked for my opinion about the speaker's presentation. Justin[2] was one of the few Black men in the program, and we had spoken periodically throughout the semester about challenges he faced navigating identity politics with both faculty and peers. I felt honored that he was comfortable sharing some of his story and struggles with me—a white middle-class ciswoman—and I was eager to be perceived as a good ally in his eyes. His question about my interpretation of the speaker felt like a test—and I was determined to perform well. I expressed frustration that a program that prided itself on the development of public interest lawyers would talk about social activism in such a capitalist and hyper-individualist way. I may have ranted about how students were being encouraged to "dabble" with community activism, to "play" with activism in their leisure time; not necessarily with the intent of supporting the Black and Brown communities advocating for social change, but with an eye toward presenting a résumé reflecting a marketable performance of social and political consciousness. By the time I finished, we'd reached my office door and were preparing to part ways. Justin caught my eye for a moment, nodded, and then said, "Ok, you've told me what you thought. Now what are you going to do about it? You work here—she's on you too."

The incident with the Justin and the career advisor has stuck with me because it provides two distinct but related examples of woke play. The advisor's was perhaps more explicit—an overt call for unserious, self-interested performances of social consciousness for the purposes of personal career promotion. In some ways, however, my play was equally if not more dangerous. I was performing for Justin, attempting to assert both my wokeness and my goodness by proving that I was different, that I "got it," and that I could be trusted. My critiques may have been valid, but I aired them for a selfish purpose and in a space where I took little risk and accomplished nothing in terms of supporting students or advocating for institutional change. Justin was right to call me out on my play, and right to push me to take my criticism into a more productive space in order to engage my colleague and fellow white student affairs practitioners in dialogue about the potential harms of such discourse. To my shame, I did not take his advice, and my equity-mindedness remained merely performative.

Writing this chapter, therefore, is a deeply personal project. I am aware that I have engaged in superficial and performative wokeness in the past and have taken advantage of my white privilege to opt in and out of conversations and activism surrounding racial justice when they felt too uncomfortable or inconvenient (DiAngelo, 2018; Leonardo & Porter, 2010; Matias, 2016). What's more, I feel confident that I will do so again in the future, particularly if I am not vigilant and self-critical about my work and my relationships. I am also confident that I am not alone in these moments of failure, or in my struggle to do better. As a white woman who both directly and indirectly benefits from anti-Black racism, I recognize that my scholarship and praxis (and my activities outside the academy entirely) are shaped by what Ibram Kendi (2019) calls the "dueling consciousness" of abolitionist and racist ideologies. In recognition of this tension, I have started to refer to the work of critical white allies as *anti/racist* in nature—using the slash[3] as a visual representation of Kendi's "duel" and a reminder of how easily well-intentioned work can become co-opted and reclaimed by white supremacy, can become mere woke play rather than effective allyship or activism. The slash is a reminder that we must remain suspicious and vigilant of our own allyship, and to be particularly self-critical when diversity, equity, and inclusion efforts begin to feel comfortable, commonplace, and habitual.

What I hope this chapter does, therefore, is provide language for recognizing and pushing back against woke play, in part by proposing reflective prompts that encourage student affairs practitioners and aspiring anti/racist allies to engage in what Leigh Patel (2016) calls a "praxis of pausing." This critical pause provides space for deeper reflection about our motivations, strategies, and expectations for engaging in coalitional politics. It reminds us to remain humble. After all, as Audrey Thompson (2003) reminds us, by "regarding ourselves as *authoritatively* antiracist, we keep whiteness at the center of antiracism" (p. 9).

Student Affairs as Woke Playground

Drawing on the prior anecdote and the framing of critically conscious anti/racism as a challenge to woke play, the next section will engage in a literature review to specifically explore this issue in relation to the research-practice of student affairs preparation programs. In particular, I am interested in connecting the phenomenon of woke play to the increased professionalization of student affairs and the socialization of student affairs graduate students into a paradigm that positions diversity, equity, and inclusion as a competency for advancement. As Dean Spade (2011) notes in his book *Normal Life: Administrative Violence, Critical Trans Politics, & the Limits of Law*, the incorporation of social justice initiatives within hegemonic (white) institutions like higher education often results in the weakening and co-optation of radical agendas. He outlines the dangers of professionalizing social movements by suggesting that these organizations center highly educated, elite, and well-compensated practitioners over the voices and leadership of those individuals and communities directly affected by stratifying policies and practices. Spade (2011) argues:

> In this context, social justice has become a career track populated by individuals with specialized training who rely on business management models to run nonprofits "efficiently." The leadership and decision-making come from these disproportionately white, upper-class paid leaders and donors, which has significantly shifted priorities toward work that stabilizes structural inequality by legitimizing and advancing dominant systems of meaning and control rather than making demands for deeper transformation. (p. 29)

Spade's critique can be easily translated to a higher education context through a transformative racial equity research-practice (TRERP) lens. In particular, he calls for constant suspicion and interrogation of the ways that Whiteness and other interlocking systems of oppression work to distract and deradicalize transformative change efforts, and calls for a centering of the voices and experiences of BIPOC stakeholders who work "on the ground" to resist and reimagine current structures. Similarly, the TRERP perspective calls for an approach to racial equity research-practice that recognizes the entanglement of knowing and doing, and calls for work that not only names but actively strives to resist and disrupt (to transform) hegemonic policies and practices that enact violence and exclusion.

This focus on merging research and practice, centering the experiences of BIPOC practitioners as knowledge co-producers and actively working to change the material conditions for minoritized and marginalized communities, leads to a particular series of questions about the current and potential role of student affairs preparatory programs. In particular, how might Whiteness be working to distract and redirect diversity, equity, and inclusion efforts as they become incorporated and mainstreamed into an increasingly "professionalized" student affairs practice? What risks come with "allies" and self-proclaimed scholar and practitioner "activists" who are educated in these preparatory programs but have no personal or professional connection to the communities most directly impacted by structural and systemic inequities? To what degree are student affairs master's programs privileging the exposure and education of privileged and majoritized students over the safety, experiences, and transformative change-efforts of their BIPOC peers? And, perhaps most importantly for readers of this volume, how might the research-practice of student affairs resist the pressures of the "woke playground" to move beyond teaching students how to *appear* socially conscious and to recognize their/our responsibility to actively disrupt and transform oppressive structures within the academy?

Demographics and the Dangers of "Diversity as Everyone's Job"

Student affairs is uniquely positioned to intersect with concerns related to student learning and development, as well as institutional policy negotiation and implementation (Hevel, 2016), particularly when it comes to issues related to racial equity. A 2016 study by the American Council on Education (ACE), for example, found that a majority of college and university presidents rely on student affairs professionals to directly engage with racial climate issues and direct campus education and transformational change projects. In fact, over three-quarters of presidents surveyed stated that they primarily relied on their VP of Student Affairs/Dean of Students to assist with "addressing issues of racial diversity among students" (Espinosa et al., 2016, para. 11). The survey also found that one of the most common institutional responses to racial tension on campus was an increase in campus-based diversity and cultural competency trainings, typically designed and offered by student affairs professionals under the guidance and oversight of their Chief Student Affairs Officer. While the demographics of the student affairs profession are changing (Pritchard & McChesney, 2018), it is significant to note that a 2014 study of Chief Student Affairs Officers by the National Association of Student Affairs Professionals (NASPA) reported that 73 percent of student affairs leaders identified as white, and the majority were over the age of 50 (Wesaw & Sponsler, 2014, p. 8).

While we have information about the social identities of top student affairs officers, D-L Stewart (2019) has noted that it is difficult to access data related to the demographics of student affairs practitioners in entry- or mid-level roles, as neither of the primary professional associations (e.g., American College Personnel Association [ACPA] and the National Association of Student Personnel Administrators [NASPA]) publish these data. It is commonly understood, however, that while the proportion of student affairs practitioners who identify as Black or Latinx is on the rise (Pritchard & McChesney, 2018), these professionals tend to be clustered in multicultural/ethnic student support roles. Stewart argues that this "ghettoizing of BIPOC professionals serves to isolate and exclude these professionals from broader inclusion and engagement with student affairs practice" (p. 21) and ensures that "general" or "mainstream" student affairs offices (e.g., residential life, student activities, conduct, and fraternity and sorority life) remain predominantly white. While it is necessary to challenge the hiring practices and unfriendly climate concerns that result in this "ghettoization," Stewart's research also highlights the importance of ensuring that emerging professionals receive strong, equity-minded socialization during their graduate school training, regardless of the practice area they plan to enter in the future.

Competencies, Checklists, and the Institutionalization of Woke Play

In response to changing demographics in higher education and the growing need for student affairs professionals to demonstrate at least a base familiarity with diversity, equity, and inclusion scholarship, many higher education and student affairs (HESA) graduate preparation programs now espouse an explicit commitment to racial equity. For many programs, this emphasis is in part informed by the guidance documents published by the field's two leading professional organizations (NASPA and ACPA). The documents—"Professional Competency Areas for Student Affairs Professionals" (2015) and "Professional Competencies Rubrics" (2016)—outline foundational dispositions, skills, and knowledges that all professionals in the field should demonstrate. The documents outline 10 competency areas for assessment: Advising and Supporting; Assessment, Evaluation, and Research; Law, Policy, and Governance; Leadership; Organizational and Human Resources; Personal and Ethical Foundations; Social Justice and Inclusion; Student Learning and Development; Technology; and Values, Philosophy, and History. Each competency is assessed in a rubric with relevant skills and knowledges evaluated on a scale with three levels—foundational, intermediate, and advanced.

The highlighting of "social justice and inclusion" (SJI) as one of 10 competencies that competent student affairs practitioners are expected to possess structures the ways that graduate programs and early career professional development programs approach issues of diversity, equity, and inclusion. The SJI competency is organized into a matrix with three levels of assessment—foundational, intermediate, and advanced—for five metrics: (1) understanding of self and navigating systems of power, (2) critical assessment and self-directed learning, (3) engaging in socially just practice, (4) organizational systemic advocacy, and (5) understanding theory (ACPA & NASPA, 2016). While these competencies represent a significant advancement in terms of their explicit engagement with power, institutional and systemic racism, and calls for action, scholars continue to critique the model for being both too individualized (focused on competencies as a strategy for personal professional development and career advancement) and vague in terms of strategies for advancing racial justice and organizational change. Practitioners are encouraged to track their advancement across the rubrics and "level up" in competency through coursework, professional development workshops, and performance evaluations.

While the guidance documents stress that "the outcomes should not be viewed as checklists, but as sets of indicators mapping development in and around each of the competency areas" (ACPA & NASPA, 2015, p. 8), the rubric structure of the competencies suggests a grading scale where practitioners "achieve" levels of competency required for professional advancement. Despite this warning, however, scholarship shows that the competencies are, in fact, used as checklists across the country and the profession, including through ACPA publications, structures for presentations at ACPA and NASPA conferences, and as organizing guidelines for student affairs graduate programs (Eaton & Smithers, 2019). This operationalization of the Social Justice and Inclusion competency as a checklist for professional development and career advancement arguably enforces a script or dominant narrative that students and professionals must perform in order to be seen as competent practitioners in the field. This scripting in turn encourages performative wokeness where students and emerging professionals learn to say and do the "right" things according to the rubric but without necessarily engaging in the reflective, and power-conscious, and context-specific praxis required for transformational change.

Competency Scripts: Racialized Labor and Confessing Privilege

The next section of this chapter examines SJI scripts as they play out in student affairs graduate programs, and the differential impacts these pedagogical discourses have for majoritized and minoritized students and practitioners. After all, despite the clear importance of introducing anti/racist and equity-minded training into higher education and student affairs (HESA) graduate programs, a number of scholars have critiqued the impact of the field's focus on multiculturalism and diversity discourses (see Flowers, 2003; Gayles & Kelly, 2007; Iverson, 2018) that works to position racially minoritized students as outsiders, at-risk participants disadvantaged by their differential access to white middle-class cultural norms, and commodities/resources for the education of white classmates. A common theme across these studies has been that HESA programs regularly espouse commitments to social justice but fall short in actualizing or enacting these commitments and may actually do harm to minoritized students. In particular, Gayles and Kelly (2007) observed that while most HESA graduate programs required a "diversity course" for graduation, syllabi for these courses focused on cultural difference and personal privilege and were dramatically lacking in structural critiques of systems of oppression. This finding suggests that diversity requirements do not always ensure that future student affairs practitioners will be able, or willing, to engage racial equity or social justice in their work. Diversity and equity courses may heighten graduate students' awareness of difference, but they do not necessarily ensure that practitioners are prepared to engage ethically or responsibly in social justice efforts that move beyond a surface-level performativity of woke awareness of difference (King & Howard-Hamilton, 2003).

More recently, Harris and Linder (2018) used a critical race theory lens to analyze narratives from racially minoritized HESA graduate students and found that the students articulate four sources of critique of the course experiences: (1) expectations that they will educate white peers, (2) invalidation of experiences and identity, (3) racial stereotypes, and (4) isolation. These students describe feeling as though their bodies and stories were used as source material for the growth and development of white peers (and, on occasion, faculty instructors) who remained largely unconscious and uncritical of their own racial identity and privileges as well as the structural and systemic ways that racial oppression, exclusion, and marginalization continue to operate in higher education and student affairs. A complementary study by Stephanie Bondi (2012) examining the experiences of white students enrolled in a student affairs master's program traced three common narratives related to experiences with race and racism: (1) At least I'm ready to learn, (2) Let me contribute, and (3) Exclusion. Bondi argues that these narratives center whiteness by claiming that institutions ought to privilege white students' desire to learn and speak candidly over the rights of minoritized peers to be cognitively and emotionally safe and to hear their experiences reflected in the classroom.

This perceived "right to enter and occupy space" is a key component of Cheryl Harris's (1993) theory of Whiteness as property, and one that has appeared frequently in conversations related to white self-described allies engaged in woke play. Sullivan (2006) refers to this sense of entitlement as *ontological expansiveness*, which she defines as the tendency for white people "to act and think as if all spaces—whether geographical, psychical [i.e., cognitive and emotional], linguistic, economic, or otherwise—are or should be available to them to move in and out as they wish" (p. 10). In higher education scholarship this concept is often used in the context of campus ecology and the ways that Whiteness "takes up space" by centering (unnamed) white interests and student organizations while marginalizing other ways of being and engaging on campus (Cabrera et al., 2016; Gusa, 2010; Harper & Hurtado, 2007). White students and practitioners are encouraged to believe that they "belong" and can speak with authority (Foste, 2020) in any space or conversation that they choose to enter, despite the fact that their curriculum often leaves them unprepared to engage in critical conversation of either personal privilege or systemic injustice in higher education or student affairs.

When majoritized students are prompted to think critically, lessons are often focused on articulating their own individual experiences of privilege (Jupp & Lensmire, 2016; Lensmire et al., 2013; Leonardo, 2004), rather than strategies for recognizing, naming, and challenging racist and oppressive practices and policies. So-called "privilege pedagogies" have been a staple in many student affairs contexts for years. Many Residential Education programs still use "Privilege Walks" as part of their programming—where students move about a room in response to prompts like "Step forward if you've never been followed by a clerk in a store due to your race," and "Step back if your K–12 schooling was conducted in a language other than that spoken in your home." Others use a "White Benefits Checklist" where participants examine a checklist of privileges and place tic marks next to the items that apply to their own life. Although this pedagogy can be useful to help prompt reflection on unearned privileges and immunities, it does not provide students and emerging student affairs practitioners with language or resources to fully grasp the complexity of white supremacy as a system of oppression operating through institutions like higher education. Indeed, Lensmire and colleagues (2013) refer to these activities as "ritual confessions" on the part of majoritized students that ultimately serve a "redemptive function" of emotional catharsis that absolves the bearer of privilege from any responsibility to action (p. 422). In other words, privilege pedagogies in student affairs programs and graduate classrooms risk teaching majorized students that they can prove their "goodness" through confessing privilege and awareness of inequities but do not provide language or skills for challenging oppression at systemic levels.

The dilemma that faces us in higher education and student affairs, therefore, is how to close the gap between our espoused values of racial equity and the scripts of performative "box-checking" to emerge through the competencies model and the persistent presence of whiteness as property. As racial equity becomes more prevalent in institutional rhetoric, critically challenging work is required to ensure that it does not become absorbed into the status quo of empty platitudes and practices that uphold white supremacist structures. In a 2018 *Change* magazine article titled "Reclaiming Racial Justice in Equity," Estela Bensimon asked us to consider whether "this embrace of equity signif[ies] an embrace of its critical and anti-racist foundations. . . . Or does the proliferation of this term instead represent the appropriation and dilution of equity" (Bensimon, 2018, p. 95). She calls for scholars and practitioners to "reclaim the 'justice' focus in racial equity and equity-mindedness" (p. 96), in part by identifying, articulating, and resisting the ways that the normalization and institutionalization of equity discourses have the potential to maintain and reinforce the very racial equity gaps that they claim to challenge. What she's asking us to do, in other words, is to reject the scripts of woke play and to engage in the more difficult reflective work of anti/racist practice.

The ACPA Strategic Imperative for Social Justice and Decolonization as Counterscript

One promising shift away from the competencies checklist model is ACPA's 2019 *Strategic Imperative for Social Justice and Decolonization* (SIRJD), which marks a significant shift for HESA programs and the student affairs profession away from concrete, stepwise rubrics of performance toward a model that stresses context, power differentials, and the importance of combining critical analysis at the individual, organizational, and systemic levels. The authors of the SIRJD engage in transformative racial equity research-practice by explicitly calling out higher education's historic and contemporary complicity with anti-Black racism and settler colonialism and insisting that "we must put the focus on institutions, institutional systems, and the people who reproduce and profit from the societal disadvantaging of Indigenous and racially minoritized communities" (Quaye et al., 2019, p. 6). While the prior model focused on assessing SJI competencies for the purposes of measuring preparation for career advancement, the SIRJD focuses instead on the work required to critique systems and dismantle structures of oppression. Personal reflection and exploration of privilege and positionality is still key; however, it is no longer the *end* of the activity/pedagogy but rather a *means* by which students and practitioners become better prepared to do the work. In other words, rather than focusing on individual privilege or cultural differences, the SIRJD insists on an orientation toward racial justice and de/colonizing practice that explicitly "seeks the critique, dismantling, and transformation of the systems and structures of white supremacy, racism, and its coordinates with nativism, colorism, and (religio)ethnocentrism" (p. 8). This refusal of stepwise or checklist models for personal/professional development is evident in the circular structure of the SIRJD framework (figure 1), which centers love and empathy and places values and strategies within a contextualizing arc of history. The guiding principles, or vanes, that emerge from the center represent possible (but not exclusive) strategies for critiquing personal, organizational, and systemic complicity with white supremacy and settler colonialism. The authors stress the fluid potentiality of these principles—they should not be seen as checklists

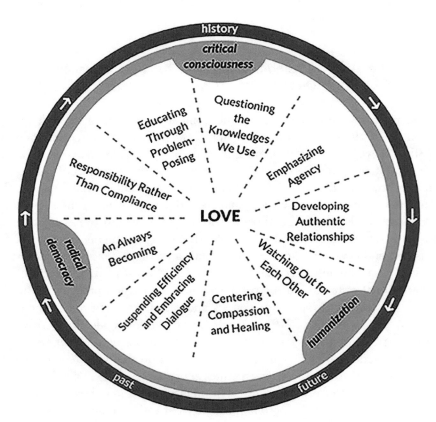

Figure 1. The SIRJD's Racial Justice and Decolonization Framework. Reprinted from *A Bold Vision Forward: A Framework for the Strategic Imperative for Racial Justice and Decolonization* (p. 11), by Quaye et al., 2019, ACPA. Copyright 2019 by ACPA-College Student Educators International.

but rather as possible starting points. They articulate a hope that "once a student affairs educator builds self-awareness; understands how love is foundational to justice; and foregrounds the recognition of history and how history informs our present, then they can begin to integrate and/or strengthen their dedication to the spirit these principles bring to their daily practice" (p. 13).

Shifting the script (or rejecting it outright) away from competency checklists and centering the work to be done toward racial justice and decolonization decenters the neoliberal focus on individual career advancement and "good ally" posturing so common in current woke play practices. The SIRJD framework is perhaps too new to have been internalized by HESA graduate programs or emerging professional development initiatives, but it provides a promising shift in rhetoric that program coordinators and department heads would be wise to consider in re/designing their pedagogy and programming. This chapter will therefore conclude with a series of reflective prompts and loose recommendations informed by the SIRJD that seek to challenge performative wokeness and the proliferation of woke play in student affairs research-practice.

Reflective Prompts for Anti/Racist Student Affairs Pedagogy and Practice

In keeping with the rejection of checklist mentalities and the centering of fluid, contextually dependent praxis, I resist offering concrete recommendations or "best practices." In keeping with the TRERP frame, the following prompts are intended to support an interpretation of anti/racist work as a "lifelong process of unlearning, rife with epistemic uncertainty and ambiguity" (Foste, 2019, p. 10) and to remind aspiring allies—particularly those in student affairs roles who are charged with implementing institutional "diversity, equity, and inclusion" initiatives—of the importance of both personal reflection *and* a commitment to transformative action that is inspired and led by the research-practice of BIPOC community members doing work "on the ground." In thinking through my envisioned anti/racist orientation, I am inspired in part by Gooden and colleagues' (2018) theory of antiracist action, which involves four cyclical and intersecting processes: (1) gaining and integrating knowledge, (2) examining self, (3) (re)envisioning the world, and (4) taking antiracist action. Combating woke play requires a focus on unlearning epistemologies of ignorance and ahistoricism (Leonardo & Manning, 2017), critically reflecting on personal complicity in the maintenance of white supremacist systems and structures, challenging taken-for-granted norms about how the world is and should be organized, and moving past the cycles of fear, shame, and guilt (Linder, 2015) that impede coalitional politics, effective risk-taking, and authentic anti/racist action.

Grounding practice in place. Following the lead of de/colonizing scholars and activists, student affairs practitioners must recognize that their work is deeply contextualized and takes place within very particular social, cultural, and historical settings. We must refuse the uncritical adoption of "best practices" and traditional approaches in favor of grappling with specificities of institutional, departmental, and individual contexts. The SIRJD encourages students and practitioners to ground themselves in the specificity of place by asking, "What is the history of my campus and how has it benefited from racism and colonization? What do I need to learn [about where and when I am] to begin to promote racial justice and decolonization in my work?" (Quaye et al., 2019, p. 19).

In HESA classrooms, this type of place-based engagement might involve in-depth study of institutional history—including investigations of the institutions' complicity with racist and settler colonial logics and the various strategies that activists have used to combat these policies and practices. Studying site-specific histories of both oppression and activism provides students with opportunities to both learn about structures and roots impacting practice today, and begin imagining how their own activism might contribute to a legacy of change.

Another site for place-informed student affairs practice would be the fraught activity of community service and service-learning programs. As scholars have noted (Cann & McCloskey, 2017; Endres & Gould, 2009; Mitchell et al., 2012), service-learning projects can easily slide into supporting deficit mindsets and the maintenance of Whiteness if they are not framed within a larger conversation of systemic power and privilege. In their 2012 article, "Service Learning as a Pedagogy of Whiteness," Mitchell, Donahue, and Young-Law argue that unless instructors and student affairs practitioners critically interrogate the cultural, historical, political, and economic realities of partnering groups, "service learning can become part of what we call a pedagogy of whiteness—strategies of instruction that consciously or unconsciously reinforce norms and privileges developed by, and for the benefit of, white people in the United

States" (p. 613). The authors recommend that service programs are scaffolded through activities of deep reflection and framing that stress explicit considerations of the social-political structures that inform race and class-based stratification. Only by engaging in dialogue and action guided by an understanding of place can these projects move beyond performative gestures of woke saviorism and into collaborative learning and support.

In all of these instances, a TRERP lens would remind us that understanding the local and structural/systemic context of a particular racial equity "problem" must always be grounded in the voices and sense-making of BIPOC practitioners who are engaged in doing the work "on the ground." It is not enough to teach students how to understand and describe these contexts or the structural forces that shape them—HESA programs must also encourage a sense of responsibility for coalition-building and knowledge co-construction that will work toward effective and equitable transformation.

Why this, why me, why now? In the framing of the SIRJD framework, the authors draw on three questions that Leigh Patel (2016) encourages all scholars and practitioners to answer before engaging in anti/racist and de/colonializing work: Why this, why me, and why now? I interpret this call, in part, to be an insistence that we consider whether and how our individual voices and bodies show up differently in this work. As a white aspiring anti/racist ally, I must recognize that there are arguments and initiatives that are not mine to take up, and that my action might better serve the movement by providing silent support or taking my voice to other (whiter) spaces. Similarly, graduate programs and student affairs programmers should remain vigilant and conscious of *why* they're taking up a particular issue/topic/program, *who* they've decided to have represent or lead it, and whether *now* is the necessary and productive time to move. For example, I am reminded of the scandal that occurred at the 2018 Association of College and University Housing Officers–International (ACUHO–I) annual conference when the planning team invited Christian Picciolini—a self-identified "former far-right extremist"—as a keynote speaker. The association believed that Picciolini's voice would provide a unique perspective to give insight into "understanding how our students may be recruited into this growing movement of hate" (DeNiro, 2018, para. 2) but failed to adequately consider how such a speech/speaker might resonate in a racially diverse setting within the context of rising visibility of white supremacist and alt-right activity. The question of *who*, in this case, can also be extended to include a series of related critical conversations, including: Who benefits from the work—a recovering alt-right extremist, White conference attendees, the association, or the minoritized communities who have been systematically othered by policies and practices and may have been victimized by the funded speaker? ACUHO–I, like other offices and organizations, would have been well served to consider whose learning and knowledges are being centered in the content, and to whom the office/program/curriculum is held accountable.

Check your privilege, but keep moving. Privilege pedagogies have undeniable power for helping majoritized students learn to recognize and critique the inequitable access to resources, opportunities, and immunities that they have accumulated; however, student affairs programs and practices must take care that these lessons of self-reflection do not end with mere confession. Identifying privilege, while difficult and painful for some students, can also become comfortable and commonplace—a process of confession and absolution that allows majoritized students and practitioners to affirm their identities as "good" while side-stepping responsibilities for bringing about change. For this reason, critical whiteness scholar Zeus Leonardo (2004) has cautioned educators to be wary of privilege pedagogies that encourage merely performative recitations or confessions of individual and institutional privilege. He argues that white privilege and white supremacy are inextricably intertwined and that naming the first without grappling with the second results in ineffectual, performative, and exclusionary teaching. Educators looking to create equity-minded and anti/racist change must make a shift toward "a critical pedagogy of white racial supremacy [that] revolves less around the issue of unearned advantages or the *state* of being dominant, and more around direct processes that secure domination and the privileges associated with it" (p. 137, italics in original).

Student affairs pedagogies and practices might *start* with explorations of privilege and personal positioning but then shift to conversations about how individual identities, values, and experiences equip us to engage differently in equity work and efforts toward institutional transformation.

The narrative I shared earlier in this chapter with Justin and the career advisor is an example of the type of woke play that would benefit from moving beyond confessions of privilege and power-consciousness to a politics of action. I knew enough, at that point, to be able to critique the career advisor's speech and recognize how her rhetoric encourages a performative, self-interested approach to "activism"—but I wasn't yet in the habit of taking the next step and leveraging my privilege and position within the institution to push for change. This intellectualization and avoidance of personal responsibility was a response that I'd learned through both my prior graduate training and my experience as a higher education administrator—an example of one of the ways that white supremacy operates in both of those spaces to distract and undermine transformative racial equity efforts by encouraging a focus on understanding rather than action.

Moving beyond performativity would have required me to mobilize my privilege—my Whiteness and my professional status—and embrace the vulnerability of calling out racist and opportunistic narratives. Closing the equity gap between espoused values (confessions of privilege and proclamations of woke social awareness) and enacted practice requires taking on the risky business of challenging power and hegemonic norms. A TRERP perspective would also require a recognition of the power and necessity of coalition-building and the centering of BIPOC practitioner voices and agendas, ensuring that policies, practices, and/or scholarship that emerged in response to this activism are focused on transforming harmful practices rather than simply creating noise and distracting from larger change efforts.

Conclusion

The goal of this chapter was to explore some of the gaps between the values and dispositions that student affairs graduate programs and practices espouse related to diversity, equity, and inclusion, and the ways that their programs and policies are enacted. I argue that if we are to work toward a transformative racial equity research-practice model that challenges the long-standing inequities and interlocking forms of systemic oppression that structure higher education generally, and the field of student affairs more specifically, we must move away from neoliberal, self-interested, and unserious engagements with competency-based "woke play." Racial equity is not a checklist for career advancement, a marketing ploy, or a strategy for enabling aspiring allies to feel good about their participation. Student affairs can't afford to play. It never could.

Notes

1. My capitalization choices throughout this chapter are intentional and deeply political. For example, I capitalize "Whiteness" when used to refer to dominant narratives and ideologies that structure institutions and systems of race-based privilege and oppression; I do not, however, capitalize "white" when it is used to refer to racial categories or identities, which is consistent with the tenets and political commitments of critical frameworks. I follow the guidance of Pérez Huber (2010), who makes a case for "rejecting the standard grammatical norm as a means to acknowledge and reject the grammatical representation of power capitalization brings to the term 'white'" (p. 93). In contrast, I do capitalize the terms Black, Latinx, Indigenous, and other minoritized groups.

2. Pseudonym. Anecdote recounted with permission.

3. This grammatical choice is also modeled after the use of the slash in recent de/colonizing work (Bhattacharya, 2009; Patel, 2016; Tuck & Yang, 2012), which recognizes that efforts to dismantle settler colonial logics occur within institutions that were built on and continue to operate under those very colonial systems. For Kakali Bhattacharya (2009), the slash is used to "denote interactions between traditional colonizing discourses and the resistance against such discourses. . . . [and identifies] spaces where multiple colonizing and resisting discourses exist and interact simultaneously" (p. 105). While I prefer to use the slash when referring to my own anti/racist efforts and theorizing, I retain other authors' choices when referencing their work.

References

ACPA & NASPA. (2015). *Professional Competency Areas for Student Affairs Practitioners.* http://search.ebscohost.com/login.aspx?direct=true&db=eric&AN=ED522920&site=ehost-live&scope=site%5Cnhttp://www2.myacpa.org/publications/internal-publications

ACPA & NASPA. (2016). *Professional Competencies Rubrics.* https://www.myacpa.org/sites/default/files/ACPA%20NASPA%20Professional%20Competency%20Rubrics%20Full.pdf?

Ahmed, S. (2012). *On being included: Racism and diversity in institutional life.* Duke Univerity Press.

Alemán, E. (2009). Through the prism of critical race theory: Niceness and Latina/o leadership in the politics of education. *Journal of Latinos and Education, 8*(4), 290–311. https://doi.org/10.1080/15348430902973351

Anderson, G. M. (2012). Equity and critical policy analysis in higher education: A bridge still too far. *Review of Higher Education, 36*(1), 133–142. https://doi.org/10.1353/rhe.2012.0051

Bensimon, E. M. (2018). Reclaiming racial justice in equity. *Change: The Magazine of Higher Learning, 50*(3–4), 95–98. https://doi.org/10.1080/00091383.2018.1509623

Bhattacharya, K. (2009). Othering research, researching the other: De/colonizing approaches to qualitative inquiry. In J. C. Smart (Ed.), *Higher education: Handbook of theory and research* (pp. 105–150). Springer.

Bondi, S. (2012). Students and institutions protecting whiteness as property: A critical race theory analysis of student affairs preparation. *Journal of Student Affairs Research and Practice, 49*(4), 397–414. https://doi.org/10.1515/jsarp-2012-6381

Cabrera, N. L., Franklin, J. D., & Watson, J. S. (2016). Whiteness in higher education: The invisible missing link in diversity and racial analysis. *ASHE Higher Education Report, 42*(6), 7–125. https://doi.org/Kriegsbild

Cann, C. N., & McCloskey, E. (2017). The Poverty Pimpin' Project: How whiteness profits from black and brown bodies in community service programs. *Race Ethnicity and Education, 20*(1), 72–86. https://doi.org/10.1080/13613324.2015.1096769

Castagno, A. E. (Ed.). (2019). *The price of nice: How good intentions maintain educational inequity*. University of Minnesota Press.

Ching, C. D. (2017). *Constructing and enacting equity at a community college* (Accession No. 10801796). Doctoral dissertation, University of Southern California. ProQuest Dissertations Publishing.

DeNiro, M. (2018, July 12). Concerns about AC&E speaker. *ACUHO-I Educational Events*. https://www.acuho-i.org/events/cid/6735?portalid=0

DiAngelo, R. (2018). *White fragility: Why it's so hard to talk to white people about racism*. Beacon Press.

Eaton, P. W., & Smithers, L. (2019). This is not a checklist: Higher education and student affairs competencies, neoliberal protocol, and poetics. *Educational Philosophy and Theory*, 1–15. https://doi.org/10.1080/00131857.2019.1679624

Endres, D., & Gould, M. (2009). "I am also in the position to use my Whiteness to help them out": The communication of Whiteness in service learning. *Western Journal of Communication, 73*(4), 418–436. https://doi.org/10.1080/10570310903279083

Espinosa, L. L., Chessman, H. M., & Wayt, L. (2016). Racial climate on campus: A survey of college presidents. https://doi.org/10.4135/9781452276151.n329

Ferguson, R. A. (2012). *The reorder of things: The university and its pedagogies of minority difference*. University of Minnesota Press.

Flowers, L. A. (2003). National study of diversity requirements in student affairs graduate programs. *NASPA Journal, 40*(4), 72–82.

Foste, Z. (2019). Reproducing Whiteness: How white students justify the campus racial status quo. *Journal of Student Affairs Research and Practice, 56*(3), 241–253. https://doi.org/10.1080/19496591.2019.1576530

Foste, Z. (2020). The enlightenment narrative: White student leaders' preoccupation with racial innocence. *Journal of Diversity in Higher Education, 13*(1), 33–43. http://dx.doi.org/10.1037/dhe0000113

Freelon, D., McIlwain, C. D., & Clark, M. D. (2017). Beyond the hashtags: #Ferguson, #Blacklivesmatter, and the online struggle for offline justice. *SSRN Electronic Journal.* https://doi.org/10.2139/ssrn.2747066

Gayles, J. G., & Kelly, B. T. (2007). Experiences with diversity in the curriculum: Implications for graduate programs and student affairs practice. *NASPA Journal, 44*(1), 193–207.

Gooden, M. A., Davis, B. W., Spikes, D. D., Hall, D. L., & Lee, L. (2018). Leaders changing how they act by changing how they think: Applying principles of an anti-racist principal preparation program. *Teachers College Record, 120*(14), 1–26.

Grzanka, P. R., Adler, J., & Blazer, J. (2015). Making up allies: The identity choreography of straight LGBT activism. *Sexuality Research and Social Policy, 12*(3), 165–181. https://doi.org/10.1007/s13178-014-0179-0

Gusa, D. L. (2010). White institutional presence: The impact of whiteness on campus climate. *Harvard Educational Review, 80*(4), 464–490. https://doi.org/10.17763/haer.80.4.p5j483825u110002

Harper, S. R., & Hurtado, S. (2007). Nine themes in campus racial climates and implications for institutional transformation. *New Directions for Student Services, 120,* 7–24. http://works.bepress.com/sharper/18/

Harris, C. I. (1993). Whiteness as property. *Harvard Law Review, 106*(8), 1707–1791.

Harris, J. C., & Linder, C. (2018). The racialized experiences of students of color in higher education and student affairs graduate preparation programs. *Journal of College Student Development, 59*(2), 141–158. https://doi.org/10.1353/csd.2018.0014

Hevel, M. S. (2016). Toward a history of student affairs: A synthesis of research, 1996–2015. *Journal of College Student Development, 57*(7), 844–862. https://doi.org/10.1353/csd.2016.0082

Iverson, S. V. (2018). Multicultural competence for doing social justice: Expanding our awareness, knowledge, and skills. *Journal of Critical Thought and Praxis, 1*(1). https://doi.org/10.31274/jctp-180810-14

Jupp, J. C., & Lensmire, T. J. (2016). Second-wave white teacher identity studies: Toward complexity and reflexivity in the racial conscientization of white teachers. *International Journal of Qualitative Studies in Education, 29*(8), 985–988. https://doi.org/10.1080/09518398.2016.1189621

Kendi, I. X. (2019). *How to be an antiracist.* Oneworld.

King, P. M., & Howard-Hamilton, M. (2003). An assessment of multicultural competence. *NASPA Journal, 40*(2), 119–133. https://doi.org/10.2202/1949-6605.1226

Lensmire, T. J., McManimon, S. K., Tierney, J. D., Lee-Nichols, M. E., Casey, Z. A., Lensmire, A., & Davis, B. M. (2013). Mcintosh as synecdoche: How teacher education's focus on white privilege undermines antiracism. *Harvard Educational Review*, 83(3), 410–431. https://doi.org/10.17763/haer.83.3. 35054h14l8230574

Leonardo, Z. (2004). The color of supremacy: Beyond the discourse of "white privilege." *Educational Philosophy and Theory*, 36(2), 137–152. https://doi.org/10.1111/j.1469-5812.2004.00057.x

Leonardo, Z., & Manning, L. (2017). White historical activity theory: Toward a critical understanding of white zones of proximal development. *Race Ethnicity and Education*. https://doi.org/10.1080/13613324.2015.1100988

Leonardo, Z., & Porter, R. K. (2010). Pedagogy of fear: Toward a Fanonian theory of "safety" in race dialogue. *Race Ethnicity and Education*, 13(2), 139–157. https://doi.org/10.1080/13613324.2010.482898

Linder, C. (2015). Navigating guilt, shame, and fear of appearing racist: A conceptual model of antiracist white feminist identity development. *Journal of College Student Development*, 56(6), 535–550. https://doi.org/10.1353/csd.2015.0057

Matias, C. E. (2016). *Feeling white: Whiteness, emotionality, and education*. Sense.

Mitchell, T. D., Donahue, D. M., & Young-Law, C. (2012). Service learning as a pedagogy of whiteness. *Equity and Excellence in Education*, 45(4), 612–629. https://doi.org/10.1080/10665684.2012.715534

Patel, L. (2016). *Decolonizing educational research: From ownership to answerability*. Routledge.

Perez Huber, L. (2010). Using Latina/o Critical Race Theory (CRT) and racist nativism to explore intersectionality in the educational experiences of undocumented Chicana college students. *Educational Foundations*, 24(1–2), 77–96.

Pritchard, A., & McChesney, J. (2018). *Focus on student affairs, 2018: Understanding key challenges using CUPA-HR data*. https://www.cupahr.org/surveys/research-briefs/

Quaye, S. J., Aho, R. E., Jacob, M. B., Domingue, A. D., Guido, F. M., Lange, A. C., Squire, D., & Stewart, D-L. (2019). *A bold vision forward: A framework for the strategic imperative for racial justice and decolonization*. ACPA. https://www.myacpa.org/sites/default/files/SIRJD_GuidingDoc2.pdf

Spade, D. (2011). *Normal Life: Administrative violence, critical trans politics, & the limits of law* (2nd ed.). Duke Univerity Press.

Stewart, D-L. (2019). Ideologies of absence: Anti-Blackness and inclusion rhetoric in student affairs practice. *Journal of Student Affairs*, 28, 15–30.

Sullivan, S. (2006). *Revealing whiteness: The unconscious habits of racial privilege*. Indiana University Press.

Thompson, A. (2003). Tiffany, friend of people of color: White investments in antiracism? *International Journal of Qualitative Studies in Education, 16*(1), 7–29. https://doi.org/10.1080/0951839032000033509

Tuck, E., & Yang, K. W. (2012). Decolonization is not a metaphor. *Decolonization: Indigeneity, Education & Society, 1*(1), 1–40. http://www.decolonization.org/index.php/des/article/view/18630

Villarreal, C. D., Liera, R., & Malcom-Piqueux, L. (2019). The role of niceness in silencing racially minoritized faculty. In A. E. Castagno (Ed.), *The price of nice: How good intentions maintain educational inequity* (pp. 127–144). University of Minnesota Press.

Wesaw, A. J., & Sponsler, B. A. (2014). *The chief student affairs officer: Responsibilities, opinions, and professional pathways of leaders in student affairs.* NASPA. https://www.naspa.org/files/dmfile/CSAO_2014_ExecSum_Download2.pdf

About the Editors

Royel M. Johnson is Associate Professor in the Rossier School of Education at the University of Southern California (USC), where he is also Director of Student Engagement in the USC Race and Equity Center. His interdisciplinary research broadly examines issues related to education access, racial equity, and student success, as they are shaped by social identities and systems of oppression. He has authored over 40 publications that appear in outlets such as the *Journal of Higher Education*, *Urban Education*, and *Journal of College Student Development*, to name a few. He serves on the editorial boards for the *Review of Higher Education* and *Journal of Diversity in Higher Education* and is associate editor for *Frontiers in Education*, higher education section. The US Department of Health Resources and Services Administration, Spencer Foundation, ACPA—College Educators International, and others have awarded him more than $5.1 million to support his work.

Uju Anya is Associate Professor in the Department of Modern Languages at Carnegie Mellon University and Research Affiliate at the Center for the Study of Higher Education at Pennsylvania State University. She conducts inquiry in postsecondary language education with a focus on race, gender, sexual, and social class identities in language classrooms and study abroad. She also has expertise in equity and inclusiveness in curriculum design, teacher education, service learning, and civic engagement in postsecondary pedagogy. Her scholarship is published in journals, teacher training program manuals, encyclopedias, and in her book, *Racialized Identities in Second Language Learning: Speaking Blackness in Brazil* (2017), winner of the 2019 American Association for Applied Linguistics (AAAL) First Book Award recognizing a scholar's first book as an exceptional contribution to the field.

Liliana M. Garces is Associate Professor at the University of Texas at Austin and Affiliate Faculty at the School of Law. Her research is grounded in the intersection of law and educational policy, with a focus on access, diversity, and equity in higher education, and the use and influence of social science research in law. Her scholarship is published in a variety of outlets, including peer-reviewed education journals, law journals, policy reports, and books. She is an associate editor for the *Journal of Higher Education* and a coeditor of *Affirmative Action and Racial Equity: Considering the Fisher Case to Forge the Path Ahead* (2015) and *School Integration Matters: Research-Based Strategies to Advance Racial Equity* (2016).

About the Contributors

Paula Adamo is Teaching Professor of Spanish and a PhD student of curriculum and instruction at the University of Denver. Her passion focuses on what constitutes excellent teaching in the higher education context. Her main research interests include aesthetic teaching and learning, inclusive and holistic pedagogies, and curriculum design. She is currently involved in various projects that invite and guide faculty members from different disciplines to think creatively about the possibilities of a college classroom.

Evelyn Ambriz is a doctoral candidate and research assistant at the University of Texas at Austin. In her research, she draws from frameworks in sociology and employs qualitative methods to investigate how organizational actors work within constrained and racialized systems of higher education to promote equitable access to capital for students and alumni. Her research has been published in *American Educational Research Journal* and *Administrative Theory & Praxis*. She holds an MPA in social policy and a BS in sociology from Cornell University, where she served as the assistant dean of students for student development diversity initiatives.

Estela Mara Bensimon is University Professor Emerita at the University of Southern California. She is the founder of the Center for Urban Education at USC. She is now leading Bensimon & Associates, a consulting firm that provides services to colleges, universities, and philanthropic organizations. Bensimon is an elected member of the National Academy of Education and a Fellow of the American Education Research Association. She is a governor appointee to the Education Commission of the States. In 2020 she received ASHE's Howard Bowen Award and the

McGraw Prize. Her most recent book is *From Equity Talk to Equity Walk: Expanding Practitioner Knowledge for Racial Justice in Higher Education*.

Mildred Boveda is Associate Professor of Special Education at the Pennsylvania State University. In her scholarship, she uses the terms "intersectional competence" and "intersectional consciousness" to describe teachers' preparedness to address intersecting equity concerns. Drawing from Black feminist theory and collaborative teacher education research, she interrogates how differences are framed across education communities to influence education policy and practice. Boveda earned an EdD in exceptional student education at Florida International University and an EdM in education policy and management from the Harvard Graduate School of Education.

Felecia Commodore is Assistant Professor of Higher Education in the Educational Foundations and Leadership Department at Old Dominion University in Norfolk, Virginia. Her research focuses on leadership, governance, and administrative practices with a particular focus on historically black colleges and universities and minority-serving institutions. She is a coeditor of *Opportunities and Challenges of Historically Black Colleges and Universities and Graduate Education at Historically Black Colleges and Universities (HBCUs): A Student Perspective* (2014). She is also the lead author of *Black College Women: A Guide to Success in Higher Education* (2018).

Liliana Diaz Solodukhin is a policy analyst at the Western Interstate Commission for Higher Education (WICHE) and a doctoral candidate in the Department of Higher Education at the University of Denver's Morgridge College of Education. Diaz Solodukhin's research explores Latinx identity formation, its relationship to civic and community engagement, and the development of equity-centered higher education policy.

Aaron T. George is a doctoral student in college student affairs administration at the University of Georgia, Athens. He received his bachelor's and master's degrees from the University of the Pacific, in Stockton, California. He has worked in student affairs for over a decade in multiple roles across the United States. Aaron's research interests include using critical and poststructural frameworks to explore the experiences of student affairs practitioners.

Judy Marquez Kiyama is Associate Vice Provost for Faculty Development and Professor in the Center for the Study of Higher Education at the University of Arizona. Kiyama's research examines the structures that shape educational opportunities for underserved groups to better understand the collective knowledge and resources drawn upon to confront, negotiate, and (re)shape such structures. Kiyama grounds her work in community knowledge and organizes her research in three interconnected areas: the role of parents and families, equity and power in educational research, and underserved groups as collective networks of change.

Román Liera is Assistant Professor of Higher Education Administration in the College of Education and Human Resources at Montclair State University. He is a qualitative researcher who conceptualizes higher education campuses as racialized organizations. Liera specifically studies how administrators, faculty, and staff leverage organizational processes to advance racial equity. He has published work in the *Journal of Higher Education*, the *American Educational Research Journal*, and *Education Policy Analysis Archives*.

Janiece Z. Mackey was born in Colorado and is a wife and mother of four children. Due to being one of the few Black folks within her academic, political, and professional spaces, she created an organization entitled Young Aspiring Americans for Social and Political Activism (YAASPA) to provide a conduit for youth of color to reclaim academic, career, and civic spaces. She is an Equitable Futures postdoctoral research fellow with Rutgers University. She earned a PhD in higher education with emphases in public policy and curriculum and instruction at the University of Denver.

Adrienne Martinez currently serves as Associate Vice President of Classroom to Careers at Metropolitan State University of Denver, a modified open-access and Hispanic-serving institution. As a practitioner-scholar, she employs an equity framework in her commitment to research-informed practice and practice-oriented research endeavors. With a broad range of higher education experience, she strives to (re)create systems that result in more equitable outcomes for underserved and historically excluded students. Her approach to this work and scholarship reaffirms the strengths inherent within such students and their respective communities.

About the Contributors

Darris R. Means is Associate Professor of Higher Education at the University of Pittsburgh. Using critical and qualitative methodologies, his research examines postsecondary education access and success for rural Black and Latinx students. Darris's research appears in the *Review of Higher Education, Journal of Research in Rural Education,* and *The Rural Educator.* His recent research on rural Black students and postsecondary education access has been supported by the National Academy of Education and Spencer Foundation.

Demetri L. Morgan is Assistant Professor of Higher Education at the Loyola University Chicago School of Education. Morgan's research interests center on the purpose and responsibilities of higher education in a diverse democracy. His governance research agenda seeks to understand and illuminate how higher education governing boards contribute to or detract from equity and inclusion efforts aimed at responding to higher education's changing demographics. His research has been published in the *Review of Research in Higher Education,* the *Journal of Diversity in Higher Education,* and the *Journal of Higher Education.*

Susana M. Muñoz is Associate Professor and Director of the Higher Education Leadership program at Colorado State University. Her scholarly interests center on the experiences of underserved populations in higher education. Specifically, she focuses her research on issues of activism and campus climate for undocumented Latinx students, while employing perspectives such as Latino critical race theory, Chicana feminist epistemology, and college persistence theory to identify and deconstruct issues of power and inequities as experienced by these populations.

Raquel M. Rall is Assistant Professor of Higher Education Administration and Policy at the University of California, Riverside. Her research is dedicated to maximizing educational outcomes for communities that have traditionally had the least opportunities. She centers her work on higher education leadership and governance. In particular, her research and practice sit at the intersection of governance, equity, diversity, and inclusion. Her research has been published in the *Journal of Higher Education,* the *Journal of Negro Education,* and *Harvard Educational Review.*

Ericka Roland is Assistant Professor in the Educational Leadership and Policy Studies Department at the University of Texas at Arlington.

Her research examines critical leadership development in postsecondary educational settings through two interconnected lines of inquiry: (1) the dynamics of dialogical relationships, and (2) the lived leadership experiences of historically minoritized persons. In the study of critical leadership development, she centers questions through problems and possibilities leading to the enactment of equity and justice.

Stephen Santa-Ramirez (he, him, his) is Assistant Professor of Higher Education at the University at Buffalo, State University of New York. His research agenda centers the lives and knowledge of historically marginalized and economically neglected college students. By employing critical and asset-based frameworks, his scholarship investigates campus racial climate, first-generation students' sense of belonging, and the various ways race, ethnicity, and im/migration inform Latinx undocu/DACAmented collegians' educational experiences.

Amanda Taylor currently serves as Assistant Vice President for Diversity, Equity, and Inclusion at American University, where she works to support and build campus-wide collaborations that advance strategic equity goals. Additionally, Taylor is a faculty member at American University's School of International Service and a faculty fellow with AU's Antiracist Research and Policy Center. She earned her doctorate in education and her master's in education at Harvard University. Taylor's research, teaching, and administrative work focus on the intersections of culture, power, and education in micro- and macropolitical contexts.

Ali Watts is a PhD candidate at Penn State University and a graduate research assistant at the Center for the Study of Higher Education. Her research interests include equity-minded institutional policy, grant-making, critical whiteness studies, and educational philosophy. Prior to beginning doctoral studies, she worked in a range of roles in education administration—including PK–12 and graduate admissions, distance education student and faculty support, residential life, and leadership development.

Jenay Willis is a Southern Black woman with rural roots in Georgia. She draws from her upbringing, which inspires her to center those experiences in her research as a scholar-practitioner. Jenay challenges how rurality is defined by creating counter-spaces for Black people. Her work foregrounds and uplifts the narratives of Black individuals within rural communities by using critical lenses in qualitative research.

Index

Adamo, Paula, 10, 85, 93, 98, 215
admissions, race-conscious, 3
Advancing Students for a Stronger Economy Tomorrow (ASSET). *See* Colorado State University
Ambriz, Evelyn, xv, 8, 43, 215
anti-Blackness, viii, 158, 190, 191, 193, 201
anti-(im)migrant rhetoric, 143, 144, 145, 147, 150, 153
anti/racism, 193, 194, 198, 203–204, 205, 206, 208
Anya, Uju, vii, 1, 213
Arizona State University, 150–153; and Undocumented Students for Education Equity (USEE), 152
asset-based approaches, 36, 85, 169, 179–180

Bensimon, Estela, vii–ix, 28, 30, 201, 215
bias: implicit, 26–27, 31, 33–34, 35; in-group, 21, 23; unconscious, 45, 52
Black Feminist thought, 103, 104, 106, 107, 111, 112, 115
Black Lives Matter, vii, 90, 145
Black rural students: *See* rural students

boards of trustees, 9; and budget allocation, 74–76; composition of, 65–66, 69, 78; and duty of loyalty, 68–69; and duty of obedience, 69; and equity-centered decision-making, 61, 64, 66, 68, 78; and fiduciary duty, 62, 63, 67; and presidential hiring, 76–77; and strategic planning, 70–76
Boveda, Mildred, 10, 103, 216

campus climate, 11, 48, 69, 90, 142, 144–146, 148, 150, 154, 158
campus-wide collaborations. *See* diversity and inclusion councils
Ching, Cheryl D., 29, 33, 34
Colorado State University, 148–150, 163–165; and Advancing Students for a Stronger Economy Tomorrow (ASSET), 149
Commodore, Felecia, 9, 61, 65, 77, 216
community cultural wealth, 169, 174–175, 180
co-teaching/co-learning, 93–96
counter-spaces of resistance, 89–91
Crash, 11, 121
critical race media literacy, 126, 127, 128, 134

221

critical race theory, 5, 169, 173–174, 199
cross-racial dialogue. *See* racial dialogues

data disaggregation, 29, 53, 72, 78
DACA. *See* Deferred Action for Childhood Arrivals
Dear White People, 121, 128, 129–130, 131–132, 133–134
de/colonial ethical considerations, 104, 106, 110–111, 112–114
Deferred Action for Childhood Arrivals (DACA), 11–12, 141, 158n2; at Arizona State University, 150–153; at Colorado State University, 148–150; and institutional support, 141–142, 143–144. *See also* undocumented students
degree attainment: by race/ethnicity, 4, 91; among rural students, 169, 173, 179
Diaz Solodukhin, Liliana, 10, 85, 89, 98, 99, 216
diversity and inclusion councils, 8; composition of, 51–52, 53; institutional stages of, 47, 53; role of administrators, 48, 50, 55; role of students, 48–49, 50–51, 53, 55, 56; university leadership, 43–44, 45, 54, 55
diversity, equity, and inclusion, 6, 62, 66, 115, 189, 193, 194, 195, 197, 203, 207
DREAMzone, 151–152, 155, 157, 164

enrollment demographics, 4, 65, 151
epistemicide, 111, 113
epistemic justice, 148, 155
epistemological equity, 87–88, 89

equity-mindedness: and competencies, 30, 32, 34, 35, 36; and inquiry, 31–38; and leadership, 8, 9, 68, 77; and practices, 6, 29–31, 71, 74–76, 78, 104, 198, 201, 206; and training, 198

facilitation. *See* racial dialogues
faculty hiring: diversification of, 8, 21–22; and equity-minded inquiry activities, 31–38; inquiry-based interventions, 28–29; and job announcements, 25–26, 32–33; strategies for, 23–28. *See also* search committees
funds of knowledge, 87, 93, 95, 96, 98n2

Garces, Liliana M., vii, 1, 214
George, Aaron T., 12, 167, 170, 216
Get Out, 11, 121
Gonzales, Leslie, 148

Hate You Give, The, 11, 128–129
Help, The, 128
higher education and student affairs (HESA) programs. *See* student affairs
Higher Learning, 128
historically white institutions (HWIs), 7, 8, 158n3, 173, 179. *See also* predominantly white institutions
hooks, bell, 108, 128

(im)migrant students, 11–12, 142, 151–158 passim
intergroup dialogues, 11, 124–125
intersectional competence, 10, 104, 107
intersectional competence construct, 107, 112

intersection competence measure (ICM), 107–108, 114
intersectional consciousness, 10, 104
intersectional consciousness collaboration protocol (ICC), 108–110, 114
intersectional consciousness collaboration protocol for teacher education (ICC-TE), 108, 109, 115
intersectionality, 103, 106, 107, 180, 183
instersectional justice, 148, 154–155
Ishiwata, Eric, 148, 149

Johnson, Royel M., vii, 1, 86, 104, 122, 175, 213

Kendi, Ibram X., 193
Kiyama, Judy Marquez, 10, 85, 92, 93, 96, 98, 217

labor justice, 148, 154
Ladson-Billings, Gloria, 87
Leonardo, Zeus, 206
Liera, Román, 8, 21, 29–30, 32, 33, 34, 35, 217

Mackey, Janiece Z., 10, 85, 98, 217
Martinez, Adrienne, 10, 85, 98, 217
Means, Darris, 12, 167, 169, 170, 175, 176, 177, 179, 181, 218
minoritized. *See* racially minoritized faculty
Morgan, Demetri L., 9, 61, 218
Muñoz, Susana M., 11, 141, 146–147, 148, 149, 218

non-Native colleges and universities (NNCUs), 145, 158n3

Orphan, Cecilia, 89, 99
Osefi-Kofi, Nana, 87

P-12 schools, 104–105, 107, 114
pedagogy: culturally responsive, 85–86, 96–97, 102; inclusive, 10, 89, 91–96; liberatory, 89; and privilege, 200, 206; and reciprocity, 87–89
Peele, Jordan, 121
performative allyship, 189–190, 193, 203, 207
positionality, 26, 87, 97–98, 112, 125, 133, 154, 169, 170, 191, 192, 201
practitioners, higher education, xi; BIPOC, 6, 89, 195, 196, 205, 207; racially minoritized, 175; student affairs, 55, 191, 194–195; and TRERP, 5–6
predominantly white institutions, 91, 106, 110, 111, 130, 176. *See also* historically white institutions (HWIs)

Quaye, Stephen John, 123–124, 201

racial dialogues, 121; and development of racial consciousness, 123, 124, 127, 133; facilitation of, 122, 123, 127, 128–134; movies as a tool for, 121, 125, 127, 128–134
racially minoritized faculty, 8, 21–27 passim, 33, 35–36, 37
racist incidents, 2–3, 8, 11
racist nativism, 153, 154, 158
Rall, Raquel M., 9, 61, 218
reparative justice, 148, 155
Roland, Ericka, 11, 121, 218
rural students, 12; and Black students, 168, 169, 171–172, 176–179, 183; of Color, 168; and education access, 171–172, 176–179, 183; and postsecondary success, 172–173, 179–181, 183

Santa-Ramirez, Stephen, 11, 141, 147, 219
search committees, 21, 23–38. *See also* faculty hiring
self-reflexivity, 92
sense of belonging, 145–146
settler colonialism, 7, 158, 191, 201, 202, 204, 208n3
social justice and inclusion competency, 197–198
Spade, Dean, 194
Stewart, D-L., 196
Strategic Imperative for Social Justice and Decolonization (SIRJD), 201–203, 204, 205
systems of oppression, 176, 190–191; and intersectional competence, 107; and intersectional justice, 154; and pedagogy, 10, 87, 90, 103, 113, 114, 121, 200; and SIRJD, 201; and student affairs, 13, 198, 200, 207; and TRERP, 5, 6, 62, 70, 87, 104, 127, 175, 180, 194; and university leadership, 43, 70
student activism, 2–3
student affairs, 191, 194–207; and higher education and student affairs (HESA) programs, 197, 198–199, 201, 203, 204

Taylor, Amanda, 8, 9, 43, 219
teacher educators, 104, 105, 109–110; of color, 105–106
transformative change: and DACA students, 12, 142, 143, 156; and pedagogy, 96, 112, 115, 127, 134; and racial equity, 6, 7, 8, 127, 190; and SIRJD, 201–203; and student affairs, 11, 13, 191, 195, 198, 201–203, 205–207; and TRERP, 22, 115, 127, 175, 190, 194–195, 201–203, 205–207; and university leadership, 8, 47, 53, 194–195
translational racial equity research-practice (TRERP), 5–7, 28–29, 31, 32, 34, 36, 38, 43, 190, 194–195, 203, 205, 207; and boards of trustees, 61, 62, 70; and DACA students, 156; and pedagogy, 86, 87, 89, 96–97; and racial dialogues, 122, 127; and rural students, 169, 175; and teacher education, 104, 115
TRERP. *See* translational racial equity research-practice
"Trump effect," 1, 3, 11, 143

undocumented students, 11–12, 141, 158n1; at Arizona State University, 150–153; at Colorado State University, 148–150; and institutional support, 141–142, 143–144. *See also* Deferred Action for Childhood Arrivals (DACA
Undocumented Students for Education Equity (USEE). *See* Arizona State University

Watts, Ali, xv, 12, 189, 219
white privilege, 123, 126, 178, 193, 199, 206
white entitlement, 199–200
white supremacy, xi, 105, 108, 110, 111, 180, 193, 207; and pedagogy, 126, 206; and reparative justice, 148, 155; and student affairs, 190, 204; and systemic oppression, 103, 200, 202; and TRERP, 6, 127, 175
whiteness: and pedagogy, 204, 206; as property, 199–200; as social

construction, 128, 174; and student affairs, 195, 204; and systems of oppression, 148, 191, 194, 208n1

Willis, Jenay, 12, 167, 170, 219

"woke play," 12, 190, 192–193, 195, 207

Yosso, Tara J., 174